Apple Pro Training Series
OS X Server
Essentials 10.9

Arek Dreyer and Ben Greisler

Apple
Certified

Apple Pro Training Series: OS X Server Essentials 10.9
Arek Dreyer and Ben Greisler
Copyright © 2014 by Peachpit Press

Peachpit Press
www.peachpit.com

To report errors, please send a note to errata@peachpit.com. Peachpit Press is a division of Pearson Education.

Apple Series Editor: Lisa McClain
Production Coordinator: Kim Elmore, Happenstance Type-O-Rama
Technical Editor: Adam Karneboge
Apple Reviewer: John Signa
Apple Project Manager: John Signa
Copy Editor: Scout Festa
Proofreader: Scout Festa
Compositor: Cody Gates, Happenstance Type-O-Rama
Indexer: Jack Lewis
Cover Illustration: Paul Mavrides
Cover Production: Cody Gates, Happenstance Type-O-Rama

Notice of Liability

The information in this book is distributed on an "As Is" basis, without warranty. While every precaution has been taken in the preparation of the book, neither the authors nor Peachpit shall have any liability to any person or entity with respect to any loss or damage caused or alleged to be caused directly or indirectly by the instructions contained in this book or by the computer software and hardware products described in it.

IMPORTANT: Some of the exercises contained in this guide can be temporarily disruptive, and some exercises, if performed incorrectly, could result in data loss or damage to system files. As such, it's recommended that you perform these exercises on a Mac computer that is not critical to your daily productivity.

Trademarks

Many of the designations used by manufacturers and sellers to distinguish their products are claimed as trademarks. Where those designations appear in this book, and Peachpit was aware of a trademark claim, the designations appear as requested by the owner of the trademark. All other product names and services identified throughout this book are used in editorial fashion only and for the benefit of such companies with no intention of infringement of the trademark. No such use, or the use of any trade name, is intended to convey endorsement or other affiliation with this book.

ISBN 13: 978-0-321-96354-3
ISBN 10: 0-321-96354-7
9 8 7 6 5 4 3 2 1 Printed and bound in the United States of America

Thanks to my lovely wife, Heather Jagman, for her cheerful support.

— Arek Dreyer

My love and appreciation to my wife, Ronit, and my children, Galee and Noam, for being there for me throughout this project.

— Ben Greisler

Acknowledgments With the memory of Steve Jobs still fresh in our minds, thank you to Tim Cook, Jonathan Ive and everyone at Apple for continually innovating, surprising, and delighting customers.

Thank you to all the people at Apple for getting Mountain Lion and OS X Server out the door.

Thank you to all the people who continue to help their users get the most out of OS X and iOS. Keep learning, and don't expect the pace of change to let up any time soon.

Thanks to the amazingly capable Lisa McClain for gently making sure these materials made it into your hands, and to Scout Festa and Kim Elmore for working their editorial and production magic.

Thank you, also, to the following people. Without your help, this book would be much less than what it is:

Craig Cohen	Nick Johnson	Mike Reed
David Colville	Adam Karneboge	Joel Rennich
Maria Coniglio	Andrina Kelly	Schoun Regan
Gordon Davisson	Andre LaBranche	Fred Reynolds
John DeTroye	Judy Lawrence	Alby Rose
Kevin Dunn	Pam Lefkowitz	John Signa
Josh Durham	Ben Levy	David Starr
Charles Edge	Tip Lovingood	Tyson Vu
Eugene Evon	Jussi-Pekka Mantere	Cindy Waller
Todd Fernandez	Jason Miller	Jeff Walling
Sam Ficke	Nader Nafissi	Simon Wheatley
Patrick Gallagher	Anita Newkirk	Kevin White
Rodrigo Gómez	Tim O'Boyle	Josh Wisenbaker
Ben Harper	Timo Perfitt	Eric Zelenka
Eric Hemmeter	John Poyner	

Contents at a Glance

Providing Network Services

Using Collaborative Services

Table of Contents

Configuring Accounts

Managing Devices with Configuration Profiles

Using Collaborative Services

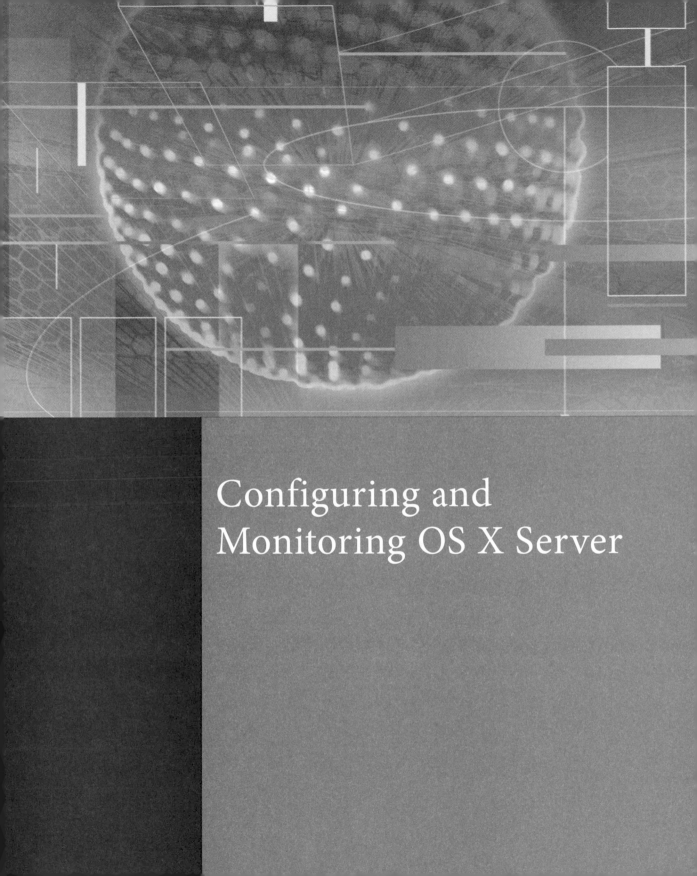

Configuring and Monitoring OS X Server

Lesson 1
About This Guide

This guide serves as a tour of the breadth of functionality of OS X Server and the best methods for effectively supporting users of OS X Server systems. In addition, this guide is the curriculum for the Apple official training course Mavericks 201: OS X Server Essentials 10.9, a three-day, hands-on course that provides an intense and in-depth exploration of how to configure and troubleshoot OS X Server for Mavericks. This course is facilitated by an Apple Certified Trainer and is organized into multiple lessons, each containing instructor presentations followed by related student exercises. In other words, this guide is for both self-paced learners working independently and those participating in an instructor-led course.

The primary goal of this guide is to prepare technical coordinators and entry-level system administrators for the tasks demanded of them by OS X Server; you will learn how to install and configure OS X Server to provide network-based services, such as configuration profile distribution and management, file sharing, authentication, and collaboration services. To help you become truly proficient, this guide covers the theory behind the tools you will use. For example, not only will you learn how to use the Server app—the tool for managing services and accounts—but you will also learn about the ideas behind profile management, how to think about access to and control of resources, and how to set up and distribute profiles to support your environment.

You will learn to develop processes to help you understand and work with the complexity of your system as it grows. Even a single OS X Server computer can grow into a very complicated system, and creating documentation and charts can help you develop processes so that additions and modifications can integrate harmoniously with your existing system.

GOALS

▶ Understand how this guide is organized to facilitate learning

▶ Set up an environment for self-paced exercises

▶ Introduce Apple Authorized Training and Certification

This guide assumes that you have some knowledge of OS X, because OS X Server is an app that you install on top of OS X (Mavericks). Therefore, you should be comfortable with basic navigation, troubleshooting, and networking in OS X. When working through this guide, a basic understanding and knowledge of OS X is preferred, including knowledge of how to troubleshoot the operating system. Refer to *Apple Pro Training Series: OS X Support Essentials 10.9* from Peachpit Press if you need to develop a solid working knowledge of OS X.

NOTE ▶ Unless otherwise specified, all references to OS X refer to version 10.9 or later, and references to OS X Server refer to version 3.0, which at the time of this writing is the most current version available. Due to subsequent upgrades, some screenshots, features, and procedures may be slightly different from those presented on these pages.

Learning Methodology

Each lesson in this guide is designed to give technical coordinators and entry-level system administrators the skills, tools, and knowledge to implement and maintain a network that uses OS X Server by

▶   Providing knowledge of how OS X Server works

▶   Showing how to use configuration tools

▶   Explaining troubleshooting and procedures

The exercises contained within this guide are designed to let you explore and learn the tools necessary to manage OS X Server for Mavericks. They move along in a predictable fashion, starting with the installation and setup of OS X Server and moving to more advanced topics such as performing multiprotocol file sharing, using access control lists, and permitting OS X Server to manage network accounts. It is required that you start from a Mac that is not yet running OS X Server, and that you do not use this server as a production server.

This guide serves as an introduction to OS X Server and is not meant to be a definitive reference. Because OS X and OS X Server contain several open source initiatives, and can be configured at the command line, it is impossible to include all the possibilities and permutations here. First-time users of OS X Server and users of other server operating systems who are migrating to OS X Server have the most to gain from this guide; still, others who are upgrading from previous versions of OS X Server will also find this guide a valuable resource.

OS X Server is by no means difficult to set up and configure, but how you use OS X Server should be planned out in advance. Accordingly, this guide is divided into seven parts:

▶ Part 1, "Configuring and Monitoring OS X Server," covers planning, installation, initial configuration, and monitoring of OS X Server.

▶ Part 2, "Configuring Accounts," defines authentication and authorization, access control, and Open Directory and the vast functionality it can provide.

▶ Part 3, "Managing Devices with Configuration Profiles," covers managing devices with the Profile Manager service.

▶ Part 4, "Sharing Files," introduces the concept of sharing files over multiple protocols and controlling access to files with access control lists.

▶ Part 5, "Implementing Deployment Solutions," teaches you how to effectively use deployment services, NetInstall, the Caching service, and the Software Update service.

▶ Part 6, "Providing Network Services," introduces the network services, including the Time Machine, VPN, DHCP, and Websites services.

▶ Part 7, "Using Collaborative Services," focuses on setting up collaboration services together, starting with Mail, moving through Wiki, Calendar, and Messages, and finishing with the Contacts service.

Lesson Structure

Most lessons in this guide contain a reference section followed by an exercise section (the lesson on the Caching service does not contain an exercise).

NOTE ▶ "Note" resources, like this one, offer important information to help clarify a subject. For example, to avoid confusion you should know that this first lesson is the only one in the guide without a specific exercise section.

The reference sections contain initial explanatory material that teaches essential concepts. The exercise sections augment your understanding of concepts and develop your skills through step-by-step instruction for both self-paced learners and the hands-on portions of an instructor-led course.

TIP ▶ "Tip" resources, like this one, provide helpful hints, tricks, or shortcuts. For example, each lesson begins with an opening page that lists the learning goals and necessary resources for the lesson.

MORE INFO ▶ The "More Info" resources, like this one, provide ancillary information. These resources are merely for your edification and are not considered essential for the coursework.

Throughout this guide you'll find references to Apple Support articles. These articles can be found at the Apple Support website (www.apple.com/support), a free online resource containing the very latest technical information for Apple products. We strongly encourage you to read the suggested articles and search the Apple Support website for answers to any problems you encounter.

We encourage you to explore two additional resources that Apple provides specifically for OS X Server: OS X Server support (https://www.apple.com/support/osxserver/) and OS X Server: Advanced Administration (https://help.apple.com/advancedserveradmin/mac/3.0/).

Lesson files and bonus materials are available online when you redeem the access code supplied with your guide at www.peachpit.com/redeem. Detailed instructions for downloading files are provided later in this guide. The "Lesson Review Questions & Answers" appendix recaps each lesson through a series of questions that reinforce the material you learned in the guide. Try to answer each question yourself before looking at the answer. You can refer to various Apple resources, such as the Apple Support website and OS X Server documentation, as well as the lessons themselves to help you answer these questions. The "Additional Resources" appendix contains a list of relevant Apple Support articles and recommended documents related to the topic of each lesson. The "Updates & Errata" document contains updates and corrections to the guide if any.

Exercise Setup

This guide is written so that both the self-paced learner and the attendee at an Apple Authorized Training Center (AATC) or Apple Authorized Training Center for Education (AATCE) can complete most of the exercises using the same techniques. Those attending Mavericks 201 at an AATC or AATCE will have the appropriate exercise setup provided as part of the training experience. On the other hand, self-paced learners attempting these exercises will have to set up an appropriate environment using their own equipment.

NOTE ▶ Some of these exercises can be disruptive—for example, turning on the DHCP service may prevent devices on the local network from being able to browse Internet—and some exercises, if performed incorrectly, could result in data loss or damage to files. As such, it's recommended that you perform these exercises on an isolated network, using OS X computers and iOS devices that are not critical to your daily productivity. Apple, Inc., and Peachpit Press are not responsible for any data loss or any damage to any equipment that occurs as a direct or indirect result of following the procedures described in this guide.

Mandatory Requirements

Here's what you will need to complete the lessons in the guide:

▶   Two Mac computers, each with OS X Mavericks. One Mac is referred to as your "administrator computer," and the Mac on which you will install OS X Server is referred to as your "server computer" or, more simply, your "server." After you are done using your server computer with this guide, you should erase and reinstall OS X on its startup volume before using it again in a production environment.

   NOTE ▶ OS X Server does not require the use of a built-in Ethernet network interface, except to provide NetInstall services; therefore, if you do not want to perform the NetInstall exercise, you can use Macs that do not have built-in Ethernet interfaces.

▶   An Apple ID that is associated with a verified email address so you can obtain Apple Push Notification service (APNs) certificates for Server app notifications and for the Profile Manager service. You can create an Apple ID at the appropriate time during an exercise if you don't already have an Apple ID.

▶   A valid licensed copy of OS X Server from the Mac App Store (or a valid licensed copy of OS X Server that was sold with a Mac).

▶   An Internet connection is required for obtaining APNs certificates for alerts and for the Profile Manager service.

▶   An isolated network or subnet with an exercise-specific configuration. This can be facilitated with something as simple as a small network Wi-Fi router with multiple Ethernet ports. For example, Apple AirPort Extreme would be a good choice (www.apple.com/airport-extreme/). You can find instructions for the general setup of an exercise network and specific instructions for the configuration of AirPort Extreme at www.apple.com/airport-extreme.

▶ A router (such as AirPort Extreme) to connect the small isolated network to the Internet.

▶ To complete the NetInstall exercises, you need two Ethernet network cables; each Ethernet cable will connect a Mac to the Ethernet switch.

▶ Student Materials demonstration files, which you can download after registering your guide with Peachpit. Instructions for registration and download are included in Exercise 2.1.

Optional Add-Ons

If a specific resource is required for an optional exercise, it will be listed as a prerequisite at the beginning of that exercise. For example:

▶ An iOS device to test access to OS X Server services, including the Profile Manager service.

▶ A Wi-Fi access point (preferably the same AirPort base station) to provide wireless access for iOS devices to your private network.

▶ For Exercise 15.2, "Create NetBoot and NetRestore Images": To make an image of your administrator computer's startup volume, your server computer and your administrator computer must both have the same kind of port—either a FireWire port or a Thunderbolt port—and you must have the appropriate FireWire cable or Thunderbolt cable to connect the two computers.

▶ For Exercise 20.1, "Configure DHCP Service (Optional)": To provide DHCP on an extra isolated network: either an additional built-in Ethernet port on your Mac (for example, if your server computer is a Mac Pro), or a USB to Ethernet adapter, or a Thunderbolt to Gigabit Ethernet Adapter; and an extra Ethernet network switch.

If you lack the equipment necessary to complete a given exercise, you are still encouraged to read the step-by-step instructions and examine the screenshots to understand the procedures demonstrated.

Network Infrastructure

As was previously stated, the exercises require an isolated network. You should replicate the instructor-led classroom environment, which is described in the next sections, as closely as possible, so that you do not need to translate between the exercise instructions and your situation.

IPv4 Addresses

The instructor-led environment provides an IPv4 network with a gateway of 10.0.0.1 and subnet mask of 255.255.255.0; if possible, configure your internal network with the same parameters.

Many consumer-level routers are configured with a gateway of 192.168.1.1 and a subnet mask of 255.255.255.0. You might not be able to change this on your router; in many cases you will be able to replace the "10.0.0" portion of an IPv4 address in the exercise with a value appropriate for your isolated network (for example, 192.168.1.171 instead of 10.0.0.171 for a server address for student 17). You will need to remember to substitute your network prefix throughout the exercises.

DHCP

The classroom DHCP service provides IPv4 addresses in the range of 10.0.0.180 to 10.0.0.254; if possible, configure your internal network's DHCP service with the same parameters.

If DHCP service is available on your isolated network, your Mac computers will use DHCP during the initial setup, but you will then configure them to use manually assigned IPv4 addresses.

If you can configure your isolated network's DHCP service, configure it to use a similar range of IPv4 addresses. If you are unable to change the range of IPv4 addresses, there is a possibility that the DHCP service will assign to a device an IPv4 address already in use by your server computer or your administrator computer. This is another reason to keep your network isolated; do not introduce new devices to it.

Domain Names

The exercises in this guide use the Internet domains pretendco.com and pretendco.private, which are for learning environments only; do not attempt to use these in your production environment.

The exercises are written in such a way that any existing DNS service on your isolated network will be ignored, so that you can experience your server setting up the DNS service for itself.

Advanced Administrators

If you already have advanced server administration skills, you may choose to use different settings, including your organization's Internet domain (instead of pretendco.com), your organization's DNS service, and a different IPv4 address scheme, but be warned that this introduces a high level of variability that the exercises cannot address in the given space, and be prepared to modify the exercises on your own as necessary.

Exercise Order

The exercises in this guide are designed to be relatively independent of each other, so that you can perform them out of order or skip exercises you are not interested in. However, some exercises you must perform in the correct order, and where appropriate, an exercise lists the prerequisites for that exercise.

▶   You must perform all the exercises in Lesson 2, "Installing OS X Server," to install OS X Server and configure your administrator computer before performing any other exercises.

▶   You must perform Exercise 9.1, "Configure Your Server as an Open Directory Master," and Exercise 10.1, "Create and Import Network Accounts," to create users that you will use in later exercises; otherwise, if the prerequisites section for an exercise lists the user accounts used in the lesson, you can simply create those user (and possibly group) accounts with the Server app's Users pane.

▶   You must create additional DNS records in Lesson 3, "Providing DNS," before performing the exercises in Lesson 21, "Hosting Websites."

Apple Training and Certification

The Apple Training and Certification program is designed to keep you at the forefront of Apple technology. Certification creates a benchmark to demonstrate your proficiency in specific Apple technologies and gives you a competitive edge in today's evolving job market.

Certification exams are delivered at Apple Authorized Training Centers around the world.

Reading this guide or attending the Mavericks 201 class will help prepare you to pass the OS X Server Essentials 10.9 exam and become an Apple Certified Technical Coordinator. Passing both this exam and the OS X Support Essentials 10.9 exam earns Apple Certified

Technical Coordinator 10.9 (ACTC) certification. This is the second level of the Apple certification program for Mac professionals, which includes:

▶ Apple Certified Support Professional (ACSP) certification verifies an understanding of OS X core functionality and an ability to configure key services, perform basic troubleshooting, and support multiple users with essential OS X capabilities. ACSP certification is designed for the help desk professional, technical coordinator, or power user who supports OS X users, manages networks, or provides technical support for the Mac. Students earn ACSP certification by passing the OS X Support Essentials 10.9 Exam. Visit training.apple.com/certification/osx to review the OS X Support Essentials Exam Prep Guide. To prepare for this exam, attend the Mavericks 101 class or read *Apple Pro Training Series: OS X Support Essentials 10.9*.

▶ Apple Certified Technical Coordinator (ACTC) certification verifies a foundation in OS X and OS X Server core functionality and an ability to configure key services and perform basic troubleshooting. ACTC certification is intended for OS X technical coordinators and entry-level system administrators who maintain small-to-medium networks of computers using OS X Server. Students earn ACTC certification by passing the OS X Support Essentials 10.9 Exam and OS X Server Essentials 10.9 Exam. Visit training.apple.com/certification/osx to review the OS X Server Essentials Exam Prep Guide.

MORE INFO ▶ To read OS X technical white papers and learn more about all Apple certifications, visit training.apple.com.

NOTE ▶ Although all the questions in the OS X Server Essentials 10.9 Exam are based on material in this guide, nothing can substitute for time spent learning the technology. After you read the guide or take the class, spend time increasing your familiarity with OS X Server on your own to ensure your success on the certification exam.

Lesson 2
Installing OS X Server

OS X Server for Mavericks helps your users collaborate, communicate, share information, and access the resources they need to get their work done, whether in business or education.

OS X Server is an app that runs on a Mac running Mavericks; if your Mac can run Mavericks, it can run OS X Server.

Although you could dive right in and install and configure OS X Server, it's recommended that you divide working with OS X Server into four phases:

GOALS

▶ Understand the requirements for OS X Server

▶ Perform the initial installation and configuration of OS X Server

1. Planning and installation—Plan how the server will be set up, verify and configure the hardware, and install the OS X Server software; this is covered in this lesson.

2. Configuration—Use the Server app to configure your server; all the lessons in this guide use the Server app to configure your server.

3. Monitoring—Use the Server app to monitor the status of your server, and optionally to specify an email address to receive notifications of specific alerts, which is covered in Lesson 6, "Using Status and Notifications."

4. Ongoing maintenance—Use the Server app to perform ongoing server and account maintenance and monitoring.

This lesson begins with planning and continues into the initial installation and configuration of OS X Server.

Reference 2.1
Evaluating OS X Server Requirements

Before you install the software, take the time to evaluate the server needs of your organization and the OS X Server hardware requirements.

Understanding Minimum Hardware Requirements

You can install the OS X Server application on any Mac computer running OS X Mavericks, with at least 2 GB of RAM and 10 GB of available disk space.

In order to run Mavericks, your Mac must be one of the following models or later:

▶   iMac (Mid 2007 or later)

▶   MacBook (13-inch Aluminum, Late 2008; 13-inch, Early 2009 or later)

▶   MacBook Pro (13-inch, Mid-2009 or later; 15-inch or 17-inch, Mid/Late 2007 or later)

▶   MacBook Air (Late 2008 or later)

▶   Mac mini (Early 2009 or later)

▶   Mac Pro (Early 2008 or later)

▶   Xserve (Early 2009)

Some features of OS X Server require an Apple ID, and some features require a compatible Internet service provider.

Verifying System Requirements

Before you install OS X Server, confirm that your system meets the hardware requirements. You can find this information on the label attached to the box of every Mac sold, or you can find it with the About This Mac and System Information applications.

To check if a Mac can run Mavericks, you can start with the About This Mac application. The next few figures are taken from a Mac running a previous version of OS X, and they walk you through the process of determining whether this Mac can run OS X Server for Mavericks.

In the About This Mac window, click More Info to move on to the System Information application, which contains all the information you need in a single application. The Overview pane displays your Mac system's model and memory.

The Storage pane displays information about available storage.

Additional Hardware Considerations

Typical considerations when choosing server systems include network and system performance, disk space and capacity, and RAM. You may find that using multiple servers, running a few services on each server, results in better performance than running all the services on a single server.

Network

Be sure to consider the speed of the network interface when making a server hardware decision. Many Apple products support Gigabit Ethernet; if your Mac ships with a built-in Ethernet port, that port supports Gigabit Ethernet. If your Mac is equipped with a Thunderbolt port, you can use the Apple Thunderbolt to Gigabit Ethernet Adapter.

You can combine two Ethernet interfaces to act as one, to aggregate network throughput for services such as File Sharing.

For learning and testing scenarios only, you could consider using Wi-Fi as your server's primary network connection. This opens the possibility of using a MacBook Air, which does not have a built-in Ethernet port. In this instance, you could use Wi-Fi, the Apple USB Ethernet adapter for MacBook Air (which provides 10/100 Base-T Ethernet), or the Thunderbolt to Gigabit Ethernet Adapter. These options are adequate for the purposes of learning and testing.

> **NOTE ▸** Ethernet is required to provide the Caching service and the NetInstall service. See Lesson 15, "Leveraging NetInstall," and Lesson 16, "Caching Content from Apple," for more information.

Disk

Be sure you have enough disk space to hold the data for the services you plan to offer. If the services you plan to offer are disk intensive—for example, the Mail service with a high volume of mail—consider using a faster physical disk or even an external disk system. Although you can change the location where your server stores the service data for many of its services, as you will learn in Lesson 4, "Exploring the Server App," it is recommended to specify a location *before* populating your server with data, because moving the service data location stops services, then moves the data, before starting services again. Your server's services are not available during this time, and the amount of data to move could impact the amount of time the process takes.

RAM

In general, more RAM results in better system performance, but exactly how much RAM is ideal for your situation is impossible for this guide to prescribe.

Availability

In order to help ensure that OS X Server stays up and running, you can enable the Energy Saver system preference setting labeled "Start up automatically after a power failure" (not available on all Macs). It is recommended that you use an uninterruptible power supply (UPS) for your server, including any external volumes, to keep your server up and running in the case of a brief power outage.

> **NOTE ▶** If you use an external volume, do not select the checkbox for "Start up automatically after a power failure," because you cannot guarantee that an external volume will be powered up correctly after a power failure.

Reference 2.2
Preparing to Install OS X Server

> **NOTE ▶** This reference section describes the process of installing OS X Server in a general way; the exercises offer detailed step-by-step instructions, so do not perform any actions until you reach the exercises, which are at the end of this lesson.

It is possible to purchase a Mac with OS X Mavericks and OS X Server preinstalled. However, you may find yourself upgrading an existing Mac. Any Mac capable of running Mavericks can run OS X Server for Mavericks. As detailed in Reference 2.4, "Upgrading or Migrating to OS X Server," the Mac App Store will not allow you to purchase OS X Server unless you are running OS X Mavericks.

Formatting/Partitioning Disks

After you confirm that your computer meets the hardware requirements, you can simply install Mavericks on your existing startup disk, or you can install Mavericks on another disk. You can also begin making decisions surrounding the devices and subsequent formatting of those devices prior to actually installing the software.

Disk Utility is located in the Utilities folder, which is in the Applications folder. Using this utility, you can divide a disk into one or more partitions. Doing so allows you to first choose a partition scheme for your disk. Your choices are as follows:

▶   GUID Partition Table—Used to start up Intel-based Mac computers

▶   Apple Partition Map—Used to start up PowerPC-based Mac computers

▶   Master Boot Record—Used to start up DOS and Windows-based computers

> **NOTE** ▶ In order to install OS X Server on a volume, that volume's disk must be formatted with the GUID Partition Table. You can examine a disk's partition scheme with the Disk Utility application, which lists this information as the Partition Map Scheme, and with the System Information application, which lists this information as Partition Map Type.

Once you choose a partition scheme, you can divide your disk into as many as 16 logical disks, each with its own format. Each logical disk is called a partition. Once you format a partition, it contains a volume. See *Apple Pro Training Series: OS X Support Essentials 10.9* for further information about the available volume formats.

In order to install OS X Server on a volume, it must have one of the two following journaled formats:

▶   Mac OS X Extended (Journaled)

▶   Mac OS X Extended (Case-Sensitive/Journaled)

Unless you have a compelling reason to use Case-Sensitive/Journaled format, use Mac OS X Extended (Journaled).

You can use the other, nonjournaled formats for data partitions, but journaling eliminates the need for a lengthy disk check on a volume after a power outage or other failure.

By using separate partitions, you can segregate your data from the operating system. You may decide to store user data on a separate volume. Having the operating system on its own volume conserves space by keeping user files and data from filling up the startup volume. In case you need to perform a clean install of OS X and OS X Server at a later time, you can erase the entire startup volume and install the operating system without touching the data on the other volumes.

NOTE ▶ OS X Server stores data for many of its services in /Library/Server on the startup volume by default, but as you will see later in this lesson, you can use the Server app to change the service data location. In any event, make sure you have a good backup of your server before erasing your server startup volume.

To create multiple partitions on a single disk, simply select your disk, choose the number of partitions from the Partition Layout menu, and choose the following for each partition:

▶ Name of partition—Using lowercase alphanumeric characters and removing spaces in volume names may help reduce troubleshooting of share points later down the road.

▶ Format of partition—See the previous list for various acceptable OS X Server partition formats.

▶ Size of partition—Again, OS X Server requires at least 10 GB of available disk space for installation.

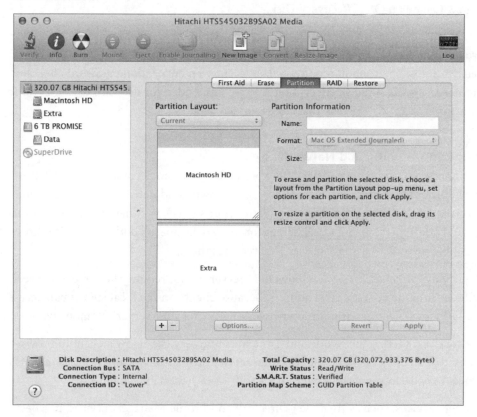

Before you click Apply, remember: *All previous data on the disk may be erased!*

Having multiple partitions does not increase speed, but installing multiple disks may increase server performance. Installing the operating system on one disk and installing additional disks to store user data can reduce connection times to the operating system and to data. If you add the second disk on a separate bus, the server can read and write to each of those buses independently.

RAID (Redundant Array of Independent Disks)

In order to provide increased availability or performance, it is possible to install OS X on a RAID volume before installing OS X Server. However, because an OS X Recovery system partition cannot exist on a RAID volume, you may want to create an external OS X Recovery system from which you can start up in order to access a variety of administration and troubleshooting utilities. For further information, you may wish to read *Apple Pro Training Series: OS X Support Essentials* Lesson 4, "OS X Recovery," particularly Exercise 4.2, "Create an OS X Recovery Disk."

FileVault 2 Full Disk Encryption

Because full disk encryption requires a user to enter an encryption password after the computer starts up, full disk encryption isn't recommended for use with OS X Server for the startup disk or for any disk that stores service data.

Configuring Naming and Networking

Traditionally, servers require a static network address and an accompanying DNS host name in order for clients to access services at a known good network address. Previous versions of OS X Server required you to verify your server's host name during its initial setup and configuration, but OS X Server for Mavericks doesn't bother you with those details unless you're starting a service that requires them.

Today, many of the services offered by OS X Server do not require the server to have a specific host name or static IPv4 address, because clients on the local subnet can access those services via zero-configuration networking (using your server's Bonjour name).

Some services, such as the Xcode and Time Machine services, allow a client to browse for the service; other services, like the Caching service, just automatically work for clients on the local network, even if the server's IPv4 address or host name changes.

For other services, such as the Open Directory and Profile Manager services, it is best practice to configure the server with a static IPv4 address and an accompanying DNS host name in order to ensure that clients can consistently access the service.

For example, if you intend to use OS X Server to provide only the File Sharing and Wiki services on the local network and have your clients access these services via your server's Bonjour name, you don't need to bother switching the server from DHCP to a static IPv4 address.

Nevertheless, it's still a best practice to manually assign your server a static IPv4 address, rather than to rely on a DHCP service to provide a dynamically assigned IPv4 address.

TIP▶ To configure the DNS server(s) that your Mac uses, in the Network system preferences, click Advanced and then click the DNS tab.

MORE INFO ▶ OS X automatically appends the contents of the Search Domains field to the DNS names you enter in apps like Safari.

Clients can access your server's services directly via IPv4 and IPv6 address or, more commonly, via various names, including:

▶   Computer Name

▶   Local Hostname

▶   Host Name

The following three sections explain each in detail.

Understanding the Computer Name

The *computer name* is used by clients on your server's local subnet when browsing using the following:

▶   Finder sidebar to access File Sharing and Screen Sharing services on the server

▶   Apple Remote Desktop (ARD)

▶   AirDrop

▶   Xcode preferences to add a new server for the Xcode service

The computer name can contain spaces.

If your server offers file- or screen-sharing services, Mac users in the same broadcast domain (usually a subnet) will see your server's computer name in the Shared section of the Finder sidebar, as in the following example.

The computer name also appears when users modify their Xcode preferences and add a new Xcode server.

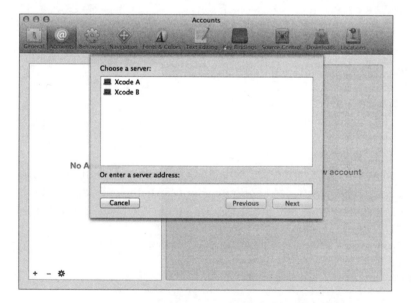

Understanding the Local Hostname

Your server uses Bonjour to advertise its services on its local subnet. The local hostname is a name that ends in .local and follows the rules for DNS names. OS X automatically removes any special characters and replaces any space character with a dash in the local hostname.

MORE INFO ▶ See www.apple.com/support/bonjour for more information about Bonjour zero-configuration networking.

Devices that use Bonjour (including PCs, Macs, and iOS devices) on the same subnet as your server can access services using your server's local hostname. The following figure is an example of using a local hostname to access a local Wiki service.

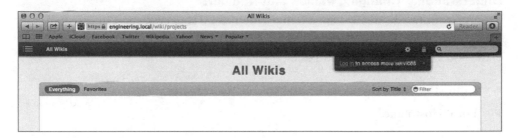

Understanding the Host Name

The *host name*, or the primary DNS host name, is a unique name for your server, historically referred to as the fully qualified domain name, or FQDN. Some services on OS X Server require a working FQDN or will work better if one is available. Computers and devices can access services on your server by using your server's DNS host name, even if they are not on the same local subnet.

If there is a DNS record for your server Mac's primary IPv4 address, OS X automatically uses DNS records to set your Mac's host name. Otherwise, OS X automatically uses your Mac's computer name to set a Bonjour-based host name, like local-admins-macbook-pro.local.

When you first configure OS X Server, it automatically creates a self-signed SSL certificate using your Mac's host name, even if the host name is something like local-admins-macbook-pro.local. so it's best practice to configure your Mac with your desired host name before initially installing and configuring the Server app. You'll learn more about certificates in Lesson 5, "Configuring SSL Certificates."

MORE INFO ▶ If you use Change Host Name Assistant, covered in the next section, to change your host name, the Server app automatically creates a new self-signed SSL certificate with your new host name.

If your environment's infrastructure already has a DNS service that provides DNS records for devices on your internal network, it's best to keep using that DNS service; create DNS records for your server using the appropriate tools for the existing DNS service.

If you don't have a DNS service already running for devices on your internal network, and you don't have DNS records available at the time you install OS X Server, that's OK, because if there are no appropriate DNS records available, your server can provide them, as you'll learn in the following section.

Understanding Changing Names and Numbers

After your initial installation and configuration of OS X Server, you can use the Server app to change the following attributes quickly (by clicking Edit next to the Computer Name attribute in the Overview pane):

▶ Computer Name

▶ Local Hostname

NOTE ▶ The Sharing pane of System Preferences also allows you to change the computer name and the local hostname.

You can also use the Server app to start Change Host Name Assistant (by clicking Edit next to the Host Name in the Overview pane) to change the following attributes:

▶ Computer Name

▶ Host Name

▶ Network Address

Connecting to your Server

Enter a computer name and host name.

Computer Name: server17

The name that users will see in Finder or when connecting on the local network.

Host Name: server17.pretendco.com

Enter the domain name you registered for this server, such as "server.example.com".

Network Address: 10.0.0.171 on Wi-Fi   Edit...

(?)

Back   Finish

When you use Change Host Name Assistant, if the DNS service you specify in the DNS Server field of the Network preferences does not supply forward and reverse DNS records for the address you specify in the IP Address field, the Server app asks if you'd like to start the DNS service. If you answer affirmatively, the Server app performs the following configuration steps:

▶ Configures the DNS service on your server computer to provide a forward DNS record for your primary DNS name and a reverse DNS record for its primary IPv4 address.

▶ Starts the DNS service.

▶ Configures your server computer's primary network interface to use its own DNS service (specifically, 127.0.0.1, which is the loopback address that always points back to the computer itself) as the primary DNS service, in addition to the DNS service that was previously specified.

▶ If appropriate, removes the old default self-signed SSL certificate and creates a new one with the new host name.

This ensures that your server will always be able to resolve its host name to its IPv4 address, and its IPv4 address to its host name.

However, other computers and devices will not necessarily use these DNS records, and therefore will not be able to access services on your server by its host name unless you configure them to use your server's DNS service. See Lesson 3, "Providing DNS," for more information about DNS.

Downloading OS X Server

If you purchased a computer with OS X Server preinstalled, the Server app is already in your Applications folder. Otherwise, download OS X Server from the Mac App Store. The Mac App Store will not allow you to purchase OS X Server unless you are running OS X Mavericks.

NOTE ▶ It's called OS X Server in the Mac App Store, and it's called Server in your Applications folder (once it finishes downloading from the Mac App Store). This guide refers to it as the "Server app."

NOTE ▶ If you purchased a computer with OS X Server preinstalled, you can use the Server app on another Mac to administer your server, but you must copy the Server app from your server to the other Mac. You will need to repeat this step whenever you update the Server app on your server. See Apple Support article HT4814, "How to administer OS X Server remotely using Server app" for more information.

Reference 2.3
Installing OS X Server

Once you have configured OS X on your server computer and have the Server app installed on your server computer, you can start installing OS X Server.

When you configure OS X Server, be sure to have an active network connection, even if it is only to a network switch that doesn't have anything else connected to it.

Open the Server app; if it isn't already in the Dock, you can click Launchpad in the Dock and then click Server, or open the Server app from your Applications folder, or you could even open it with a Spotlight search. From the introductory window, when you click Continue, you start the process of installing and configuring OS X Server.

> **NOTE ▶** If you want to use the Server app to manage another server that has already been installed and configured (rather than installing and configuring OS X Server on this Mac), instead of clicking Continue click Other Mac.

As soon as you click Continue, you have to agree to the terms of the software license agreement. As with all software, carefully read the software license agreement.

Once you click Agree, you need to provide local administrator credentials. After your credentials have been confirmed, the Server app configures itself. When the process is complete, the Server app displays the Overview pane.

NOTE ▶ The previous version of OS X Server (for Mountain Lion) prompts you to confirm and possibly change the computer name and host name during its initial configuration. In comparison, the initial configuration of OS X Server for Mavericks is much more streamlined.

Reference 2.4
Upgrading or Migrating to OS X Server

If you have an existing Mac with Snow Leopard Server, Lion Server, or OS X Server for Mountain Lion, and your computer meets the hardware requirements for OS X Mavericks, you can *upgrade* to OS X Server for Mavericks. Otherwise, you can *migrate* from your old server to OS X Server for Mavericks on a Mac that meets the hardware requirements for Mavericks by first installing OS X Mavericks, then using OS X Setup Assistant or Migration Assistant, and then installing OS X Server.

To upgrade to OS X Server for Mavericks, first you need to upgrade to Mavericks, and then you can install OS X Server. Remember that it is always best practice to back up any existing setup prior to running the upgrade so you can restore should anything go wrong.

Use the following steps:

1   Make sure your Mac can run Mavericks.

2   Make sure you have OS X Server for Mountain Lion, Lion Server, or the latest version of Snow Leopard Server. Use Software Update to update to the latest version of the appropriate software.

3   Download OS X Mavericks from the Mac App Store.

4   Open Install Mac OS X Mavericks to perform the upgrade to OS X Mavericks.

5   Once running Mavericks, download OS X Server from the Mac App Store.

6   Open Server from Launchpad or the Applications folder to install OS X Server.

NOTE ▶ Upgrading the server software should be a planned event. Always run updates on a test system before rolling out into production. In some cases, third-party solutions have not continued to operate smoothly with the new software. You should preflight the update in isolation first and roll out the update once you have tested your implementation.

MORE INFO ▶ See Apple Support articles HT5381, "OS X Server: Upgrade and migration from Lion Server or Snow Leopard Servers" and HT5996, "OS X Server: Upgrade and migration from Mountain Lion" for detailed instructions.

Reference 2.5
Updating OS X Server

When an update for OS X Server becomes available, you can download and install it using the Mac App Store.

You may notice that the App Store icon in the Dock displays a badge with a number indicating the number of updates available.

To install the update, open the App Store, click Updates in the toolbar, and then click Update for the OS X Server update.

If you haven't already signed in to the Mac App Store, you will be prompted to do so.

Even though you see a message that services have been stopped, you'll find that all your services are still running.

To complete the update of OS X Server, open the Server app and, at the update pane, click Continue and provide local administrator credentials.

Wait while your services are updated.

Reference 2.6
Troubleshooting

One common problem found in server installations is incompatibility with third-party hardware and software configurations. Isolate the changes to your system when you run into problems, and keep the variables to a minimum.

Inspecting Logs

Mavericks and OS X Server log events to various log files. You can view logs in the Console application or select Logs in the sidebar of the Server app. In the following figure, the Console app displays the contents of system.log.

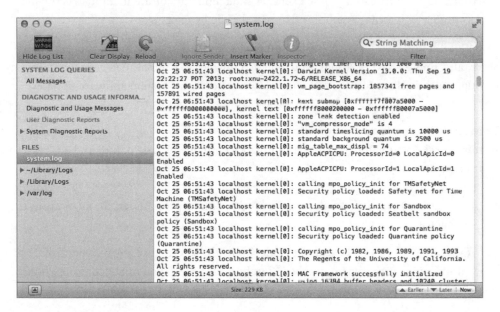

Throughout this guide, you will view various logs with the Console application or the Logs pane of the Server app.

Exercise 2.1
Configure OS X Before Installing OS X Server on Your Server Computer

▶ **Prerequisite**

 ▶ You must have a Mac that is running OS X Mavericks, that has never had OS X Server installed on its startup volume, and that is qualified to run OS X Server.

In this exercise, you will configure your server computer in preparation for installing OS X Server on it.

You'll use one of two options to configure a local administrator account, depending on whether you are performing these exercises independently or are in an instructor-led environment with a Mac computer that has already been set up.

In both situations, you'll use System Preferences to configure Network, Sharing, App Store, and Energy Saver settings. You will also download student materials that you'll use throughout this class. Finally, you will apply any necessary system software updates.

Establish Your Student Number

In this exercise you will use a student number to provide unique names and addresses for your computers.

1   If you are in an instructor-led environment, obtain your student number from the instructor.

If you are performing the exercises independently, you can use any number from 1 to 17, but this guide uses student number 17 in its examples, so you might consider choosing 17 as your student number.

Configure OS X

It is most convenient to start out with a fresh installation of OS X. If your Mac is at the Welcome pane when you turn it on, you can use the Option 1 section that follows. If you need to use an existing OS X system, you should skip to Option 2 so your Mac will be configured as expected for rest of the exercises.

Option 1: Configure OS X on Your Server Computer with Setup Assistant

This option is necessary if your server computer has not already been set up, which is the situation in an instructor-led environment. If you are using a Mac with existing accounts, perform Option 2, "Configure an Existing OS X System for Your Server Computer," instead.

Ensure that you have Mavericks installed on your server computer. If it isn't already installed, install it now using the Mac App Store, the Recovery HD, or a method specified by your instructor, and then continue when you reach the Welcome pane.

In this section, you'll step through OS X Setup Assistant for initial system configuration of your server computer.

1   Ensure that your computer is connected to a valid network connection.

2   If necessary, turn on the Mac that will run OS X Server.

3   In the Welcome pane, select the appropriate region and click Continue.

4   Select the appropriate keyboard layout and click Continue.

    Setup Assistant will evaluate your network environment and try to determine if you are connected to the Internet. This can take a few moments.

5   If asked to Select Your Wi-Fi Network or "How Do You Connect to the Internet," this indicates that either there is no active Ethernet connection or there is no connection to the Internet.

    If you are performing the exercises in an instructor-led environment, ask your instructor how you should configure your computer; it is possible that the classroom DHCP service is not enabled, or that your server computer is not connected to the classroom network.

    If you are performing the exercises independently and you plan to use Wi-Fi as your primary network connection, select an appropriate Wi-Fi network and click Continue. Keep in mind that in order to perform the NetInstall exercises, both your server and your administrator computer need an Ethernet connection.

6   When asked about transferring information to this Mac, select "Don't transfer any information now" and click Continue.

7   At the Sign in with Your Apple ID pane, select "Don't sign in," click Continue, and then click Skip to confirm that you want to skip signing in with an Apple ID. Note that if you do provide Apple ID credentials, some figures may look slightly different, and there may be extra steps. In an instructor-led environment, it is recommended that you not enter an Apple ID at this time.

8   In the Terms and Conditions pane, when you have finished reading, click Agree.

9   In the dialog to confirm that you have read and agree to the OS X Software License Agreement, click Agree.

Create your local administrator account.

NOTE ▶ It is important that you create this account as specified here. If you do not, future exercises may not work as written. Highlighted text is used throughout this guide to indicate text that you should enter exactly as shown.

1   In the Create Your Computer Account pane, enter the following information:

▶ Full Name: Local Admin

▶ Account Name: ladmin

▶ Password: ladminpw

▶ (verify field): ladminpw

▶ Hint: Leave blank.

▶ Leave the checkbox "Require password to unlock screen" selected.

▶ Deselect the checkbox "Set time zone based on current location."

▶ Deselect the checkbox "Send Diagnostics & Usage data to Apple."

If you are performing the exercises independently, and if your server is accessible from the Internet, you can select a more secure password for the Local Admin account. Be sure to remember the password you have chosen, as you will need to reenter it periodically as you use this computer.

If you are performing the exercises independently, you may provide a password hint if you want to.

If you entered your Apple ID, you can select or deselect the checkbox "Allow my Apple ID to reset this user's password"; it does not have a major effect on the exercises.

NOTE ▶ In a production environment, you should always use a strong password.

2   Click Continue to create the local administrator account.

3   If you see the Select Time Zone pane, click your time zone in the map, or choose the nearest location in the Closest City pop-up menu, and then click Continue.

4   At the Register Your Mac pane, select "Don't register," then click Continue; you won't be entering registration information at this time.

5   When asked if you are sure you don't want to register, click Skip.

6   If you are prompted to install software updates, click Not Now.

Please skip the Option 2 section, and continue at the section "Confirm Your Computer Is Qualified to Run OS X Server."

Option 2: Configure an Existing OS X System for Your Server Computer

This option is designed only for those who are performing the exercises independently and who have a computer that is already set up with an existing administrator account.

> **NOTE ▶** You may not use a Mac whose startup volume has already had OS X Server installed.

If your computer has not been set up (that is, if the initial administrator account has not been created), perform Option 1, "Configure OS X on Your Server Computer with Setup Assistant," instead.

Create a new administrator account in System Preferences.

1   If necessary, log in with your existing administrator account.

2   From the Apple menu, choose System Preferences.

3   In System Preferences, click Users & Groups.

4   In the lower-left corner, click the lock icon.

5   In the dialog that appears, enter the password for your existing administrator account and click Unlock.

6   Click the Add (+) button under the user list.

7   In the dialog that appears, enter the following information:

> **NOTE ▶** It is important that you create this account as specified here. If you do not, future exercises may not work as written. If you already have an account named Local Admin or ladmin, you will have to use a different name here and then remember to use your substitute name throughout the rest of the exercises. Highlighted text is used throughout this guide to indicate text that you should enter exactly as shown.

> ▶ New Account: choose Administrator
> ▶ Full Name: Local Admin
> ▶ Account Name: ladmin

If your server is not accessible from the Internet, enter ladminpw in the Password and Verify fields.

If you are performing the exercises independently, you can select a more secure password for the Local Admin account. Be sure to remember the password you have chosen, as you will need to reenter it periodically as you use this computer.

You may provide a password hint if you want to.

If you entered your Apple ID, you can select or deselect the checkbox "Allow my Apple ID to reset this user's password"; it does not have a major effect on the exercises.

NOTE ▶ In a production environment, you should always use a strong password.

8   Click Create User.

9   At the bottom of the user list, click Login Options.

10 If an account is selected for Automatic Login, use the pop-up menu to switch it to Off.

11 Close System Preferences and log out.

12 At the login screen, select the Local Admin account and enter its password (ladminpw, or whatever you specified earlier).

13 Press Return to log in.

This is the end of Option 2; everyone should continue with the next section.

Confirm Your Computer Is Qualified to Run OS X Server

Before you go to the trouble of installing OS X Server, make sure your computer meets the technical requirements to run OS X Server. The first requirement is a Mac computer running Mavericks. The other two requirements are 2 GB of memory and 10 GB of available disk space.

1   From the Apple menu, choose About This Mac.

2   Confirm that you have at least 2 GB of memory.

3   If your Mac computer has more than one volume, About This Mac displays the name of your startup disk. Make a note of the name of your startup disk.

4   Click More Info.

5   Click the Storage tab.

6   For your Startup Disk, confirm that you have at least 10 GB free disk space.

7   If your Mac computer has only one volume, make a note of its name—it is the name of your startup volume.

8   Press Command-Q to quit System Information.

Change Your Startup Volume Name

In the last section, you made a note of your startup volume name. Before you install OS X Server, confirm that your server computer's startup volume is what you would like it to be. You can change that name now, because you should avoid changing your startup volume name after you install OS X Server. If you need to change your server computer's startup volume name after you install OS X Server, you should restart your server after making the change.

1   In the Finder, choose Go > Computer.

   The Finder window displays the volumes.

2   Select your startup volume.

3   Press Return to edit the name.

4   Enter Server for the new startup volume name.

5   Press Return to save the name change.

6   Press Command-W to close the Finder window.

Set the Computer Name and Turn On Remote Management

In an environment with more than one student, because every student has entered the same account name information and because OS X uses the account name and computer model name as the basis for the initial computer name and local hostname, all student computers may have the same computer name. To distinguish your computer on the network, you need to set a unique computer name. Additionally, OS X won't allow duplicate local hostnames on the same subnet, so you may see an alert message indicating that your local hostname has been incremented from Local-Admins-*computer model*.local to Local-Admins-*computer model-n*.local, where *n* is a semirandom number (not your student number).

You will specify a computer name associated with your student number.

You will also enable Remote Management, which will allow the instructor to observe your computer, control your keyboard and mouse, gather information, copy items to your computer, and otherwise help you if necessary.

> **NOTE ▶** Even though you know administrator credentials for other students' computers and have the technical ability to remotely control their computers, please do not use that ability to interfere with their classroom experience.

1 In your Dock, open System Preferences.

2 Open Sharing.

3 Set the Computer Name to servern, replacing *n* with your student number.

   For example, if your student number is 17, the computer name should be server17, all lowercase and no spaces.

4 Press Return.

   Notice that the name listed under the Computer Name field, which is the Local Hostname, updates to match your new computer name.

Enable your instructor (and yourself) to remotely manage your server computer from another Mac computer using Apple Remote Desktop or Screen Sharing.

5 Select the Remote Management checkbox.

6 In the dialog that appears, leave all the checkboxes deselected and click OK for now, as this controls access for all local users, and you will configure access for one user only next.

7 In "Allow Access for," select "Only these users."

8 Click the Add (+) button, select Local Admin, and click Select.

9   In the dialog that appears, hold down the Option key while selecting the Observe checkbox, which results in automatically selecting all the checkboxes, as shown in the following figure.

10 Click OK.

11 Click Show All to return to the main System Preferences pane.

Set Energy Saver Preferences

Prevent your server computer from going to sleep while you use it for the exercises. You can set the display sleep to whatever setting you prefer.

1   In System Preferences, open Energy Saver.

2   If you have a portable computer, you have two tabs: Battery and Power Adapter. Click Power Adapter to configure the settings while using the power adapter.

3   Set the computer to never sleep by dragging the "Computer sleep" slider to the far right.

    This prevents the computer from going to sleep while installing software updates.

4   When the "Your computer may use more energy with these settings" message appears, click OK.

5   Drag the "Display sleep" slider to a value of your choice. You can leave the other settings at their defaults.

6 Select the "Start up automatically after a power failure" checkbox if it is available.

7 Click Show All to return to the main System Preferences pane.

Configure App Store Software Update

If you are performing the exercises in an instructor-led environment, you should disable the App Store from automatically checking for updates, so that you do not unnecessarily use bandwidth.

1 In System Preferences, click App Store.

2 Deselect the "Automatically check for updates" option.

3 If necessary, deselect the "Automatically downloads apps purchased on other Macs" option.

4 Click Show All to return to the main System Preferences pane.

Configure Network Interfaces

It is best practice to configure your network settings before you initially install and configure OS X Server. To get started now, you will use your environment's DNS service, but keep in mind that during the course of these exercises, you will eventually use Change Host Name Assistant to configure, turn on, and use your server's DNS service.

> NOTE ▶ The exercises are written for only one network interface to be active, but if you decide to use multiple network interfaces, this will not significantly impact your ability to complete the exercises.

1 In System Preferences, click Network.

2 In the instructor-led environment, configure your Mac computer's built-in Ethernet port to be the only active network service.

> NOTE ▶ You may leave your Wi-Fi network interface enabled, but not joined to any network, in order to use AirDrop.

If you are performing the exercises independently, you may leave additional interfaces active, but be aware that this may cause differences between the way the exercises describe the windows and what you actually see.

In the list of network interfaces, select each network interface you will not use in the exercise (which should be all interfaces except one Ethernet port), click the Action (gear icon) pop-up menu, and choose Make Service Inactive.

3   If you will use multiple network interfaces, click the Action (gear icon) pop-up menu, choose Set Service Order, drag services to an appropriate order so that your primary interface is at the top of the list, and click OK.

4   Select the active Ethernet interface.

5   In the Configure IPv4 pop-up menu, choose Manually.

6   In the instructor-led environment, enter the following information to manually configure the Ethernet interface (IPv4) for the classroom environment:

   ▶   IP Address: 10.0.0.n1 (where n is your student number; for example, student1 uses 10.0.0.11, student 6 uses 10.0.0.61, and student 15 uses 10.0.0.151.)

   ▶   Subnet Mask: 255.255.255.0

   ▶   Router: 10.0.0.1

   If you are performing the exercises independently and choose to use different network settings, see the "Exercise Setup" section in Lesson 1.

7   Click Advanced, and then click the DNS tab.

8   Even though you just switched from DHCP to Manual, you did not yet apply the change, so values assigned by DHCP are listed, but they are dimmed. Values manually assigned are not dimmed.

   If there are any values in the DNS Servers field that are not dimmed, select each entry that is not dimmed, then click Delete (–) to delete the entry, until there are no non-dimmed values listed.

9   In the instructor-led environment, under the DNS Servers field, click Add (+) and enter 10.0.0.1.

   If you are performing the exercises independently, under the DNS Servers field, click Add (+) and enter the value or values appropriate for your environment.

10 In the Search Domains field, values assigned by DHCP are listed, but they are dimmed. Values manually assigned are not dimmed.

If there are any values in the Search Domains field that are not dimmed, select each entry that is not dimmed, then click Delete (–) to delete the entry, until there are no non-dimmed values listed.

11 Under the Search Domains field, click Add (+) and enter pretendco.com.

If you are performing the exercises independently, enter a value appropriate for your environment.

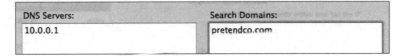

12 Click OK to save the change and return to the list of network interfaces.

13 Review the settings, and then click Apply to accept the network configuration.

14 Quit System Preferences.

Update Software

Run Software Update. If a local Caching service is available, your Mac will automatically use it.

1   From the Apple menu, choose Software Update.

2   Click Update next to any update for OS X, if there are any listed.

   You do not need updated versions of other software, such as iTunes, in order to use the exercises in this guide, but you are free to update any items you wish to update.

Download Student Materials

There are some files that are necessary for the completion of some of the exercises. If you are in an instructor-led environment, you can use the Option 1 section that follows. Otherwise, you should skip to Option 2.

Option 1: Download Student Materials in the Instructor-Led Environment

If you are performing the exercises independently, skip to Option 2, "Download Student Materials for the Independent Reader."

If you are in an instructor-led environment, you will connect to the classroom server and download the student materials used for the course. To copy the files, you'll drag the folder to your Documents folder.

1   In the Finder, choose File > New Finder Window (or press Command-N).

2   In the Finder window sidebar, click Mainserver.

   If Mainserver does not appear in the Finder sidebar, in the Shared list click All, and then double-click the Mainserver icon in the Finder window.

   Because Mainserver allows guest access, your server computer logs in automatically as Guest and displays the available share points.

3   Open the Public folder.

4   Drag the StudentMaterials folder to the Documents folder in the Finder window sidebar.

5   Once the copy is complete, disconnect from Mainserver by clicking Eject next to the Mainserver listing.

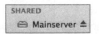

In this exercise you configured your server computer in preparation for installing OS X Server. You have completed this exercise; skip the Option 2 section that follows.

Option 2: Download Student Materials for the Independent Reader

If you are in the instructor-led environment, skip this section.

If you are performing the exercises independently, download the materials from Peachpit's site, place them in your Documents folder, and then run Software Update.

You will use a redemption code—provided on the card in the back of the printed version of this guide or on the "Where Are the Lesson Files?" page in the electronic version of this guide—to access the student materials.

After you enter the provided redemption code on the Peachpit.com website, the related files will be added to your Peachpit account on the "Lesson & Update Files" tab.

1   Using Safari, open www.peachpit.com/redeem, enter the code provided, and click Redeem Code.

   NOTE ▶ If you do not already have a free Peachpit account, you will be prompted to create one.

   NOTE ▶ If you purchase or redeem a code for the electronic version of this guide directly from Peachpit, the lesson file link will automatically appear on the "Lesson & Update Files" tab without the need to redeem an additional code.

2   Click the "Lesson & Update Files" tab.

3   Click the lesson file links to download the appropriate files to your computer, which places the material in your Downloads folder.

4   In the Finder, choose File > New Finder Window (or press Command-N).

5   Choose Go > Downloads.

6   Double-click the StudentMaterials.zip file to decompress the file.

7   Drag the StudentMaterials folder from your Downloads folder to your Documents folder in the Finder window sidebar.

8   Drag the StudentMaterials.zip file from your Downloads folder to the Trash in the Dock.

In this exercise you used About This Mac, System Preferences, and the Finder to configure OS X on your server computer in preparation for installing OS X Server.

Exercise 2.2
Perform the Initial Installation of OS X Server on Your Server Computer

▶ **Prerequisite**

  ▶   Exercise 2.1, "Configure OS X Before Installing OS X Server on Your Server Computer"

Now that you have OS X configured on your server computer, it's time to install OS X Server on it and configure it so you can administer it remotely.

Install Server
It's recommended to download the latest version of OS X Server from the Mac App Store.

If you are in an instructor-led environment, use the Option 1 section that follows. Otherwise, you should skip to Option 2.

Option 1: In the Instructor-Led Environment, Copy Server

In the instructor-led environment, the classroom server has the Server app available in the StudentMaterials folder; move the Server app to the Applications folder on your server computer with the following steps:

1   In the Finder on your server computer, open a new Finder window, click Documents in the Finder window sidebar, open the StudentMaterials folder you downloaded, and then open the Lesson02 folder.

2   Drag the Server app into the Applications folder in the Finder window sidebar.

Please skip the Option 2 section, and continue at the section "Open Server."

Option 2: For the Independent Reader, Download or Purchase Server in the Mac App Store

If you are performing the exercises independently, download OS X Server from the Mac App Store, which automatically places the Server app in your Applications folder.

Open Server

Once you have the Server app installed in the Applications folder, open the Server app.

1   In your Dock, click Launchpad.

2   You may need to swipe to the next page in Launchpad to see the Server app (hold down the Command key and press the Right Arrow key, or if you have a trackpad, swipe to the left with two fingers to get to the next page in Launchpad).

3   Click Server to open the Server app.

4   At the "To set up OS X Server on this Mac, click Continue" pane, click Continue.

5   At the license agreement pane, click Agree.

6   Provide local administrator credentials (User Name Local Admin and Administrator Password ladminpw) and click Allow.

7   Wait while the Server app configures itself.

After its initial installation, the Server app displays the Overview tab in the server pane of the Server app.

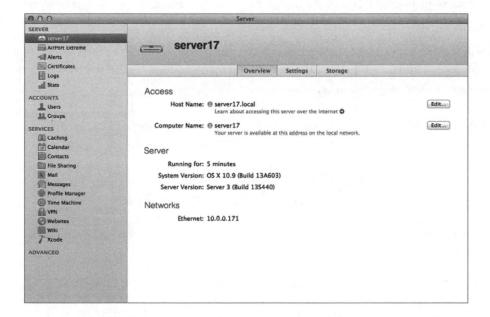

8   The Server Tutorials window opens. You can explore its content, but to continue with the exercise, close the Server Tutorials window.

You have successfully installed OS X Server. Congratulations!

Configure Your Server's Host Name and DNS Records

In many production environments, DNS is already provided. This guide is carefully designed to be useful for students in an instructor-led environment as well as for independent readers, who may have any of a variety of different combinations of network infrastructure. This guide is written so that your server provides DNS, and your administrator computer uses your server's DNS; in production environments, it is common to have different configurations.

Before you installed OS X Server, if you followed this guide, you configured your Mac to use a DNS service that does not have DNS records for the IPv4 address that you manually assigned for your Mac, so OS X automatically assigned the host name server*n*.local (where *n* is your student number).

> **NOTE** ▶ It is recommended that you configure your server computer and your administrator computer according to the instructions in this guide, even if your environment provides DNS records, in order to experience what happens when the Server app configures your DNS service.

You will change your server's host name, which causes the Server app to offer to automatically configure, start, and use the DNS service, then you will use the Alerts to address the "Host name changed" notification.

> **NOTE** ▶ It is best practice to set up OS X Server with appropriate DNS records in place. This exercise illustrates a common scenario.

1   If the Server app window is not already displaying the Overview tab, select your server in the Server app sidebar and then click the Overview tab.

2   Confirm that your server's Host Name is server$n$.local (where n is your student number).

3   Confirm that your server's Computer Name is server$n$ (where n is your student number).

4   Next to the Host Name field, click Edit to change the host name.

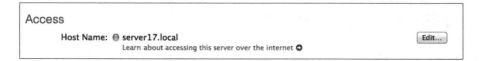

5   In the Change Host Name pane, click Next.

6   If you see the Multiple Networks Detected pane, choose the network interface that you would like to use to configure your server's identity; the Server app will create forward and reverse records using the IPv4 address assigned to the network interface you choose (it should be 10.0.0.n1, where n is your student number). Click Next.

7   In the Accessing Your Server pane, select Domain Name and click Next.

    You will learn more about these options in Lesson 3, "Providing DNS."

8   If necessary, set the Computer Name to server$n$, where n is your student number.

9   In the Host Name field, enter server$n$.pretendco.com, where n is your student number.

10 Next to the Network Address field, click Edit to review your network settings.

11 If you have multiple interfaces, first select, then drag, your intended primary network interface to the top of the network interface list, if it is not already at the top of the list.

12 Select your primary network interface, and confirm that it is configured as you want it configured; the settings should be as follows:

  ▶ Configure IPv4: Manually

  ▶ IP Address: 10.0.0.*n*1 (where *n* is your student number)

  ▶ Subnet Mask: 255.255.255.0

  ▶ Router: 10.0.0.1

  ▶ DNS Server: 10.0.0.1

  ▶ Search Domains: pretendco.com

13 If you made any changes, click Apply to accept the network configuration changes. Otherwise, click Cancel to return to the Connecting to your Server window.

14 At the Connecting to your Server pane, click Finish to accept the new names and network address settings.

15 At the "Do you want to set up DNS?" dialog, click Set Up DNS.

16 in the Overview pane, confirm that your Host Name and Computer Name fields are configured as you expect.

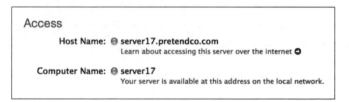

17 In the Server app sidebar, hold your pointer above the word Advanced, then click Show to display the list of advanced services.

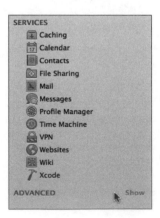

18 Confirm that there is a green status indicator next to DNS, which indicates that DNS is running on this server.

19 Open System Preferences and click Network.

20 Click your primary network interface, click Advanced, and click DNS.

Configure the DNS Servers field to contain only 127.0.0.1.

Note that 10.0.0.1 is also listed in the DNS Servers field. The Server app automatically adds your original DNS servers after adding 127.0.0.1 as a first entry, as a fallback in case your server's DNS service is stopped or does not forward requests to other DNS servers properly. However, because other DNS servers may not reply with DNS records your server expects (for instance, replying with a public IPv4 address instead of a private IPv4 address), you should remove all entries other than 127.0.0.1 from the DNS Servers field.

21 Highlight the 10.0.0.1 entry, then click Remove (–).

22 Confirm that the DNS Servers field contains 127.0.0.1 only, and that the Search Domains field contains pretendco.com.

23 Click OK to save the change and return to the list of network interfaces.

24 Review the settings, and then click Apply to accept the network configuration.

25 Quit System Preferences.

View the Host Name Change Alert

After you change the server's host name, the server generates an alert about the change.

1 Click Alerts in the Server app sidebar.

2 Double-click to open the "Host name changed notification" alert.

3 Review the information in the Alert.

4 Click Done.

Configure Your Server to Allow Remote Administration

Configure your server so that you can administer it with the Server app on your administrator computer.

1 In the Server app window, click the Settings tab.

2 If necessary, select the checkbox "Allow remote administration using Server."

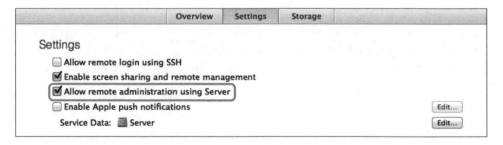

3 Because you're going to open the Server app on your administrator computer next, press Command-Q to quit the Server app.

It's recommended that you administer your server with only one instance of the Server app at a time; if you have the Server app open while logged in on your server, quit the Server app before opening the Server app on your administrator computer.

In this exercise you used the Server app to configure your server with OS X Server, and you enabled remote administration using the Server app, which leads nicely to the next exercise, which is to configure your administrator computer.

Exercise 2.3
Configure Your Administrator Computer

▶ **Prerequisites**

- ▶ Exercise 2.1, "Configure OS X Before Installing OS X Server on Your Server Computer"
- ▶ Exercise 2.2, "Perform the Initial Installation of OS X Server on Your Server Computer"
- ▶ You must have a Mac that is running OS X Mavericks and that has never had OS X Server installed on its startup volume.

Your "administrator computer" is a Mac on which you will open the Server app and use it to administer your computer running OS X Server. Remember that your administrator computer must be running OS X Mavericks in order to administer OS X Server for Mavericks.

In this exercise, you will configure your administrator computer in preparation for using it to administer your server and to remotely access services from your server.

This exercise is very similar to Exercise 2.1, but you will configure your administrator computer to use:

- ▶ A different computer name
- ▶ A different primary IPv4 address
- ▶ Your server's DNS service

You'll use one of two options to configure a local administrator account, depending on whether you are performing these exercises independently or are in an instructor-led environment.

In both situations, you'll use System Preferences to configure Network, Sharing, and Energy Saver settings. You will also download student materials that you'll use throughout this class. Finally, you will apply any necessary system software updates, and then use the Server app to confirm that you can use it to connect to your server.

If your administrator computer has not yet been set up, and is at the Welcome pane, use the Option 1 section that follows. Otherwise, you should skip to Option 2, "Configure an Existing OS X System for Your Administrator Computer."

Option 1: Configure OS X on Your Administrator Computer with Setup Assistant

This option is only necessary if your administrator computer has not already been set up, which is the situation in an instructor-led environment. If you are using a Mac with existing accounts, perform Option 2, "Configure an Existing OS X System for Your Administrator Computer," instead.

Ensure that you have Mavericks installed on your administrator computer. If it isn't already installed, install it now using the Mac App Store, the Recovery HD, or a method specified by your instructor, and then continue when you reach the Welcome pane.

In this section, you'll step through OS X Setup Assistant for initial system configuration of your administrator computer.

1   Ensure that your administrator computer is connected to a valid network connection.

2   If necessary, turn on your administrator computer.

3   In the Welcome pane, select the appropriate region and click Continue.

4   Select the appropriate keyboard layout and click Continue.

   Setup Assistant will evaluate your network environment and try to determine if you are connected to the Internet. This can take a few moments.

5   If asked to Select Your Wi-Fi Network or "How Do You Connect to the Internet," this indicates that you don't have an active Ethernet connection or you don't have a connection to the Internet.

   If you are performing the exercises in an instructor-led environment, ask your instructor how you should configure your computer; it is possible that the classroom

DHCP service is not enabled, or that your administrator computer is not connected to the classroom network.

If you are performing the exercises independently and you plan to use Wi-Fi as your primary network connection, select an appropriate Wi-Fi network and click Continue. Keep in mind that in order to perform the NetInstall exercises, both your administrator computer and your server need an Ethernet connection.

6   When asked about transferring information to this Mac, select "Don't transfer any information now" and click Continue.

7   At the Sign in with Your Apple ID pane, select "Don't sign in," click Continue, and then click Skip to confirm that you want to skip signing in with an Apple ID. Note that if you do provide Apple ID credentials, some figures may look slightly different, and there may be extra steps.

8   In the Terms and Conditions pane, when you have finished reading, click Agree.

9   In the dialog to confirm that you have read and agree to the OS X Software License Agreement, click Agree.

Create your local administrator account.

> **NOTE ►** It is important that you create this account as specified here. If you do not, future exercises may not work as written. Highlighted text is used throughout this guide to indicate text that you should enter exactly as shown.

1   In the Create Your Computer Account pane, enter the following information:

> ► Full Name: **Local Admin**
>
> ► Account Name: **ladmin**
>
> ► Password: **ladminpw**
>
> ► (verify field): **ladminpw**
>
> ► Hint: Leave blank.
>
> ► Leave the checkbox "Require password to unlock screen" selected.
>
> ► Deselect the checkbox "Set time zone based on current location."
>
> ► Deselect the checkbox "Send Diagnostics & Usage data to Apple."
>
> **NOTE ►** In a production environment, you should always use a strong password.

If you entered your Apple ID, you can select or deselect the checkbox "Allow my Apple ID to reset this user's password"; it does not have a major effect on the exercises.

2 Click Continue to create the local administrator account.

3 If you see the Select Time Zone pane, click your time zone in the map, or choose the nearest location in the Closest City pop-up menu, and then click Continue.

4 At the Register Your Mac pane, select Don't register, then click Continue; you won't be entering registration information at this time.

5 When asked if you are sure you don't want to register, click Skip.

6 If you are prompted to install software updates, click Not Now.

Please skip the Option 2 section, and continue at the section "Set the Computer Name and Turn On Remote Management."

Option 2: Configure an Existing OS X System for Your Administrator Computer

This option is designed only for those who are performing the exercises independently and who have a computer that is already set up with an existing administrator account.

NOTE ▶ You may not use a Mac whose startup volume has already had OS X Server installed.

If your computer has not been set up (that is, if the initial administrator account has not been created), perform Option 1, "Configure OS X on Your Administrator Computer with Setup Assistant," instead.

Create a new administrator account in System Preferences.

1 If necessary, log in with your existing administrator account.

2 From the Apple menu, choose System Preferences.

3 In System Preferences, click Users & Groups.

4 In the lower-left corner, click the lock icon.

5 In the dialog that appears, enter the password for your existing administrator account and click Unlock.

6   Click the Add (+) button under the user list.

7   In the dialog that appears, enter the following information:

> **NOTE ▶** It is important that you create this account as specified here. If you do not, future exercises may not work as written. If you already have an account named Local Admin or ladmin, you will have to use a different name here and then remember to use your substitute name throughout the rest of the exercises. Highlighted text is used throughout this guide to indicate text that you should enter exactly as shown.

> ▶   New Account: choose Administrator
> ▶   Full Name: Local Admin
> ▶   Account Name: ladmin

If you are performing the exercises in an instructor-led environment, enter ladminpw in the Password and Verify fields.

If you are performing the exercises independently, you can select a more secure password for the Local Admin account. Be sure to remember the password you have chosen, as you will need to reenter it periodically as you use this computer.

You may provide a password hint if you want to.

If you entered your Apple ID, you can select or deselect the checkbox "Allow my Apple ID to reset this user's password"; it does not have a major effect on the exercises.

> **NOTE ▶** In a production environment, you should always use a strong password.

8   Click Create User.

9   At the bottom of the user list, click Login Options.

10   If an account is selected for Automatic Login, use the pop-up menu to switch it to Off.

11   Close System Preferences and log out.

12   At the login screen, select the Local Admin account and enter its password (ladminpw, or whatever you specified earlier).

13   Press Return to log in.

This is the end of Option 2; everyone should continue with the next section.

Set the Computer Name and Turn On Remote Management

You will specify a computer name associated with your student number. If you are performing the exercises independently, you can choose to skip this section.

You will also enable Remote Management, which will allow the instructor to observe your computer, control your keyboard and mouse, gather information, copy items to your computer, and otherwise help you if necessary.

1   In your Dock, open System Preferences.

2   Open Sharing.

3   Set the Computer Name to clientn, replacing *n* with your student number.

For example, if your student number is 17, the computer name should be client17, all lowercase and no spaces.

4   Press Return.

Notice that the name listed under the Computer Name field, which is the local hostname, updates to match your new computer name.

Enable yourself and your instructor to remotely manage your administrator computer; this also allows you to use Screen Sharing from another Mac.

5   Select the Remote Management checkbox.

6   In the dialog that appears, leave all the checkboxes deselected and click OK for now, as this controls access for all local users, and you will configure access for one user only next.

7   In "Allow Access for," select "Only these users."

8   Click the Add (+) button, select Local Admin, and click Select.

9   In the dialog that appears, hold down the Option key while selecting the Observe checkbox, which results in automatically selecting all the checkboxes.

10 Click OK.

11 Click Show All to return to the main System Preferences pane.

Set Energy Saver Preferences

Prevent your administrator computer from going to sleep while you use it for the exercises. You can set the display sleep to whatever setting you prefer.

If you are performing the exercises independently, you can choose to skip this section.

1 In System Preferences, open Energy Saver.

2 If you have a portable computer, you have two tabs: Battery and Power Adapter. Click Power Adapter to configure the settings while using the power adapter.

3 Set the computer to never sleep by dragging the "Computer sleep" slider to the far right.

   This prevents the computer from going to sleep while installing software updates.

4 When the "Your computer may use more energy with these settings" message appears, click OK.

5 Drag the "Display sleep" slider to a value of your choice. You can leave the other settings at their defaults.

6 Click Show All to return to the main System Preferences pane.

Configure App Store Software Update

If you are performing the exercises in an instructor-led environment, you should disable the App Store from automatically checking for updates, so that you do not unnecessarily use bandwidth.

1 In System Preferences, click App Store.

2 Deselect the "Automatically check for updates" option.

3 If necessary, deselect the "Automatically downloads apps purchased on other Macs" option.

4 Click Show All to return to the main System Preferences pane.

Configure Networking

Configure your administrator computer to use your server's DNS service.

> **NOTE** ▶ The exercises are written for only one network interface to be active, but if you decide to use multiple network interfaces, this will not significantly impact your ability to complete the exercises.

1   In System Preferences, click Network.

2   In the instructor-led environment, configure one of your Mac computer's Ethernet ports to be the only active network service.

> **NOTE** ▶ You may leave your Wi-Fi network interface enabled, but not joined to any network, in order to use AirDrop.

In the list of network interfaces, select each network interface you will not use in the exercise (which should be each interface except for one Ethernet interface), click the Action (gear icon) pop-up menu, and choose Make Service Inactive.

If you are performing the exercises independently, you may leave additional interfaces active, but be aware that this may cause differences between the way the exercises describe the windows, and what you actually see.

3   If you will use multiple network interfaces, click the Action (gear icon) pop-up menu, choose Set Service Order, drag services to an appropriate order so that your primary interface is at the top of the list, and click OK.

4   Select the active Ethernet interface.

5   In the Configure IPv4 pop-up menu, choose Manually.

6   Enter the following information to manually configure the Ethernet interface (IPv4) for the classroom environment:

   ▶ IP Address: 10.0.0.n2 (where n is your student number; for example, student1 uses 10.0.0.12, student 6 uses 10.0.0.62, and student 15 uses 10.0.0.152.)

   ▶ Subnet Mask: 255.255.255.0

   ▶ Router: 10.0.0.1

If you are performing the exercises independently and choose to use different settings, see the "Network Infrastructure" section in Lesson 1, and be prepared to substitute network values that are appropriate for your environment throughout all the exercises in this guide.

7   Click Advanced, and then click the DNS tab.

8   Even though you just switched from DHCP to Manual, you did not yet apply the change, so values assigned by DHCP are listed, but they are dimmed. Values manually assigned are not dimmed.

If there are any values in the DNS Servers field that are not dimmed, select each entry that is not dimmed, then click Delete (–) to delete the entry, until there are no non-dimmed values listed.

9   Under the DNS Servers field, click Add (+) and enter the IPv4 address of your server computer (10.0.0.n1, where n is your student number; for example, student1 uses 10.0.0.11, student 6 uses 10.0.0.61, and student 15 uses 10.0.0.151.)

10 In the Search Domains field, values assigned by DHCP are listed, but they are dimmed. Values manually assigned are not dimmed.

If there are any values in the Search Domains field that are not dimmed, select each entry that is not dimmed, then click Delete (–) to delete the entry, until there are no non-dimmed values listed.

11 Under the Search Domains field, click Add (+) and enter pretendco.com.

If you are performing the exercises independently, enter a value appropriate for your environment.

DNS Servers:	Search Domains:
10.0.0.171	pretendco.com

12 Click OK to close this pane.

13 Click Apply to accept the network configuration.

14 Quit System Preferences.

Confirm DNS Records

Use Network Utility to confirm that your administrator computer can access your server's DNS service. Network Utility is located in /System/Library/CoreServices/Application, which is automatically indexed by Spotlight.

1 Click the Spotlight icon in the upper-right corner of the screen (or press Command-Space bar) to reveal the Spotlight search field.

2 Enter Network Utility in the Spotlight search field.

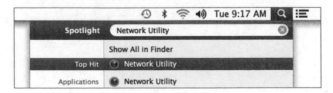

3 Press Return to open the "Top Hit" from your Spotlight search, which is Network Utility.

NOTE ► If you cannot enter text in the Spotlight search field because the disk is still indexing, then in Finder, choose Go > Go to Folder, enter /System/Library/CoreServices/Applications, click Go, and then open Network Utility.

4   In Network Utility, click the Lookup tab.

5   Enter your server's primary IPv4 address in the field (10.0.0.*n*1, where *n* is your student number) and click Lookup.

6   Confirm that your server's host name appears in the results field.

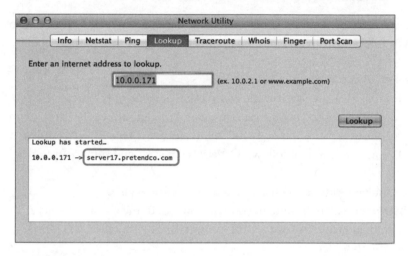

7   Enter your server's host name in the field and click Lookup.

8   Confirm that your server's primary IPv4 address appears in the results field.

9   Press Command-Q to quit Network Utility.

Update Software

Run Software Update. If a local Caching service is available, your Mac will automatically use it.

1   From the Apple menu, choose Software Update.

2   Click Update next to any update for OS X, if there are any listed.

You do not need updated versions of other software, such as iTunes, in order to use the exercises in this guide, but you are free to update any items you wish to update.

Download Student Materials

There are some files that are necessary for the completion of some of the exercises. You have already downloaded them to your server computer, but you should also have them available on your administrator computer. If you are in an instructor-led environment, you can use the Option 1 section that follows. Otherwise, you should skip to Option 2.

Option 1: Download Student Materials in the Instructor-Led Environment

If you are in an instructor-led environment, you will connect to the classroom server and download the student materials used for the course. To copy the files, you'll drag the folder to your Documents folder.

If you are performing the exercises independently, skip to Option 2, "Download Student Materials for the Independent Reader."

1   In the Finder, choose File > New Finder Window (or press Command-N).

2   In the Finder window sidebar, click Mainserver.

If Mainserver does not appear in the Finder sidebar, in the Shared list click All, and then double-click the Mainserver icon in the Finder window.

Because Mainserver allows guest access, your administrator computer logs in automatically as Guest and displays the available share points.

3   Open the Public folder.

4   Drag the StudentMaterials folder to the Documents folder in the Finder window sidebar.

5   Once the copy is complete, disconnect from Mainserver by clicking Eject next to the listing for Mainserver.

Skip the Option 2 section that follows, and resume with the section "Install the Server App."

Option 2: Download Student Materials for the Independent Reader

If you are performing the exercises independently, copy the Student Materials from your server (or download the materials from Peachpit's site), place them in your Documents folder, and then run Software Update.

If both of your Macs have AirDrop enabled, you can use AirDrop to copy the StudentMaterials folder from your server to your administrator computer. Click AirDrop in a Finder window on each Mac. On your server computer, open a new Finder window, open your Documents folder, drag the StudentMaterials folder to the picture for your administrator computer in the AirDrop window, then click Send. On your administrator computer, click Save, then once the transfer has completed, open the Downloads folder and drag StudentMaterials to your Documents folder in the Finder window sidebar. Finally, close the AirDrop window on your server computer and on your administrator computer.

Another option is to use a removable disk. If you have a USB, FireWire, or Thunderbolt disk, you can connect it to your server, copy the StudentMaterials folder from your local administrator's Documents folder to the volume, eject the volume, connect the volume to your administrator computer, and drag the StudentMaterials folder to your Documents folder in the Finder window sidebar.

Alternatively, you can download the files from Peachpit again using the following steps.

These directions assume that you redeemed the provided code for the lesson files in Exercise 2.1. If you have not already done so, see Exercise 2.1, "Option 2: Download Student Materials for the Independent Reader" for details.

1   Using Safari, open www.peachpit.com and click the Account link or the Account Sign In link at the top right of the home page to access your Peachpit account.

2   Click the "Lesson & Update Files" tab.

3   Click the lesson file links to download the appropriate files to your computer, which places the material in your Downloads folder.

4   In the Finder, choose File > New Finder Window (or press Command-N).

5   Choose Go > Downloads.

6   Double-click the StudentMaterials.zip file to decompress the file.

7   Drag the StudentMaterials folder from your Downloads folder to your Documents folder in the Finder window sidebar.

8   Drag the StudentMaterials.zip file from your Downloads folder to the Trash in the Dock.

Everyone should continue with the next section, "Install the Server App."

Install the Server App

On your server computer you ran the Server app to configure your server computer as a server. However, on your administrator computer, you will run the Server app to remotely administer your server.

Option 1: In the Instructor-Led Environment, Copy Server

In the instructor-led environment, the classroom server has the Server app available in the StudentMaterials folder; move the Server app to the Applications folder on your server computer with the following steps:

1   In the Finder on your server computer, open a new Finder window, click Documents in the Finder window sidebar, open the StudentMaterials folder that you downloaded, then open the Lesson02 folder.

2   Drag the Server app into the Applications folder in the Finder window sidebar.

Option 2: For the Independent Reader, Download or Purchase Server in the Mac App Store

If you are performing the exercises independently, you should have already purchased OS X Server by the time you completed Exercise 2.2; if this is the case, open the Mac App Store from your Dock or from the Apple menu, log in with the Apple ID you used to purchase OS X Server, and download OS X Server, which automatically places the Server app in your Applications folder.

Use the Server App to Administer Your Server

Using your administrator computer, open the Server app, connect to your server, and accept its SSL certificate.

1   On your administrator computer, open the Server app.

2   Click Other Mac.

3   In the "Choose a Mac" window, select your server and click Continue.

4   Provide the administrator credentials (Administrator Name ladmin and Administrator Password ladminpw).

5   If necessary, deselect the "Remember this password in my keychain" checkbox so the credentials you provide will not be saved in your keychain (a secure store of passwords) which means that you must provide administrator credentials each time you connect to your server with the Server app. This facilitates using different administrator credentials, as is required for Exercise 8.1, "Create and Configure Local User Accounts."

6   Click Connect.

7   Because your server is using a self-signed SSL (Secure Sockets Layer) certificate that has not been signed by a Certificate Authority (CA) that your administrator computer is configured to trust, you'll see a warning message that you are connecting to a server whose identity certificate is not verified. See Lesson 5, "Configuring SSL Certificates," for more information on SSL.

> **NOTE ▶** In a production environment, you might want to address this situation as soon as possible by using Keychain Access on your server computer to configure your server to use a valid SSL certificate for the com.apple.servermgrd identity, which is used to communicate with a remote instance of the Server app. This is outside the scope of this guide.

8   Click Show Certificate.

9 Select the checkbox to always trust com.apple.servermgrd when connecting to your server.

10 Click Continue.

11 You must provide your login credentials in order to modify your keychain.

Enter your password (ladminpw) and click Update Settings.

After you click Update Settings, the Server app connects to your server.

In this exercise you prepared your administrator computer to remotely administer your server and to access services from your server.

Lesson 3

Providing DNS

The Domain Name System (DNS) is a critical service. It is so critical in fact that OS X Server will set up its own DNS service if one is not provided for it in certain circumstances. Without proper working DNS, problems will occur with certain services, and as a result, it is important to understand what DNS is and how to manage it for OS X and other computers.

Although there are many aspects of DNS, this lesson concentrates on what is needed to make OS X work properly.

Reference 3.1
What Is DNS?

In its most basic form, DNS is the system that helps identify computers, servers, and other devices on a network via an IPv4 number or name. For example:

server17.pretendco.com = 10.0.0.171 (a forward lookup)

10.0.0.171 = server17.pretendco.com (a reverse lookup)

UNIX operating systems such as OS X rely on DNS to keep track of resources on the network, including themselves. They are constantly doing "lookups" or finding out about the IP addresses and host names they need to contact, including their own information. The lookups can be triggered by authentication requests, access to resources, or almost anything else a server may be asked to do.

The flow of a DNS request goes like this:

1. A computer makes a DNS request to find out the IP address of a resource such as a web server or file server. That request is sent to the DNS server that the computer is configured to use. It got that information via DHCP or a manual configuration of the DNS server. Example: Where is www.apple.com?

2. The DNS server receives the request and determines whether it has the answer to the question. If it has the answer, it will return the answer to the requesting computer. It may have the answer because it has cached the answer from an earlier request, or it is "authoritative" for that domain (apple.com) and is configured with the answer. If not, it might forward the request to another DNS server it has been configured to use. This is known as the forwarding server, and it now has the responsibility to get the result and report back to the requesting DNS server.

3. If there is not a forwarding server, the DNS server will consult a list of root servers located at /Library/Server/named/named.ca and send a request to a root server.

4. The root server will send a response telling the DNS server where to find the DNS servers that handle .com requests, as the original request was for a domain that had ".com" as the top-level domain (TLD).

5. The DNS server then asks the TLD server where the domain "apple.com" is, and the server will respond with that answer.

6. Now knowing where the DNS server that is authoritative for "apple.com" is, the DNS server will ask for the answer to www.apple.com and the server will provide the answer.

7. The DNS server does two things with that answer, including passing the answer along to the original requestor and caching the answer in case another request comes in for that. The cached answer will live on the requesting server for a time specified in the DNS record, called Time To Live (TTL). After that time expires, the cached answer is purged.

As you can see, having the answer close at hand will speed up the lookup process, so it is handy to host your own DNS server for your own users' computers and mobile devices.

Typical trouble caused by bad or nonexistent DNS includes:

▶ Resources that can't be connected to over the network, such as websites, wikis, calendars, and file shares

▶ Not being able to log in to a computer that uses Open Directory hosted by the server

▶ Single sign-on (SSO) via Kerberos not working

▶ Authentication problems

There are a number of pieces to the DNS system, including but not limited to:

▶ Requestor—The computer looking for information

▶ DNS server—The service that provides all or some of the information the requestor asks for

▶ Records—The information-defining information relating to the DNS zone, such as machines and nameservers

▶ Zone files—The text-based files that contain the DNS records. In Mavericks, these files reside in a new location, /Library/Server/named/.

▶ Primary zone—A group of records for a domain

▶ Secondary zone—A replica of a primary zone, typically on another DNS server, that has its records created by a zone transfer

▶ Zone transfer—Sending a copy of a primary zone to another server for use with a secondary zone

▶ Forwarding server—Where requests are sent if the DNS server doesn't have the zone information to answer the request

Reference 3.2
Evaluating OS X DNS Hosting Requirements

When first configuring OS X Server, the Server app checks to see if a DNS host name correlating to the computer's IPv4 address is being provided by the DNS server listed in Network preferences. If it is, the computer is named with the host name information contained in the DNS records.

If DNS information for the computer's IPv4 address is not provided, OS X Server will set up the DNS service on that computer if the Host Name is edited. This is different from the previous version of OS X Server, which handled that task at the initial server configuration. This process guarantees that at least enough DNS information is available to the server to function properly. You can tell if the DNS service was turned on by a green status indicator next to the DNS service in the Server app list of services, and by the fact that in Network preferences, the value for the DNS server is 127.0.0.1.

Here are three typical scenarios for DNS services as they relate to OS X Server:

▶ Automatically configured DNS—If the server has its own DNS running and working, leaving it that way and not configuring the DNS service beyond that point may be appropriate. This may be when the server is the only server on the network, as might be the case in a small office. The client computers will contact the server via Bonjour for those services that support it. This assumes that the server is on the same segment (subnet) of the network as the client. This configuration is viable and might work very well.

▶ Externally provided DNS—Other configurations may require externally provided DNS. An example of this is when the server will be connected to an Active Directory (AD) system for user and groups information. In this situation it is best to place a record for the server into the DNS service used by the Windows server hosting the AD. Make sure there is an A record, used for forward lookups, server17.pretendco. com = 10.0.0.171, and a reverse or PTR record, 10.0.0.171 = server17.pretendco.com. Check these details using Network Utility or command-line tools before configuring your server to use this external DNS server.

NOTE ▶ Windows DNS service prior to 2008 R2 commonly doesn't provide a reverse zone. While making an A record there is a checkbox to automatically make a PTR record, but unless the appropriate reverse zone exists, the PTR record will not be made.

▶ OS X Server hosted DNS—This differs from the automatically configured DNS in that it is manually set up by the administrator and can be used by other computers and devices on the network to get DNS information. The DNS service on the server has new DNS zones set up and populated with records representing the computers, servers, and other devices on the network. This style of providing DNS is used when there are larger needs than simply identifying one server on the network, and all computers on your network will use your server for DNS information.

Dealing with Internal and External DNS

As more users expect to access their data from wherever they are, we need to consider how to handle requests from both inside our own networks and from the outside world networks that aren't under our control. Services such as Mail, Calendar, Websites, and device management are used from both types of networks, and we need to know how to handle DNS in both cases. These cases call for a technique called split DNS.

The concept is simple: When your users are in your network, the DHCP server provides an IP address to the client, plus the address of your internal DNS server. Your internal DNS server gives the client information for internal resources via internal IPs. Clients outside your network use an external DNS server that will give them the outside IP address that reaches your server.

Internal request:

www.pretendco.com = 10.0.0.171

External request:

www.pretendco.com = 203.0.113.10

For this to work, you need to populate the external DNS host server with the proper external IP address for your servers and allow the services access through your firewall. This allows you to provide the same services for users wherever they may be.

Let's use some examples to show when to use what DNS service:

▶ Outside DNS only—If you don't have to serve clients internal to your network, you may not have to set up internal DNS except for the server itself. If you are hosting email, profile management, or websites that users access from outside your network, there is no need to configure extra DNS records for internal usage. You just need to use a DNS hosting company to provide your DNS and set up your domain to point to the authoritative DNS servers.

▶ Outside DNS, self hosted—This is the same idea as the first one, but instead of using a commercially hosted DNS server, you configure your DNS service in OS X Server to provide the external DNS records. You will need to populate the DNS zones with the appropriate records and allow outside requests to be answered by your server. You will still need to configure the domain to point to your DNS service.

▶ Internal DNS only—If you are not exposing any of your services to the outside world, you only need to configure an internal DNS service that provides answers for internal resources. You can limit the requests that the DNS service will reply to to clients on your internal network. This allows you to have full control over your internal DNS system.

▶ Split DNS—If you are providing services to both internal clients and external clients, it is a good idea to have your own internal DNS server and configure a separate external DNS server or use a hosted service. Depending on where the client is, they will get answers to DNS queries either from your internal DNS server with internal resources if they are inside your network, or from your external DNS service with external resources if they are outside your network.

Reference 3.3
Configuring DNS Service in OS X Server

Prior to setting up DNS services in OS X Server, you need to collect certain information. This includes:

▶ The domain you want to host. In this guide you'll be using pretendco.com.

▶ The host names you want to have records for. Most of the examples in this guide use server17 as the host name, but it could also include records for devices like printer01 or winserver02. These are used for the A records or forward lookups, which map a DNS name to an IPv4 address.

▶ The IPv4 addresses for all the host names you want to include. These are used for the PTR records or reverse lookups, mapping IPv4 addresses to DNS names.

▶ The IPv4 address of upstream DNS servers that will answer DNS requests the DNS server you are setting up doesn't have the answers for. This is called a forwarder. If you don't provide a forwarder, top-down lookups involving the root DNS servers get used. It is more practical and better practice to use forwarding servers to reduce the load on the root DNS servers.

▶ The range of IPv4 addresses or networks you want your DNS server to provide DNS lookups for. This prevents unwanted networks from using your DNS server.

▶ The information for any other type of record you want to include, such as the email server needed for MX records, the server you want to make an alias for when setting up a Cname, or servers that need to advertise their services via a SRV record.

The general flow of setting up a DNS server includes defining the domain or domains that the server will be responsible for. The DNS service that is responsible for the "official" DNS information about a domain is called the Start of Authority (SoA) of the domain and is contained in the DNS records. If you are hosting DNS records strictly for your internal domains, this is not a critical piece of information, but if you are hosting DNS for a domain that is accessible to the Internet, it is critical.

Since OS X Server can create its own default zone if an external DNS record isn't available for the server's IP address, you will end up with a zone that is authoritative for the fully qualified name of your server. This is fine if you never plan to add more DNS records, but if you do you will want to add the new zones based on your domain and remove the generated zones.

Reference 3.4
Troubleshooting DNS Service in OS X Server

Since DNS is a critical service, it helps to understand the basics of troubleshooting it:

▶ Is the server, computer, or device set up to use the proper DNS server? Many problems are related to the wrong information being delivered via a wrongly defined DNS server.

▶ Are DNS services available on the defined DNS server? Check that the DNS service is running on the defined server. In Terminal, run the command telnet <IPv4 address of server> 53 and see if a connection is made (after a successful connection, press Control-], then type quit to close the connection). Port 53 is the port used by DNS.

▶ Are the proper DNS records available from the DNS server? Check all the pertinent records, forward and reverse, using Network Utility or command-line tools. Make sure both the forward and reverse records are available and match.

Exercise 3.1
Configure DNS Services

▶ **Prerequisites**

  ▶ All exercises in Lesson 2, "Installing OS X Server"

When you performed the initial installation and configuration of OS X Server in Lesson 2's exercises, the DNS service you configured OS X to use did not contain records for your server's primary IPv4 address. When the host name was changed, the DNS service was turned on and automatically configured a domain called server*n*.prctendco.com (where *n* is your student number) with one A (forward) record in it. While this is fine for a single host system, if you want to host multiple devices in your DNS, you need to build a new zone to host the pretendco.com domain. In this exercise, you will configure your DNS service to multiple host names.

Collect DNS Configuration Data

Prior to setting up the DNS service, gather the following information:

▶ Domain name (such as pretendco.com)

▶ IPv4 addresses and associated host names

▶ Forwarder server address

Configure Forwarding Servers

A forwarding server is a configuration that hands off DNS lookups to another DNS server if the DNS server does not have the information regarding the requested domain. The forwarding server is often the DNS server provided by the ISP, which has a much larger cache of entries from the Internet, but can be any other DNS that can do successful lookups.

> **NOTE ▶** In a classroom situation, your instructor will provide you with the proper IPv4 address and explain why it is being used. If you are performing the exercises independently, use the IPv4 address of a DNS server provided by your ISP.

1   On your server, open the Server app and choose the DNS service in the Advanced Services section.

2   To the right of Forwarding Servers, click Edit.

3   Click the remove (–) button to delete any existing record, and then click the Add (+) button.

4 Enter the IPv4 address of the upstream DNS server you want to use and click OK. A common DNS server to use would be the one provided by the ISP. If you are in a classroom, your instructor will provide the proper IPv4 address to use.

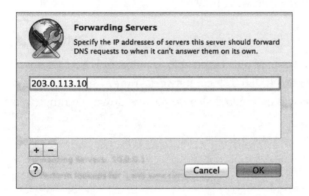

The forwarders are listed in the main DNS service pane.

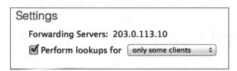

Configure Lookup Restrictions

You can control what computers or devices can use your DNS server by defining their IPv4 addresses or networks. Any computer or device not having an IPv4 address in the defined accepted ranges or hosts will not be granted DNS lookup information. Use the following steps to configure the DNS service to respond to requests from another network; you'll use 192.168.0.0 just as an example.

1 If not already selected, select the "Perform lookups for" checkbox.

2 Choose "only some clients" from the pop-up menu, which allows you to define networks that can be served by your server's DNS service.

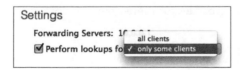

3   If necessary, to the right of "Perform lookups for," click Edit.

4   If not already selected, select the checkboxes for "The server itself," "Clients on the local network," and "Clients on the following networks."

5   Click the Add (+) button and enter 192.168.0.0/24.

This defines the 192.168.0.0 network as also being able to perform DNS lookups using this server, in addition to the 10.0.0.0 "local network" range the server is currently in. A single IPv4 address can be entered also, to narrow down the range to a single device.

6   Click OK to save the change.

Configure DNS Hosts

You will replace the limited primary zone of server*n*.pretendco.com (where *n* is your student number) with a new zone for pretendco.com, which can contain a broader set of records. You will also create and configure another primary zone, pretendco.private, to reemphasize the process of configuring zones. Additionally, the machine records you create in the pretendco.private zone are required for the exercises in Lesson 21, "Hosting Websites," which demonstrate the ability to host websites for more than one domain.

1 Click the Action (gear icon) menu at the bottom of the DNS pane and choose Show All Records. This changes the simplified view into a more standard view illustrating the various zones configured.

2 Review the records listed in the pane; you can drag the bottom edge of the Server app window to expand the Records field and expose more records. In the following figure, there are two zones: a primary named server17.pretendco.com and a reverse named 171.0.0.10.in-addr.arpa. Each zone has a nameserver record, which defines your server as the authoritative DNS service for that zone. The primary zone has one machine record, and the reverse zone has one mapping record that corresponds to the primary zone's one machine record.

3 Click the Add (+) button and choose Add Primary Zone. A primary zone holds the records for a domain in this example.

4   In the Name field enter pretendco.com and keep the "Zone data is valid for 24 hours" setting. Do not select the "Allow zone transfers" option. Click Create.

5   In the main DNS pane, click the Add (+) button and choose Add Machine Record.

6   From the Zone menu, choose pretendco.com.

7   In the Host Name field, enter servern (where n is your student number). Note that you should not enter the domain, just the first part of the host name.

8   Click the Add (+) button and enter your server's IPv4 address, 10.0.0.n1 (where n is your student number).

9   Click Create.

10 Add a mail exchanger (MX) record. Click the Add (+) button and choose Add Mail Exchanger Record. From the Zone menu, choose pretendco.com. In the Mail Server field, enter servern.pretendco.com (where *n* is your student number) and set Priority to 10. The Priority number reflects an order of preference when there are multiple MX records. The lower the number, the higher in the preference order.

11 Click Create to save the change.

Note that there is now a primary zone for pretendco.com, with machine, mail exchanger, and nameserver entries in it. There is also a reverse zone for 0.0.10.in-addr.arpa, with reverse mapping and nameserver entries.

Create an Additional Zone

Use the following steps to create another zone, specify its nameserver value, and create records in the zone. This new zone will be used in later exercises.

1   In the main DNS pane, click the Add (+) button and choose Add Primary Zone.

2   In the Name field, enter pretendco.private. Leave the other settings at their defaults, and click Create

3   In the main DNS pane, click the Add (+) button and choose Add Nameserver Record.

4   Click the Zone pop-up menu and choose pretendco.private.

5   In the Nameserver field, enter servern.pretendco.com (where *n* is your student number), then click Create. Notice that the nameserver is your server, as it contains the records for all of the zones so far.

6 In the main DNS pane, click the Add (+) button and choose Add Machine Record.

7 Click the Zone pop-up menu and choose pretendco.private.

8 In the Host Name field, enter www.

9 In the IP Addresses field, click the Add (+) button and enter 10.0.0.n5 (where n is your student number).

10 Click Create to save the new record.

11 In the main DNS pane, click Add (+) and choose Add Machine Record.

12 Click the Zone pop-up menu and choose pretendco.private.

13 In the Host Name field, enter ssl.

14 In the IP Address field, click Add (+) and enter 10.0.0.*n*3 (where *n* is your student number).

15 Click Create to save the new record.

Your records should look similar to those contained in the following figure.

Remove the Redundant Zone and Confirm Records

To prevent confusion in the future, remove the limited zone that the Server app originally created. Currently there are two zones that can answer the query for server*n*.pretendco.com, and we only want the more full-featured of the two, so we will remove the zone created during the host name configuration. Once it is removed, use Network Utility to confirm that your server and your administrator computer can successfully perform lookups on the records you just created.

1   Remove the server*n*.pretendco.com primary zone by choosing it and clicking the Delete (–) button. When prompted, confirm that you do want to delete the zone by clicking Delete. Notice that the corresponding reverse zone, *n*.0.0.10.in-addr.arpa (where *n* is your student number), was automatically removed.

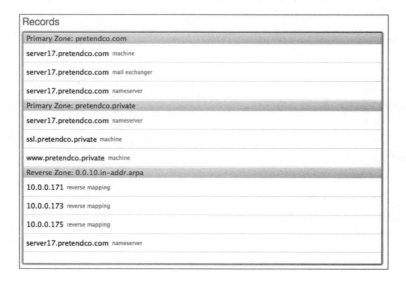

2   On your server, open Network preferences and make sure the DNS Servers field is set to 127.0.0.1 and the Search Domain field is set to pretendco.com. If they are not, change the entries to look like the following figure.

3   Using Network Utility, check that DNS is resolving properly by performing a lookup on server*n*.pretendco.com (where *n* is your student number).

4   Using Network Utility, check that DNS is resolving properly by running a lookup on 10.0.0.n1 (where n is your student number). The associated machine record is returned, server$n$.pretendco.com.

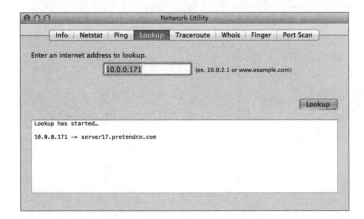

5   Using Terminal, check the returned information on just the domain pretendco.com by entering **host pretendco.com**. In the returned information are the MX record and the priority number.

```
server17:~ ladmin$ host pretendco.com
pretendco.com mail is handled by 10 server17.pretendco.com.
```

6   Using Network Utility, perform a lookup for ssl.pretendco.private, and confirm that the answer section returns 10.0.0.n3 (where n is your student number); perform a lookup for that same IPv4 address and confirm that the answer section returns ssl.pretendco.private.

7   On your administrator computer, open Network preferences and confirm that the DNS Server field is set to 10.0.0.n1 (where n is your student number) and the Search Domain field is set to pretendco.com. The server uses 127.0.0.1, known as a loop-back address, so the server will always look back at itself for DNS queries.

8   On your administrator computer, repeat steps 3–6 to use Network Utility to confirm DNS records.

Clean Up

No changes are required for this lesson, as the work you have just done creating new records and zones will be needed in later lessons and exercises.

Lesson 4

Exploring the Server App

Once you've completed your initial installation of OS X Server, the Server app opens its main configuration pane and you can continue configuring it. In this lesson you'll learn about the various panes available in the Server app. You will learn how to enable remote access to the Server app and how to move the location your server uses to store much of its service data.

Reference 4.1
Allowing Remote Access

You can certainly administer your server on your server computer, but it's not recommended to use your server for your daily productivity applications.

You can use the Server app on any Mac with Mavericks to manage OS X Server running on a remote Mac, but only if the checkbox "Allow remote administration using Server" is selected. It is recommended that you do not simultaneously use the Server app on more than one Mac to administer a given server.

MORE INFO ▶ When you select the "Allow remote administration using Server" checkbox, you enable other Macs to use the Server app to configure your server using TCP port 311.

	Overview	Settings	Storage	

Settings

☐ Allow remote login using SSH for [administrators ⌄]
☐ Enable screen sharing and remote management
☑ Allow remote administration using Server
☐ Enable Apple push notifications   [Edit...]
Service Data: 🖥 Server   [Edit...]

Unlike earlier versions of Mac OS X Server, you cannot perform a remote initial installation of OS X Server with the Server app; you have to use the Server app on the Mac on which you want to install OS X Server, at least for the initial installation and configuration.

However, sometimes you need direct control of your server computer; for example, to perform a series of file or folder copy operations using the Finder. If you select the checkbox "Enable screen sharing and remote management," you can use tools like Screen Sharing (available from the Tools menu in the Server app, and located in /System/Library/CoreServices) and Apple Remote Desktop (available from the Mac App Store) to take control of the Mac running OS X Server.

When you select the "Enable screen sharing and remote management" option, by default this allows access for all local accounts on the server computer that you configure as an administrator (if you have used Sharing preferences to configure specific users for specific levels of access, that configuration information will be preserved when you select or deselect the checkbox). If you want to allow access for other accounts, or specify a password for software that uses the VNC protocol, configure this with Sharing preferences on the server computer.

> **NOTE ▶** If you have Sharing preferences open when you use the Server app to configure remote access, you may need to quit System Preferences and reopen the Sharing pane to see the updated settings.

The following figure illustrates the checkbox in Sharing preferences that is selected when you select the checkbox for "Enable screen sharing and remote management." Note that the checkbox for Screen Sharing is unavailable; if you click Screen Sharing, you will see the message "Screen Sharing is currently being controlled by the Remote Management service."

MORE INFO ► If you use Sharing preferences to deselect Remote Management and select Screen Sharing, then in the Server app, the "Enable screen sharing and remote management" checkbox will display a dash (–) instead of a checkmark.

The "Allow remote login using SSH" checkbox in the Server app has the same effect as the Remote Login checkbox in Sharing preferences; selecting or deselecting either checkbox has the same effect on the checkbox in the other tool.

When you run the Server app on a remote administrator computer, if the "Allow remote login using SSH" option is selected, an arrow appears next to it. If you click this arrow, the Server app opens Terminal and attempts to connect to your server using the SSH protocol, with the user name of the administrator account that you provided to the Server app to connect to your remote server computer. You must provide the password to successfully open an SSH connection.

Similarly, there is also a shortcut to open a Screen Sharing session with your server. This opens the Screen Sharing application, which allows remote observation and control of the remote server computer.

Of course, the checkbox for "Allow remote administration using Server" is not available for you to configure unless you use the Server app directly at the server.

The following figure illustrates the arrows that are shortcuts to open a connection to the server.

NOTE ▶ If you upgrade from Snow Leopard (10.6.8) or any version of Lion or Mountain Lion, your Mac with OS X Mavericks inherits the Sharing settings from the system you upgraded.

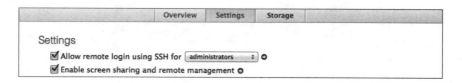

Reference 4.2
Using Server Sidebar Elements

The Server app's sidebar contains four sections, which you'll use over and over throughout this guide:

▶ Server

▶ Accounts

▶ Services

▶ Advanced Services

Server

The Server section displays your server and items that are not services or accounts:

▶ Your server

▶ An AirPort device, if there is one on your subnet

▶ Alerts

▶ Certificates

▶ Logs

▶ Stats

Lesson 5, "Configuring SSL Certificates," covers using SSL certificates to prove your server's identity and provide encryption for the network traffic associated with its services.

Lesson 6, "Using Status and Notifications," covers using the Alerts, Logs, and Stats panes to proactively monitor your server.

The following sections address the server and AirPort items in the Server section of the Server sidebar.

Your Server

Once you select your server in the Server app sidebar, you see three tabs:

▶ Overview

▶ Settings

▶ Storage

Overview Pane

The Overview pane is the first thing you see after your initial installation and configuration of OS X Server. It displays information about how clients can access services; it displays your server's host name and computer name. Note that clients in your local subnet can also use the local hostname, which is not displayed here.

The Server section of the Overview pane displays information about how long the server computer has been running since last starting up, as well as version information for OS X and OS X Server.

The bottom of the Overview pane contains a list of each active network interface and its IPv4 address.

Settings Pane

The Settings pane offers a number of options to configure the following:

► Remote access and administration

► Push notifications

► The location to store service data

The "Enable Apple push notifications" option is covered in Lesson 6, "Using Status and Notifications."

The last option in the Settings pane allows you to configure your server to store data for various services on a volume other than the startup volume.

Moving Service Data Location

By default, most service data is stored in /Library/Server on your server's startup volume. Whether you want more space or more speed or simply want service data segregated from your OS, you can change the service data location. When you click Edit next to the Service Data field, you have the opportunity to change where your server stores most of its service data. Here's what the pane looks like for a server with two internal volumes and one external volume:

If you use the Server app to choose a different service data volume, it does the following:

▶ Automatically stops the appropriate services

▶ Creates a new folder on the volume you choose (/Volumes/*volume_name*/Library/Server)

▶ Copies the existing service data to the new folder

▶ Configures services to use the new location

▶ Starts the services again

Not all the service data is moved. For example, configuration and temporary files (like the Mail spool file) remain on the startup volume, and many services, like Caching, File Sharing, FTP, NetInstall, Time Machine, Websites, and Xcode, offer separate interfaces to choose where to store data for those services.

Just as you should not change the name of your server's startup volume after you start offering services, you should not change the name of the service data storage volume after you designate it in the Server app.

MORE INFO ▶ If you choose to share the Websites root via FTP, it will share the /Library/Server/Web/Data/Sites/ folder on your server's startup volume, even if you choose a different data volume for your server's service data.

Storage Pane

The Storage pane displays an alphabetical list of the disks connected to your server computer; you can also drill down and edit file ownership, permissions, and access control lists (ACLs). You'll see more about this pane in Lesson 14, "Understanding File Access."

TIP If you have multiple volumes attached to your server, only the startup volume has special folder icons for the Applications, Library, System, and Users folders. Other volumes have regular folder icons in the Storage pane.

AirPort

If you select an AirPort device in the Server app sidebar, you have the opportunity to provide authentication to manage the AirPort device. The AirPort pane is very useful when the AirPort device sits between your internal network and your Internet connection; the option to expose services modifies the Network Address Translation (NAT) rules on your AirPort device to allow specific network traffic from the Internet to your server.

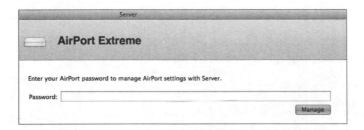

Once you authenticate to the AirPort device, you see the option to require users to provide network user credentials before gaining access to the wireless network (using RADIUS). See Lesson 9, "Configuring Open Directory Services," for more information about network accounts.

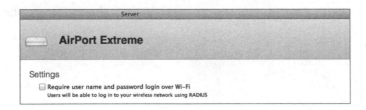

You can expose services manually by clicking Add (+) in the Airport pane, or you can have the Server app automatically expose the service when you start a service.

The following figure illustrates the menu that's available when you click Add (+):

And here's what it looks like when you start some services for the first time:

The AirPort pane displays the list of services that are exposed. In the following figure, the File Sharing service is listed.

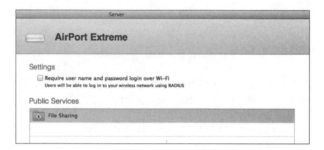

This view of exposed services simplifies some complexity. The following figure from editing the NAT rules via Airport Utility illustrates that File Sharing consists of two protocols: 139 (Windows file sharing) and 548 (AFP for Mac clients).

Accounts

The Accounts section of the Server app sidebar contains the Users and Groups panes. Lesson 8, "Managing Local Users," and Lesson 10, "Managing Local Network Accounts," make extensive use of the Users and Groups panes.

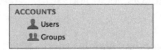

Services

This is a list of the services that OS X Server offers. A green status indicator appears next to the services that are currently running. Select any service to configure it.

Table 4.1 describes the available services.

TABLE 4.1 Basic OS X Server Services

Service Name	Description
Caching	Automatically speed up the download of software and other assets distributed by Apple for Windows PCs, Macs, and iOS devices.
Calendar	Share calendars, book conference rooms and meeting-related resources, and coordinate events using the CalDAV protocol.
Contacts	Share and synchronize contacts information among multiple devices using the CardDAV protocol.

TABLE 4.1 **Basic OS X Server Services** (continued)

Service Name	Description
File Sharing	Share files among Windows PCs, Macs, and iOS devices, using standard file sharing protocols, including SMB2, AFP, and WebDAV.
Mail	Provide mail service for multiple email clients using SMTP, IMAP, and POP standards.
Messages	Securely provide the collaborative power of instant messaging, including audio and video conferencing, file transfer, and sharing presentations with the ability to archive chat transcripts.
Profile Manager	Configure and manage iOS devices and Macs over the air via configuration profiles.
Time Machine	Provide centralized backup location for Macs that use Time Machine.
VPN	Provide secure encrypted Virtual Private Network services to facilitate secure access to local resources by remote Windows PCs, Macs, and iOS devices.
Websites	Host websites based on the combination of host name, IP address, and port number.
Wiki	Enable groups to quickly collaborate and communicate using wiki-powered websites, blogs, and calendars, including QuickLook for viewing attachments and WebDAV support for iOS.
Xcode	Allow developer teams to automate the building, analyzing, testing, and archiving of Xcode projects.

Advanced Services

By default, the list of advanced services is hidden. This list includes services that are not used as often as the other services, and it includes services, like Xsan, that are a little more advanced than the regular services. To display the list of advanced services, hover your pointer above the word Advanced, then click Show. To hide the list, hover your pointer above the word Advanced, then click Hide.

TABLE 4.2 Advanced OS X Server Services

Service Name	Description
DHCP	Dynamic Host Configuration Protocol assigns networking information to networked computers and devices.
DNS	Domain Name Service provides resolution of names to IP addresses, and IP addresses to names.
FTP	File Transfer Protocol is a legacy protocol but is widely supported for uploading files to, and downloading files from, a server.
NetInstall	Allow multiple Macs to Install OS X, install software, restore disk images, or start up (boot) from a common OS configuration by starting from a network disk rather than a locally attached disk.
Open Directory	Provide a centralized location to store information about users, groups, and other resources, and integrate with existing directory services.
Software Update	Host and manage software updates for OS X clients.
Xsan	Provide a shared storage area network (SAN) using Fibre Channel storage for clients on your local network.

MORE INFO ▸ The "Additional Resources" Appendix, Lesson 2, "Installing OS X Server," section contains a list of Apple Support articles that address services that have been offered in previous versions of Mac OS X Server but do not appear in this list of services.

Reference 4.3
Using the Manage Menu

The Server app's Manage menu offers two main menu items.

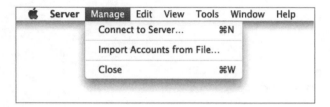

When you choose "Connect to Server" on a Mac that is not yet configured as a server, it opens a window that offers the following buttons:

▶ Other Mac: to open the Choose a Mac window

▶ Cancel: to close the window and quit the Server app

▶ Continue: to set up OS X Server on this Mac

▶ Help: to open Server Help in the Help Center

When you choose "Connect to Server" on a Mac that is already configured as a server, it opens the "Choose a Mac" window that includes the following:

▶ Your Mac

▶ Servers in your broadcast domain that allow remote administration

▶ "Other Mac," which allows you to specify another Mac by its host name or IP address

The "Import Accounts from File" menu item is covered in Lesson 8, "Managing Local Users," and Lesson 10, "Managing Local Network Accounts."

Reference 4.4
Using the Tools Menu

The Tools menu allows you to quickly open four administration applications:

▶   Directory Utility

▶   Screen Sharing

▶   System Image Utility

▶   Xsan Admin

The first three applications are located in /System/Library/CoreServices on every Mac with OS X Mavericks. Xsan Admin is located inside a folder in the Server app itself.

Reference 4.5
Using Help and Server Tutorials

A new feature that arrived with OS X Server for Mavericks is Server Tutorials. Server Tutorials offers information and step-by-step instructions for several OS X Server services. From the Help menu, choose Server Tutorials.

In the Server Tutorials window, select one of the topics, then scroll through the content.

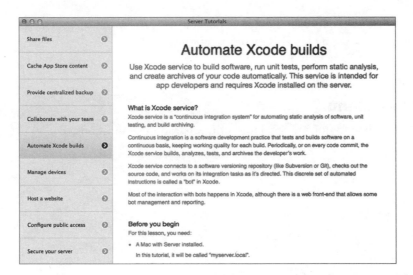

You can close the Server Tutorials window when you're done using it.

Don't underestimate the power of Server Help. After you enter search terms into the Search field, Help displays a list of Server Help resources that match your query.

Once you choose a topic from the list of results, the Help Center window stays in the foreground until you close it.

Reference 4.6
Troubleshooting

If you attempt to administer to a remote server via its host name, but your administrator computer does not have DNS records available for that remote server, you will not be able to authenticate to that server with the Server app. A simple workaround is to use its local hostname; for example, server17.local.

On your server, do not delete the Server app or move the Server app from the Applications folder on your startup volume. If you do, you will see a dialog that all your services have stopped; when you reinstall OS X Server (or just move the Server app back into the Applications folder of the server's startup volume), you will have the opportunity to reenter your Apple ID to renew your Apple Push Notification service certificates, and then your services will start again.

It is recommended that you do not change the name of any volume associated with your server after you've configured your Mac as a server.

You can provide feedback about OS X Server by choosing Server > Provide Server Feedback.

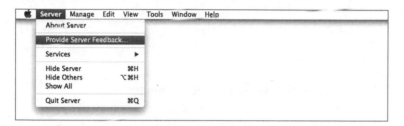

Exercise 4.1
Enable Screen Sharing And Remote Management

In Exercise 2.2, you confirmed that your server allows remote administration using the Server app. Now you will enable screen sharing and remote management as well. If you had a copy of Apple Remote Desktop, performing this action would allow you to use it to control your server. In this exercise you will use Screen Sharing to control your server.

Open a connection to your server with the Server app if you don't already have one open.

Perform these exercises on your administrator computer. If you do not already have a connection to your server computer with Server app on your administrator computer, then connect to it with the following steps: Open the Server app on your administrator computer, choose Manage > Connect to Server, click Other Mac, select your server, click Continue, provide administrator credentials (Administrator Name ladmin and Administrator Password ladminpw), deselect the "Remember this password" checkbox, and then click Connect.

Enable screen sharing and remote administration.

1   If your server isn't already selected in the Server app sidebar, select your server now.

2   Click the Settings tab.

3   Confirm that the "Enable screen sharing and remote management" checkbox is selected.

Open a Screen Sharing connection.

1 Click the arrow next to the "Enable screen sharing and remote management" checkbox.

2 Enter local administrator credentials for your server computer.

NOTE ▶ If you provided your Apple ID when setting up OS X, you will see "Connect as a registered user" and "Using an Apple ID" as two different options in the window. If this is the case, select "Connect as a registered user" and enter credentials for the local administrator on your server.

NOTE ▶ The Name field automatically contains the value of the Full Name attribute of the currently logged-in user on your administrator computer.

3 Click Connect.

4 If necessary, provide local administrator credentials to unlock the server's screen.

5 For the purposes of these exercises, click Cancel to close the window.

6 In the Screen Sharing window, click the close button.

Because you selected the checkbox for "Enable screen sharing and remote management," you were able to take control of your remote server computer using Screen Sharing, right from the Server app's shortcut.

Exercise 4.2
Inspect the Service Data Volume

▶ **Prerequisite**

    ▶   Exercise 4.1, "Enable Screen Sharing and Remote Management"

In this exercise, you will go through the procedure to relocate your service data volume, but you will not actually change it.

Moving the Service Data to a Different Volume

Using the Server app, you can choose a different volume for service data. It's a good idea to perform this task as early as possible, so that you don't have to wait with services disabled while a large amount of data is moved to the new volume.

1   On your administrator computer, if you are not already connected to your server, open the Server app, connect to your server, and authenticate as a local administrator.

2   In the Server app sidebar, select your server and click Settings.

3   Next to the Service Data field, click Edit.

4   Inspect the current Service Data Size, as well as how much space is available on any listed volume. If you have another volume available on which to store the service data, you could select that volume and click Choose.

    Because it is possible that you do not have any extra volumes in your test environment, the rest of the exercises for this guide are written with the assumption that the service data is stored on the startup volume.

5   For the purposes of these exercises, click Cancel to close the window.

Even though you went through the procedure to relocate your service data volume, you didn't actually change it in this exercise. You can use this procedure in a production environment with an additional storage volume.

Lesson 5

Configuring SSL Certificates

You can definitely use OS X Server without doing any additional work to secure its services. However, you can use SSL (Secure Socket Layer) technology to prove your server's identity to client computers and devices, and to encrypt communication between your server and client computers and devices. This lesson starts out with the basics of SSL, and then shows you how to configure SSL certificates for use with OS X Server.

Reference 5.1
Understanding SSL Certificates

Here's a problem: You want the users who use your server's services to trust your server's identity, and to be able to encrypt network traffic with your server.

The OS X solution is to use Secure Sockets Layer, or SSL, which is a system for the transmission of data securely between hosts. You can configure your server to use an SSL certificate, which will provide the ability to use the SSL system.

An *SSL certificate* (also referred to as simply a *certificate*) is a file that identifies the certificate holder. A certificate specifies the permitted use of the certificate, and has an expiration date. Importantly, a certificate includes a *public key infrastructure* (*PKI*) public key.

GOALS

▶ Understand the basics of SSL certificates

▶ Create a certificate signing request

▶ Create a self-signed SSL certificate

▶ Import a certificate signed by a certificate authority

▶ Archive your certificate

▶ Renew your certificate

▶ Configure which certificate your OS X Server services use

PKI involves the use of public and private *keys*. Grossly simplified, a key is a cryptographic blob of data, and within PKI, public and private keys are created in a way that they are mathematically linked: Data encrypted with one key can be decrypted only by using the other key. If you can decrypt data with one key, it proves that the data was encrypted with the other key. The public key is made publicly available, and the private key should be kept private. Fortunately, all of this encryption and decryption happens behind the scenes, and is the basis for establishing secure communications.

Back to definitions:

A *digital identity* (or more simply, *identity*) is an electronic means of identifying an entity (such as a person or a server). An identity is the combination of a certificate (which includes the public key) and the corresponding private key. If you don't have your private key, you can't prove your identity. Similarly, if another entity has your private key, that other entity can claim your identity, so be sure to keep your private key private!

Again simplifying, a *digital signature* is a cryptographic scheme that uses PKI private and public keys to demonstrate that a given message (a digital file such as an SSL certificate) has not been changed since the signature was generated. If a message, which has been signed, changes or is otherwise tampered with, it will be clear that the signature no longer matches the underlying data. Therefore, you can use a digital signature on a certificate to prove its integrity.

Coming back to certificates: a certificate must be either self-signed, or signed by a *certification authority* (also known as a certificate authority, or more simply, a CA). In other words, you can sign your own certificate, using your private key (remember that a certificate is a file that identifies the holder of the certificate, and includes the public key), or you can have someone else, namely a CA, use their private key to sign your certificate.

An *intermediate CA* is a CA whose certificate is signed by another CA. So it's possible to have a hierarchical *chain* of certificates, where an intermediate CA, which in turn is signed by yet another CA, signs a certificate.

In the following figure, the certificate for www.apple.com is signed by an intermediate CA with the name of Cybertrust Public SureServer SV CA, and that intermediate CA is signed by a CA with the name of Baltimore CyberTrust Root.

You can follow a chain of certificates, starting with a signed certificate, following it up to the intermediate CA, and ending at the top of the chain. The certificate chain ends with a CA that signs its own certificate, which is called a *root CA*. It is not required to have an intermediate CA involved—you could simply have a root CA sign your certificate—but in practice, an intermediate CA is often involved.

How does one know if she can trust a CA? After all, since a root CA has signed its own SSL certificate, this effectively means that the organization in control of a root CA simply asserts that you should trust that it is who it *claims* to be.

The answer is that trust has to start somewhere. In OS X and iOS, Apple includes a collection of root and intermediate CAs that Apple has determined are worthy of trust (see the Apple Root Certificate Program page in the Additional Resources Appendix for more information on the process Apple uses to do so). Out of the box, your Mac computers and iOS devices are configured to trust those CAs. By extension, your Mac computers and iOS devices also trust any certificate or intermediate CA whose certificate chain ends with one of these CAs. In OS X, these trusted CAs are stored in the System Roots keychain. (See Lesson 9, "Keychain Management," in *Apple Pro Training Series: OS X Support Essentials 10.9* for more information about the various keychains in OS X.) You can use Keychain Access to view this collection of trusted root CAs. Open Keychain Access (in the Utilities folder). In the upper-left Keychains column, click System Roots. Note that in the following figure, the bottom of the window states that there are over 200 trusted CAs or intermediate CAs by default in Mavericks.

MORE INFO ► Some third-party software companies, like Mozilla, do not use the System Roots keychain, and have their own mechanism to store CAs that their software is configured to trust.

In Lesson 9, "Configuring Open Directory Services," you will learn that when you configure your server as an Open Directory master, the Server app automatically creates a new CA and a new intermediate CA, and uses the intermediate CA to sign a new SSL certificate with your server's host name as the Common Name (the Common Name value is part of what identifies the certificate holder). It is recommended that if you haven't engaged a widely trusted CA to sign an SSL certificate for your server, you should use the SSL certificate signed by your Open Directory intermediate CA, because in Lesson 11, "Configuring OS X Server to Provide Device Management," you will learn how to use the Trust Profile to configure your iOS devices and OS X computers to trust your Open Directory CA, and by extension, the intermediate CA, and the new SSL certificate.

But what about computers and devices that are outside your control and which you cannot configure? When people use computers and devices that are not configured to trust your server's self-signed SSL certificate, or your server's Open Directory CA or intermediate CA, and they try to securely access services on your server, they will still see a message that the identity of your server cannot be verified.

One solution to the problem of proving your identity is for your server to use an SSL certificate that's signed by a CA that most computers and devices are configured to trust.

Deciding What Kind of Certificate to Use

Before going to the trouble of getting a widely trusted CA to sign a certificate for you, consider the services you'll use with the certificate, as well the computers and devices that will access those services.

If you use a self-signed certificate, there is no additional server configuration to install the certificate on your server, but you do need to configure each client to trust that self-signed certificate. For a Mac client, this involves not only distributing the certificate to the Mac and adding it to the System keychain, but also configuring how the OS will trust the certificate.

> **NOTE** ▸ If you use a self-signed certificate and are not able to configure all devices to trust that self-signed certificate, when a user encounters a service that uses the self-signed certificate, they will be presented with a dialog informing them that the certificate may not be trustworthy and that to access services they must click "Continue." This may undermine your efforts to train users not to automatically trust untrusted, expired, or otherwise invalid certificates.

If you use a certificate signed by a widely trusted CA, you need to generate a certificate signing request (CSR), submit the CSR to a CA, and then import the signed certificate.

Of course, it is possible to use a mix of certificates for different services; if your Websites service responds to multiple host names, you'd want a certificate for each host name that you use for web service secured by SSL.

In all cases, you need to configure your server's services to use the appropriate certificate(s).

The next section shows you how to obtain a certificate that's signed by a widely trusted CA, so that you can use it to prove the identity of your server, and use it to encrypt communications between your server and the users of your server's services.

Reference 5.2
Configuring SSL Certificates

Your server has a default SSL certificate that's self-signed. That's a good start, but no other computers or devices will trust services that use that certificate without additional configuration. In order to get a CA to sign a certificate, start by using the Server app to create a certificate signing request. Specific steps to accomplish this objective follow in more detail, but generally, they include the following:

▸ Generating a new CSR

▸ Submitting your CSR to a CA that is generally trusted

▶   Importing the signed certificate

▶   Configuring your server's services to use your newly signed certificate

The CA's process of using your CSR and signing your SSL certificate with its own private key includes verifying your identity (otherwise, why would anyone trust the CA if it signed certificates from unverified entities?) and optionally charging you money.

To finish the story, computers and devices can now use your server's services without getting a warning that your SSL certificate is not verified (as long as those computers and devices trust the CA you've chosen to sign your certificate). Additionally, your server and the users of its services can use your server's SSL certificate in the process of encrypting communications for services that use that SSL certificate.

Before you start creating new certificates, take a moment to inspect what you already have.

Viewing Your Server's Default Certificate

You can use the Server app to display certificates (if you're logged in at the server, you can also use the Keychain Access app). By default, the Server app doesn't display the default certificate. To display all certificates, select Certificates in the Server app sidebar, and then from the Action (gear icon) pop-up menu, choose Show All Certificates.

Once "Show All Certificates" is selected, you see your default certificate. In the following figure, the certificate has the server's host name and expires in two years.

MORE INFO ▶ When you use the Server app's Change Host Name Assistant to change your server's host name, it automatically creates a new self-signed certificate for the new host name.

To get more details, double-click the certificate (or select it, click the Action (gear icon) pop-up menu, and choose View Certificate). When you choose View Certificate, the details of the certificate are displayed.

There is so much information about the certificate that you'll need to scroll to inspect all of the certificate's information.

Click OK to return to the Certificates pane.

The figure below illustrates what you'd see after you configure your server as an Open Directory master or replica. At first glance, it looks like there is just one additional certificate, the code signing certificate, but the certificate with the server's host name is no longer a self-signed certificate, but a certificate signed by your open Directory CA; that certificate icon is blue, whereas the original self-signed certificate was bronze.

Understanding Options for Adding New Certificates

In the Server app Certificates pane, if "Show All Certificates" is not selected in the Action (gear icon) pop-up menu, then the text in the Trusted Certificates field instructs you to "Click (+) to get a trusted certificate." This is the path to getting a CA to sign a certificate for you.

> **NOTE ▶** In order to reveal the menu choice to create a new self-signed certificate, you must first click the Action (gear icon) pop-up menu and choose Show All Certificates.

After "Show All Certificates" has been selected, click Add (+) to reveal three menu commands:

- ▶ Get a Trusted Certificate has the same effect as clicking Add (+) if "Show All Certificates" is not selected; it allows you to quickly generate a certificate signing request (CSR).
- ▶ Create A Certificate Identity is the command to choose to create a new self-signed certificate.
- ▶ Import a Certificate Identity allows you to import a signed certificate or a certificate and private key that you've archived.

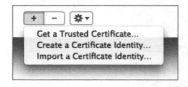

Obtaining a Trusted Certificate

You can choose to get a CA to sign a certificate for you, so that users around the world can use your server's services without being notified that your server's identity is not verified.

> **NOTE ▶** In versions of Server previous to 2.2, you need to first create a self-signed certificate, and then create a CSR from that certificate. This process has been streamlined as of Server version 2.2. However, be aware that when you use the following procedure to generate a CSR, the Server app generates a public and private key pair, but it doesn't generate a self-signed certificate.

The path to generating a self-signed certificate depends on whether or not "Show All Certificates" is selected in the Action (gear icon) pop-up menu:

- ▶ If "Show All Certificates" is not selected, simply click Add (+) in the certificates pane.
- ▶ If "Show All Certificates" is selected, click Add (+) and then choose Get a Trusted Certificate.

After that, you'll see the Get a Trusted Certificate pane.

In the next pane you can enter all the information that is necessary to establish an identity. A CA uses these details to verify your identity.

In the Host Name field, enter the host name you'll use for the services that will use this certificate. Use your organization's full legal name for the Company or Organization field, or if it's for personal use, just use your full name. The Department field is flexible; you can enter information like your department name, but you should enter some value. To be fully compliant with standards, do not abbreviate your state or province. The following figure illustrates all of the fields completed.

The next pane displays the text of your CSR, which you will submit to the CA of your choice. You can wait and access this text later, or you can select and copy this text, or click Save, now.

After you click Finish, the Server app displays the pending request.

If you didn't copy the text of your CSR earlier, you can access it again: Select the certificate that's marked "Pending," click the Action (gear icon) pop-up menu, and choose View Certificate Signing Request (or just double-click the pending certificate item).

Your course of action depends on how your CA accepts CSRs. If your CA allows you to upload a text file, then use the Save dialog to save the CSR as a text file. If your CA requires you to paste the text of the CA into a web form, click the disclosure triangle and then copy the text of the CSR.

You need to choose an appropriate CA for your organization's needs (choosing a CA is outside the scope of this guide), send the CSR to the CA, and prove your identity to the CA. After some period of time, you will receive a signed certificate from the CA.

Importing a Signed Certificate

Once you receive the signed certificate from the CA, it's time to import it with the Server app. If you are still at the list of certificates, double-click your pending certificate to reveal the field into which you can drag your signed certificate.

> **NOTE** ▶ If the CA provides you with the certificate in text form rather than in a separate file, you'll need to convert that text into a file. A quick way to do this is to select and copy the text, open TextEdit, press Command-N to create a new file, choose Format > Make Plain Text (if that is an available command). Paste the text into the text file, and save it with a suffix of cer.

Double-click the pending CSR, and drag the file containing a signed certificate, as well as any ancillary files provided by the CA, into the Certificate Files field (this is also where you could import a certificate and private key that you've exported with Keychain Access). Once the certificate is in the Certificate Files field, its color will be blue, as long as the top of the certificate chain is a root CA that your server trusts.

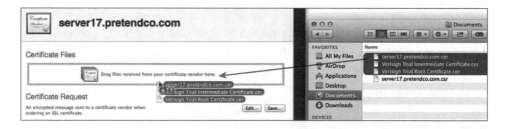

> **NOTE** ▶ If you click Edit next to "Certificate Request", then click Edit in the confirming dialog, a new public and private key pair and a new CSR will be generated, and you'll lose the original CSR.

Click OK to save your changes.

Generating a Self-Signed Certificate

In addition to generating a CSR, you can also use the Server app to generate a new self-signed certificate. This is useful if your server offers services at an alternative host name that corresponds to your server's IPv4 address or another IPv4 address that your server is configured to use, and you have the ability to configure computers and iOS devices to trust the self-signed certificate.

> **MORE INFO** ▶ In versions of the Server app prior to version 2.2, the workflow was to create a self-signed certificate, then generate a CSR, then replace the self-signed certificate with the signed certificate. In Server version 2.2 and later, the Server app does not offer a way to replace a self-signed certificate with a signed certificate.

In the Certificates pane, when you click Add (+) and choose "Create a Certificate Identity" you see a blank Name field.

> **NOTE** ▶ The "Show All Certificates" option must be selected in the Action (gear icon) pop-up menu in order for the "Create a Certificate Identity" command to be available from the Add (+) button.

Enter the host name for the self-signed certificate, then click Create.

> **NOTE** ▶ You can select the "Let me override defaults" checkbox if you have more specific needs, but for most purposes, the defaults will suffice.

At the warning that you are about to create a self-signed certificate, click Continue.

At the Conclusion window, click Done. Finally, click either Always Allow or Allow to allow the Server app to copy the public and private key pair and the certificate from your login keychain to the System keychain and to /etc/certificates.

You'll see the certificate in the Certificates field, as long as the "Show All Certificates" option is selected in the Action (gear icon) pop-up menu.

Inspecting a Certificate

You can inspect your certificates with the Server app, as well as with the System keychain of your server computer (the System keychain contains items that are not user specific and that are available to all users of a system). The following figure is an example of a certificate that's been signed by a CA for test purposes. Note that the OS has not yet been configured to trust the CA that signed this certificate.

You can also use Keychain Access to inspect a certificate and its associated private key. Because the certificate and private key are stored in the System keychain on the server, you need to log in directly on your server (or use a screen sharing method to control your server) to use Keychain Access to access the private key.

Keychain Access is in the /Applications/Utilities folder on your startup volume; you can use Spotlight or Launchpad to search for it (in Launchpad, it is in the folder named Other). Select the My Certificates category to filter the items that Keychain Access displays. If necessary, toggle the show/hide button in the lower-left corner of the Keychain Access window until you can see all keychains. Select the System keychain to show items that are for the entire system, not just for the user who is currently logged in.

At least three items are listed (if you provided an Apple ID for push notifications, you will see more items):

▶ com.apple.servermgrd, which is used for remote administration with the Server app

▶ A certificate named "Server Fallback SSL Certificate," which the Server app automatically uses if the default SSL certificate is removed

▶ An SSL certificate with the host name of your server

When you select a certificate that is not signed by a trusted CA, Keychain Access displays a warning icon, along with the text that explains the issue. In the following figure, the warning for the self-signed certificate is, "This certificate has not been verified by a third party."

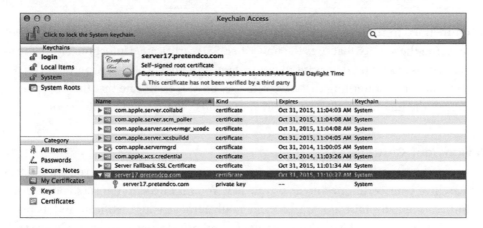

If you double-click your default self-signed SSL certificate to open it, you'll see a warning icon and the text "This certificate has not been verified by a third party."

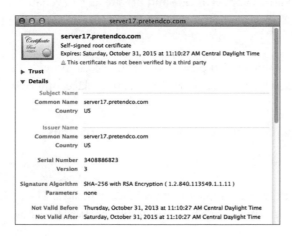

If a service on your server uses this self-signed certificate, when users attempt to use services that use that SSL certificate, they may be warned that your SSL certificate is not trusted, as shown in the following figure:

It's recommended to train your users that when they see an SSL warning, they should *not* continue using the service that uses the unverified SSL certificate. Unfortunately, the reality is that because users need or want to use certain sites, they will click Continue even when they encounter a warning that a website uses an SSL certificate that their browser cannot verify the identity of, that has expired, or that is otherwise misconfigured.

Archiving Your Certificate

Whether you have a self-signed certificate or a certificate signed by a CA, you should take steps to archive your certificate and its private key. You may need to reinstall your server in the future, or an administrator might accidentally remove your certificate and its private key; if you have an archive of your certificate and private key, you can easily use the Server app to re-import your certificate and its private key.

You use the Keychain Access app to export your certificate and private key. Keychain Access prompts you to specify a password to protect your private key; it is recommended that you use a strong password.

You use the Server app to import the certificate and private key. You need to provide the password that was entered when the certificate was exported in the first place; otherwise, you will not be able to import.

See the optional Exercise 5.3, "Archive Your Certificate," for detailed instructions.

Renewing Your Certificate

SSL certificates do not last forever. Luckily, it is simple to renew SSL certificates. The Server app issues an alert when an SSL certificate expiration date approaches. To renew a self-signed SSL certificate, simply click Renew when viewing the certificate in the Certificates pane or when viewing the alert.

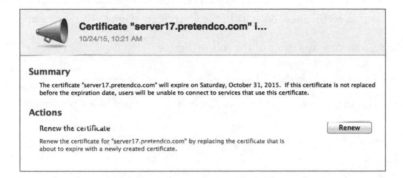

Once you click Renew, the Server app takes care of renewing the certificate, and the alert displays that the issue has been resolved.

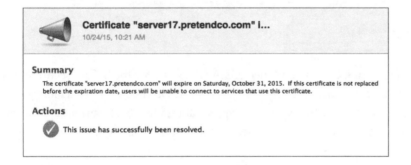

NOTE ▶ Do not click Renew for an Open Directory CA, because this causes changes to the CA properties, and your OD Intermediate CA will no longer be signed by a trusted authority.

If you have a certificate signed by a widely trusted CA, when you click Renew you will see the message that you need to generate a new CSR. See the section "Obtaining a Trusted Certificate" earlier in this section for more details.

Configuring OS X Server Services to Use a Certificate

Once you have taken steps to obtain a signed certificate or create a new self-signed certificate, or have configured your server as an Open Directory server, you should use the Server app to configure services to use that certificate. You start in the Certificate pane of the Server app.

With the pop-up menu, you can do either of the following:

▶   Choose one certificate to specify that all services use that certificate.

▶   Choose Custom to configure each service separately to use or not use a certificate.

Here's an example of choosing Custom and then editing the value for the default secure site of the Websites service. Note that there are some extra certificates in the figure. This illustrates that you can configure your server to respond to requests at multiple host names, create a certificate for each host name, and configure each secure site to use the appropriate certificate.

You can use the Server app to configure the following OS X Server services to use SSL:

▶   Calendar and Contacts

▶   Mail (IMAP and POP)

▶   Mail (SMTP)

- ▶ Messages
- ▶ Open Directory (only appears after starting Open Directory services)
- ▶ Websites

You will see in Lesson 21, "Hosting Websites," that you can granularly specify an SSL certificate for each website you host, and you can use the Profile Manager pane to specify the SSL certificate to use for the Profile Manager service.

A few other services use SSL but are not shown in the Server app:

- ▶ com.apple.servermgrd (for remote administration with the Server app)
- ▶ VPN
- ▶ Xcode

See Exercise 5.4, "Configure Your Server to Use Its New SSL Certificate," for complete instructions.

Following the Certificate Chain

When choosing a CA to use, make sure that it's a root CA that most computers and devices are configured to trust. It's not very useful for you to have a CA sign your certificate if not many computers or devices will trust that certificate. As an example, here's how an SSL certificate signed by a trial CA appears in Keychain Access:

You can see that the "Issued by" field near the top of the window shows VeriSign Trial Secure Server CA – G2. Note the red X icon and the text "This certificate was signed by an untrusted issuer." This is a CA that is by default not trusted by computers and devices, so even if you used this signed certificate for OS X Server services, the people who access your services would experience trouble. In some cases, the service might silently fail, or the user may be alerted that the identity of the service cannot be verified. The following figure illustrates that on a client Mac, Safari notifies the user that Safari can't verify the identity of the website.

If you click Show Certificate, Safari displays the certificate chain. The following figure shows what you see when you select the server's certificate at the bottom of the certificate chain: that the certificate was signed by an untrusted issuer.

The following figure illustrates that if you click the Details disclosure triangle, you'll see information about the identity of the certificate holder, as well as information about the issuer (the entity that signed the certificate). In this case, the issuer's Common Name is VeriSign Trial Secure Server CA – G2.

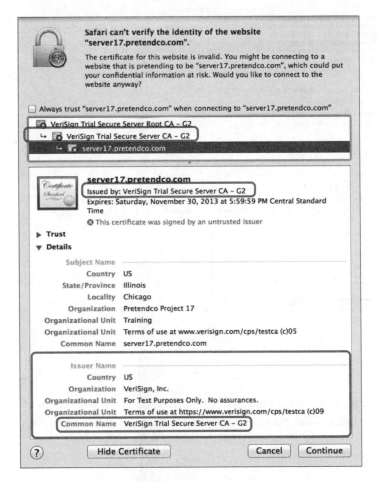

When you select the certificate in the middle of the certificate chain, you see that this is an intermediate CA; the window states "Intermediate certificate authority," and the Issuer Name information shows you that the Common Name of the issuer (or signer) is VeriSign Trial Secure Server Root CA – G2.

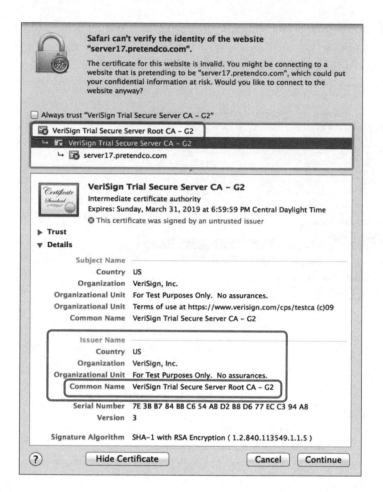

Finally, when you select the certificate at the top of the certificate chain, you see that this is a root CA; the window states, "This root certificate is not trusted." Because this root CA is not in this computer's System Root keychain, Safari doesn't trust the intermediate CA, and it doesn't trust the server17.pretendco.com certificate either.

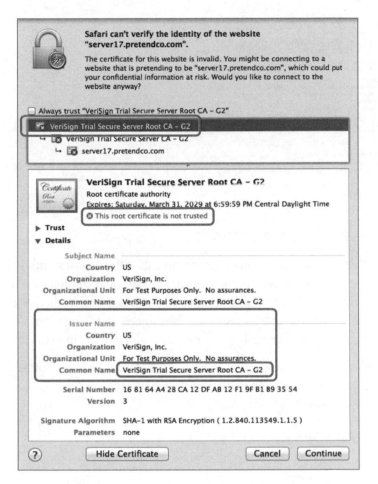

Since that example root CA is for trial use only, it is not recommended to configure your Mac to always trust it outside of a learning and testing environment.

Configuring Trust

You can configure your Mac to always trust a certificate for the currently logged-in user. Using the previous example of your server using its self-signed SSL certificate for a website, you can click Show Certificate, then select the "Always trust" option:

After you select "Always trust," OS X asks for your login credentials. After you successfully authenticate, OS X adds the certificate to your personal login keychain, and configures your system to always trust the certificate for SSL purposes, so that your Mac trusts it when you are logged in with the account that you were logged in as when you clicked "Always trust". This will not affect any other computers or devices, or any other users that log in to that Mac.

In Keychain Access, you can open and inspect the self-signed certificate you just added. Note that the blue plus (+) icon with the text that states that the certificate is marked as trusted for "server17.pretendco.com."

After you visit the site again in Safari, if you click the https icon in the Location field, then click Show Certificate, you see similar information.

A further option for Mac computers is to download and install the certificate in the System keychain, with a configuration to "Always trust" for SSL. Keep in mind that this would need to be done for *every* Mac that uses SSL-enabled services from your server.

For an iOS device, when you open Safari to a page protected by the server's self-signed certificate, you can tap Details:

Then click Accept.

Now your iOS device is configured to trust that certificate.

Note that you can use a configuration profile to distribute a certificate to Mac computers and iOS devices. This automatically configures the device to trust the certificate. See Lesson 12, "Managing with Profile Manager" for more information about profiles.

See Exercise 5.5, "Configure Your Administrator Computer to Trust an SSL Certificate," for complete instructions.

Reference 5.3
Troubleshooting

Certificate Assistant uses the IPv4 address of the Mac from which you run the Server app, so if you're using an administrator computer to configure a remote server and generate a new self-signed certificate, be sure to use the server's host name and IP address where appropriate.

When you configure your server as an Open Directory server, if you have a self-signed certificate with your server's host name in the certificate's Common Name field, the Server app will replace the original self-signed SSL certificate with a new certificate. This new certificate will be signed by a newly created intermediate CA associated with your server's Open Directory service.

However, if you have a certificate with your server's host name in the certificate's Common Name field, and the certificate is signed by a CA or an intermediate CA (that is not associated with your Open Directory service), then the Server app will not replace it with a new one signed by the Open Directory intermediate CA (however, the Server app will still create the OD CA and intermediate CA).

Each certificate has an expiration date; if the current date is later than a certificate's expiration date, the certificate is not valid.

> **MORE INFO ▸** Some files associated with certificates are stored in /etc/certificates, and possibly /var/root/Library/Application Support/Certificate Authority, on your server.

Exercise 5.1
Create a Certificate Signing Request

In this exercise, you will generate a self-signed SSL certificate, and then you will go through the steps of preparing a CSR.

If you are reading this guide in order, your server is not yet running any services other than DNS. In this lesson you will not verify that your server services actually use the SSL certificate created in this lesson. However, the lessons in this guide that cover services that do use SSL certificates will refer back to the self-signed SSL certificate that's created in this lesson.

Unfortunately, you will not be able to receive a valid signed certificate for pretendco.com for production use, but you will become familiar with the necessary steps.

1   On your administrator computer, if you are not already connected to your server, open the Server app, connect to your server, and authenticate as a local administrator.

2   In the server sidebar, click Certificates.

3   At the lower left of the Certificates pane, click the Add (+) button to get a Trusted Certificate.

    If the Show All Certificates option is selected in the Action (gear icon) pop-up menu, then when you click Add (+), choose Get a Trusted Certificate.

4   At the Get a Trusted Certificate pane, click Next.

5   In the Host Name field, enter your server's host name:

server*n***.pretendco.com** (where *n* is your student number).

NOTE ▶ If you click the arrow on the right side of the Host Name field, you will see that the Server app automatically populates the menu with the server's host name. If you choose the host name, it is automatically entered into the Host Name field.

6   In the rest of the fields, enter information appropriate for your situation.

In the Contact Email Address, enter **ladmin@server***n***.pretendco.com** (where *n* is your student number).

In a production environment, consider specifying an email address for your organization that will remain active even if you leave the organization, rather than your personal email address.

Normally you should enter valid information for every single field, because part of this information may be used as verification of your identity before a CA will sign your certificate. But for this exercise, to actually submit a CSR to a CA is optional, so the information does not need to be real—but it should at least be valid.

7   In the Company or Organization field, enter **Pretendco Project** *n* (where *n* is your student number).

8   In the Department field, enter **Training**.

9   Enter information appropriate for your Town or City.

10 Enter information appropriate for your State of Province. To be perfectly compliant with the standards, enter the full name of your state or province, not an abbreviation.

11 Modify the Country field if necessary.

12 After you have completed all the fields and confirmed that the information is correct, click Next.

13 At the pane that displays the text of your certificate signing request, click Finish (you will save it in the next exercise).

14 In the Certificates pane, confirm that your certificate request is displayed as "Pending."

In this exercise, you generated a self-signed SSL certificate, and then you went through the steps of preparing a CSR. Because this guide cannot control the next step—getting a CA to sign your CSR—the next exercise, importing a signed certificate using the Server app, is optional.

Exercise 5.2
Import a Signed Certificate (Optional)

> **Prerequisites**
>
> ▶ Exercise 5.1, "Create a Certificate Signing Request"
> ▶ A certification authority must have signed your CSR.

In this optional exercise, you use the Server app to replace your self-signed SSL certificate with the signed SSL certificate you received from a certification authority.

Several certification authorities offer to sign your CSR on a trial basis for a limited amount of time; at the time of this writing, at least one CA will sign a CSR for a domain that you do not control, for testing purposes, with a CA that is not trusted. This is fine for the purposes of this exercise. Choosing the CA is outside the scope of this guide.

Even if you do not submit your CSR to a CA for a test signed certificate, you can follow along with these steps, but you will not have anything to import, and you will be instructed to skip the last steps of the exercise.

> **NOTE ▶** Once you send your CSR to a CA to sign, the CA sends you a signed certificate. The procedure varies between each certification authority and is beyond the scope of this guide.

1   On your administrator computer, if you are not already connected to your server, open the Server app, connect to your server, and authenticate as a local administrator.

2   In the Server app certificates pane, double-click the certificate that is listed as pending.

3   Drag the signed certificate (and any intermediate certificates that your CA instructs you to download and install) into the Certificate Files field.

    If you did not submit your CSR to a CA, you will not have any signed certificates, so you can simply click Cancel and skip to the end of this exercise.

    > **NOTE ▶** Some CAs also instruct you to download and install one or more intermediate certificates. If this is the case, follow their instructions.

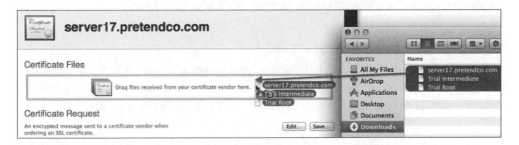

4   Click OK.

5   If you don't see your certificate, click the Action (gear icon) pop-up menu, and choose Show All Certificates.

In the following figure, both the default self-signed certificate and the signed certificate are displayed.

In this optional exercise, you used the Server app to import a signed CSR.

Exercise 5.3
Archive Your Certificate (Optional)

> ▶ **Prerequisite**
>
> ▶ Exercise 5.1, "Create a Certificate Signing Request"

In this exercise, you use Keychain Access to create a secure archive of your certificate, including your private key, and learn to reimport it if needed later.

Archiving Your SSL Certificate

Making a backup of your SSL certificate and private key is a good idea in case you lose your server and need to reimport your certificate and private key. Luckily, Keychain Access makes it easy to archive your certificate and private key in a secure way.

1 On your server computer, open Keychain Access, select System in the Keychains column, select My Certificates in the Category column, and select the certificate with your server's host name.

NOTE ▶ If you enabled the Apple Push Notification service, you will also see certificates that start with the string "APSP" listed.

2 Click the disclosure triangle to illustrate that this item includes both the certificate and its associated private key.

3 Choose File > Export Items.

4 Enter a name for the archive, such as your host name, and specify a location, such as the desktop.

5 In the File Format pop-up menu, choose Personal Information Exchange (.p12).

6 Click Save. Provide your local administrator credentials and click OK.

7 Type private! as the password to protect your private key, move into the Verify field, and then type private! again to verify (because you cannot see the characters you enter).

Note that Keychain Access evaluates the strength of the password you enter.

NOTE ▶ In a production environment, you should use a strong password.

8 Click OK.

Reimporting the Exported Certificate

NOTE ▶ The following steps are for information only. Do not delete and reimport your certificate and private key.

1   If you later need to reimport the certificate, ensure that Show All Certificates is selected in the Action (gear icon) pop-up menu, click Add (+), and choose Import a Certificate Identity

2   Drag the .p12 file into the appropriate field.

3   Provide the passphrase you used when you exported the certificate (**private!**), and click Decrypt.

If the certificate is self-signed, the pane looks like the following figure:

If the certificate is signed by a CA that requires you to also download and import an intermediate certificate, then drag those items into the field as well.

Afterward, the pane will look like the following figure. Notice that the "Issued by" field contains information about the CA that signed your CSR. The trial root CA and trial intermediate root CA items were also dragged into the field, which is indicated in the figure by the text "2 non-identity certificates will be added."

4 In either case, click Import to import the items.

You used Keychain Access to create a secure archive of your certificate, including your private key. The archive is protected by a password, but it's recommended to keep this archive file in a secure location.

Exercise 5.4
Configure Your Server to Use Its New SSL Certificate

▶ **Prerequisite**

    ▶ Exercise 5.1, "Create a Certificate Signing Request"

NOTE ▶ If you did not obtain a new SSL certificate, you can use any certificate, such as the default self-signed certificate.

Because you do not control the domain pretendco.com, you cannot get a widely-trusted CA to sign a CSR for your server's SSL certificate for production use. Because your server's SSL certificate is not in a certificate chain anchored by a CA that is configured in the System Roots keychain, computers and devices will not trust your server's SSL certificate; you can address this in Exercise 5.5, "Configure Your Administrator Computer to Trust an SSL Certificate."

Use the Server app to configure your server's Websites service to use a certificate.

1 On your administrator computer, if you are not already connected to your server, open the Server app, connect to your server, and authenticate as a local administrator.

2 In the Certificates pane, click the popup menu next to the text "Secure services using."

Choose Custom. This means that you can separately configure each service to use a different certificate, or no certificate at all.

3 For the Websites service, click the pop-up menu, and then choose a certificate.

4 Click OK to save the change and dismiss the Service Certificates pane.

Turn on the Websites service.

5 In the Server app sidebar, select the Websites service.

6 Click the On/Off switch to turn the service on.

You just configured your server to use a self-signed certificate for the Websites service, and turned on the Websites service. The next step is to confirm that the service actually uses the certificate; this is covered in Exercise 5.5.

Exercise 5.5
Configure Your Administrator Computer to Trust an SSL Certificate

▶ **Prerequisites**

- ▶ Exercise 5.1, "Create a Certificate Signing Request"
- ▶ Exercise 5.4, "Configure Your Server to Use Its New SSL Certificate"

NOTE ▶ If you obtained a certificate from a widely trusted CA, you do not need to perform this exercise.

In a production environment, it is best to use a valid SSL certificate that's been signed by a trusted CA. If that isn't possible, you should configure your users' computers and devices to trust your server's self-signed SSL certificate, so that your users do not get into the habit of configuring their devices to trust unverified SSL certificates.

This lesson shows you how to configure an individual computer to trust your server's self-signed SSL certificate; it is beyond the scope of this lesson to show you how to replicate the end result on multiple computers and devices.

Verify That the Web Service Uses the New Certificate

On your administrator computer, confirm that you are using your server's DNS service; otherwise, you will not be able to connect to its web service using its host name. Then open Safari to your server's default HTTPS website. Finally, configure your administrator computer to trust the SSL certificate.

1   On your administrator computer, open System Preferences.

2   Open the Network pane.

3   Select the active network service, and confirm that your server's IP address is listed for the DNS Service value.

   If you are using Wi-Fi, you need to click Advanced and then click the DNS tab to view the DNS Service value.

4   Quit System Preferences.

5 On your administrator computer, open Safari, press Command-L to set the insertion point in the location field, and enter https://servern.pretendco.com (where *n* is your student number).

6 Press Return to open the page.

Your certificate is not signed by a trusted CA, and you'll see the message that Safari can't verify the identity of the website.

Configure Your Administrator Computer to Trust This SSL Certificate

Once you see the dialog that Safari can't verify the identity of the website, you can click Show Certificate and configure the currently logged-in user to trust the SSL certificate used by the website.

1 Click Show Certificate.

2 Click the Details disclosure triangle and inspect the information.

3 Click the Trust disclosure triangle.

Note that the pop-up menus for Secure Sockets Layer (SSL) and X.509 Basic Policy are set to "no value specified," which means that your administrator computer does not trust this certificate for SSL.

4 Select the checkbox "Always trust 'server*n*.pretendco.com' when connecting to 'server*n*.pretendco.com'" (where *n* is your student number).

Note that this changes the pop-up menus in the Trust section to Always Trust.

5 Click Continue.

6 Provide your login credentials and click Update Settings.

This updates the settings for the currently logged-in user; this does not affect any other user on this computer.

7 Confirm that Safari opens the page using SSL, with the Safari location field displaying an icon that contains the text "https" and a lock icon.

8 Keep Safari open for the next section of this exercise.

Confirm That Your Mac Trusts the SSL Certificate

To view the SSL certificate the Websites service is using, perform the following steps.

1 In the Location field, click the "https" icon.

2 In the pane that informs you that Safari is using an encrypted connection, click Show Certificate.

3 Click the Trust disclosure triangle to display the contents of the Trust section.

4 Click the Details disclosure triangle to display the contents of the Details section.

5 Confirm that the Subject Name section contains the information you expect.

6 Click OK to close the pane.

7 Press Command-Q to quit Safari.

You confirmed that the Websites service actually uses the SSL certificate you configured in the previous exercise.

You did not get a CA to sign your certificate for production use, so you needed to configure your administrator computer to trust the certificate.

Exercise 5.6
Clean Up

To ensure that the rest of the exercises are consistent, turn off the Websites service.

1   In the Server app sidebar, select the Websites service, and click the switch to turn the service off.

2   Confirm that no green status indicators appear next to the Websites service. This indicates that the service is off.

You are ready to complete the tasks of any other lesson's exercises.

Lesson 6

Using Status and Notifications

A server can only perform its functions when it is in good health and has the resources it needs. OS X Server, via its Server app, provides monitoring and issues notifications if something triggers a threshold or condition. Using the monitoring and notifications features can help keep the server running properly.

GOALS

▶ Monitor OS X Server

▶ Set up notifications

Reference 6.1
Monitoring and Status Concepts

Servers, even OS X Server computers, need some attention from time to time and can't be left to their own devices. It is inefficient to regularly peruse all the operating parameters to make sure the server is healthy. We can utilize the built-in capabilities of the server to tell us when things go wrong or show us when certain trigger points are reached. When these points are reached, OS X Server can notify us via an alert. This doesn't remove the need to look over the server once in a while, but it can help us recognize that a situation is happening or could happen shortly.

Four major sections in the Server app help you monitor the server:

▶ Alerts—Set up what is considered a trigger point and add the email address(es) of those who will get the alerts.

▶ Logs—Quickly access and search logs for the services provided by OS X Server.

▶ Stats—View graphs for processor and memory usage plus network traffic for time periods ranging from 1 hour to 7 days. New is the ability to view Caching usage.

▶ Storage—See a list of all visible volumes available to the server and the amount of storage space left.

Screen Sharing can be used to view the server remotely, and the Server app can be installed on a non-server computer (as you did on your administration computer). This allows you to monitor and manage the server from a different computer.

Reference 6.2
OS X Server Alerts

In the Server section of the Server app, the Alerts pane allows you to configure both the list of email addresses to receive alerts and what alerts will be sent. The Alerts pane has two tabs:

▶ Alerts—Where the messages are shown.

▶ Delivery—Where the email recipients are listed and what will be delivered to them. There is also the choice for push notifications.

NOTE ▶ Push notification is available only once the Apple Push Notification service is configured and enabled on the server.

When choosing an email address for notifications, it is recommended to create a separate email account that can link to multiple people rather than sending it to specific users from the Server app. This prevents a situation where a person responsible for the server leaves the group and notifications go unnoticed. An account like alerts@pretendco.com could be used for multiple purposes and decouples the alerts from individuals.

After you use the Server app to enable Apple push notifications, and supply an Apple ID for push notifications, your server sends alerts to any Mac with Mavericks on which you use the Server app to manage your server. These alerts appear in the Server app and in the Notification Center of these computers. In the following figure, the server is configured to send alerts to the administrator account on client17.

Alert messages will be displayed with a brief description of what has occurred. You can filter the result by adding a term at the bottom of the pane. Double-click the alert, or click the Action (gear icon) menu and choose View Alert, to get additional information regarding the alert. In some cases a button is available to help rectify the error, but you must understand what caused the error and how clicking the button may help or hurt the server. Sometimes the alert is not a problem but a message that a software update is available, and the action is to run the update.

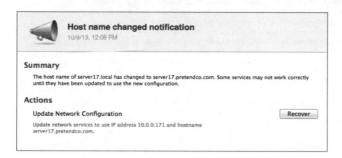

Reference 6.3
Logs in OS X Server

In the Server section of the Server app, the Logs pane allows quick access to the logs for the various services running on the server. A search box allows you to track down specific items in the logs.

Certain logs will always be available, but others become available once the service has been turned on.

Additional logs are available using the Console app, located at /Applications/Utilities.

Reference 6.4
Stats in OS X Server

In the Stats pane, four performance graphs are available:

▶ Processor Usage—Divided into System CPU and User CPU to help determine what is using the most CPU cycles.

▶ Memory Usage—Shows how much physical RAM is being used.

▶ Network Traffic—Shows outbound and inbound traffic.

▶ Caching, Bytes Served—Shows Caching service data transfer.

All four graphs are adjustable to show time intervals from the past hour to the past 7 days.

When using the graphs, realize that the actual numbers reflected on the graph don't tell the whole story. Often, the shape of the graph is most important. Review the graphs once in a while to get used to what is normal and be able to identify when a change is happening.

A normal Processor Usage graph might show a certain percentage during the workday, with spikes corresponding to heavy server utilization. It may indicate a problem when the graphs show a higher than usual percentage with no usage changes to account for it. This might indicate that it is time to do some more research.

Memory usage might creep up over time if an application isn't releasing RAM. The graph might also show that all available RAM is being used continuously, which may indicate that the server needs a RAM upgrade.

Network traffic should also follow the usage patterns. Heavy access will be shown in the graphs, but traffic at night or other times of low usage might indicate a backup process or access that isn't planned.

Reviewing the Caching service in Stats can give you an idea of the network usage associated with it.

Reference 6.5
Storage

Storage is listed under the server's name in the Server section of the Server app. Select the server in the sidebar and then click the Storage tab. Each volume attached to the server is listed, and the available amount of storage capacity is listed next to it with a bar graph for quick review. Each volume can be reviewed and permissions viewed and changed (covered further in Lessons 13 and 14).

Exercise 6.1
Use the Server App to Monitor Your Server

▶ **Prerequisites**

    ▶ All exercises in Lesson 2, "Installing OS X Server"

You use the Server app to manage OS X Server locally while logged in on the server, or to manage it remotely from another Mac running OS X Mavericks.

You can use the Server app to configure your server to send an email message, a push notification, or both, when any of the following conditions occur:

▶ An SSL certificate is about to expire.

▶ A disk that OS X Server uses is unreachable.

▶ The S.M.A.R.T (Self-Monitoring, Analysis and Reporting Technology) status of a disk anticipates failure.

▶ A disk is low on available space.

▶ Mail storage quota has been exceeded.

▶ An email message has a virus.

▶ The network configuration has changed.

▶ Software updates for your server are available.

▶ Time Machine issues.

▶ Caching issues.

1 Perform these exercises on your administrator computer. If you do not already have a connection to your server computer with Server app on your administrator computer, then connect to it with the following steps: Open the Server app on your administrator computer, choose Manage > Connect to Server, click Other Mac, select your server, click Continue, provide administrator credentials (Administrator Name ladmin and Administrator Password ladminpw), deselect the "Remember this password" checkbox, and then click Connect.

2 To allow push notifications, select the server in the sidebar. Click the Settings tab.

3 If the "Enable Apple push notifications" checkbox is not already selected, select it now.

4 If you haven't already configured an Apple ID to be used for push notifications, in the dialog, enter your Apple ID to obtain the push notification certificate. In a leader-led class, your instructor will provide one. Click OK when done.

To configure the email address that is the recipient of alerts from the Server app:

1 In the Server app sidebar, select Alerts.

2 Click the Delivery tab, and click the Email Addresses Edit button.

3   Click the Add (+) button.

4   Enter an email address (you can use your own) that will receive alerts; you can add a second email if you wish. Click OK.

It's a good idea to use the Server app to proactively monitor your server, so you can address any issues that crop up, rather than reacting to an alert in a crisis situation.

Configure which alerts you want to be sent:

1   In the Server app sidebar, select Alerts.

2   Click the Delivery tab, and select the alert types you want to be sent out.

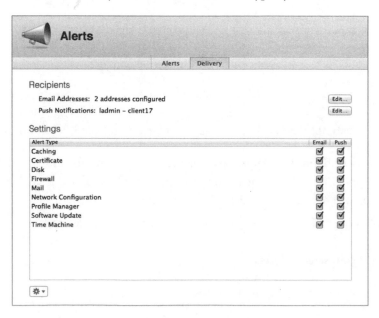

One of the alerts is for low disk space; instead of waiting for an alert, regularly use the Server app to display information about available disk space.

1   In the Server app sidebar, select your server.

2   Click the Storage tab and review the amount of available space.

Although no alert exists for an abnormally high amount of processor usage, memory usage, or network traffic, monitoring these occasionally is still a good idea. The Server app displays a graph of the following categories of information:

▶   Processor Usage (including System CPU and User CPU)

▶   Memory Usage

▶   Network Traffic (including Outbound Traffic and Inbound Traffic)

▶   Caching — Bytes Served

To use the Server app to display the available graphs:

1   In the Server app sidebar, select Stats.

2   Click the pop-up menu to choose, in turn, Processor Usage, Memory Usage, Network Traffic, and Caching.

3   Click the menu on the right to choose the duration of time to include for the graph.

Monitoring Using Screen Sharing

To view the server via Screen Sharing from your administrator computer, Screen Sharing must first be enabled in Settings. To view the server:

1   In the Server app menu, choose Tools and then Screen Sharing.

2   Enter the host name of the server, servern.pretendco.com, where *n* is your student number.

3   Enter ladmin and ladminpw to authenticate and start the viewing session.

Trigger an Alert (Optional)

Use the following optional steps to temporarily change your server's network configuration. This causes the server to send you an alert. For this you must have a wireless network, your server must be connected to the Internet, and the server app must be configured with a valid email address that you can access.

> **NOTE** ▸ The resulting alert email will be sent from root@servern.pretendco.com (where *n* is your student number) and might be considered spam by an email filter. You may need to configure your spam filters to accept email from that address.

1   Unplug the Ethernet cable, enable wireless networking, and then connect the server to a wireless network if possible. In a leader-led environment, your instructor will tell you which wireless network to use. Leave the cable unplugged for at least one minute and then disconnect from the wireless network by turning off AirPort. Plug the Ethernet cable back in.

2   In the alerts, note that the notice "The network configuration has changed" has appeared. Double-click the alert to read the details. Click Done when finished.

3   If an alert has not been registered, you can send a test alert by selecting the Delivery tab in Alerts, clicking the Action (gear icon) pop-up menu at the bottom of the pane, and choosing Send Test Alert.

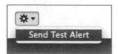

4   Within a few moments, you will receive an email alert regarding the change. It is possible for the email to be caught in spam filters, so check if you haven't received the alert.

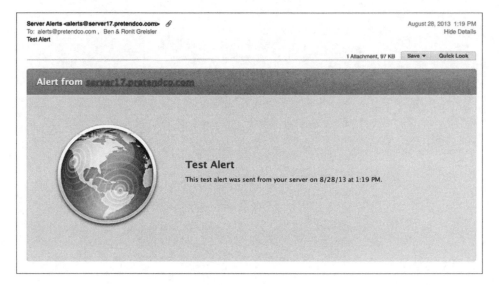

Clean Up

No changes are required for this lesson, as the work you have just done creating alerts and setting up monitoring is recommended for all servers.

Backing Up OS X Server

As much as we might hope otherwise, problems do occur, and sometimes that leads to the need to recover a server whose hardware or software has failed. To help protect against failures, a proven backup system needs to be utilized. Although there are many backup choices on the market, OS X since v10.5 has had Time Machine built in. When used with OS X Server, it can provide a functional, low-cost, and simple backup solution.

GOALS

▶ Back up OS X Server

▶ Restore OS X Server

Reference 7.1
Backup Concepts

There are a number of considerations when it comes to backing up a computer. You need to decide when and how often it gets backed up, where it gets backed up to, and how often the backup media is rotated.

The commercial products available to back up OS X Server offer a wide range of backup techniques and choice of media. With these products you can define exactly how often the server gets backed up and what gets backed up. You can decide if you are going to back up to tape, hard drives, or cloud storage. You get to decide what style of backup to use, such as:

▶ Full image—The entire server's drive is replicated block by block, but it requires that the server be stopped and started from another volume.

▶ Full file-level copy—The entire volume is copied file by file. This takes longer and doesn't require the server to be started from another volume, but unless certain services, especially ones that use a database, are stopped, the backup may not be totally valid.

▶ Incremental—Only the changes from the previous backup are copied. This takes less time and space, but it can take longer to restore, as it may need to read from multiple incremental copies to get the full amount of data.

▶ Continuous—Also known as continuous data protection (CDP), where changes are committed to the backup in short intervals rather than waiting for the end of the day. This allows for more granular backups. This is the technology that Time Machine uses.

When deciding on the media, consider capacity, lifespan, and portability. Some popular choices include:

▶ Tape—While tape's death has been reported on for years, it stays viable by offering large capacities, portability, and increasing speed. The downside is that the tape drives and libraries tend to require care and effort to keep running.

▶ Disk—The cost of disk has decreased to the point where its capacity and speed are a balance to the concerns of lifespan and lack of portability when installed in a large array of drives. Individual drives are portable, of course.

▶ Cloud-based storage—Storing data on a remote host over the Internet is becoming extremely popular and viable with increasing bandwidth and the availability of inexpensive data storage plans. The downside is the reliance on a third party to keep your data safe and the length of time to restore data over the Internet. Some hosts will allow you to make a local backup and send it to them for "seeding," where they copy your data from disk to their infrastructure and send you a disk for restores.

Regardless of the choice of backup technique and media, testing the restores is immensely critical. Data has been lost because a trusted backup turned out to have a problem when a restore was needed. Backups should be tested on a regular basis and verified as valid.

Backup Diversity

It is wise to have a backup of your backup. Backups sometimes fail or can't be recovered, so it is a good idea to use different techniques to provide additional coverage. Maybe use a local backup plus a cloud backup. Each has its advantages and disadvantages, but you can cover multiple bases by using multiple techniques.

Local backups are great because they are fast and easy to recover with, but if there is a problem at that location that damages those backups along with the original source, such as a fire or flood, you are no better off.

Cloud backups or remote backups are good because they protect against local damages, but they take longer to both back up and recover. This could make them inappropriate for situations in which time is of the essence. Just be careful that you don't exclude information that you can't recover from the loss of.

Combining the local and remote backups can give you the best of both worlds as long as you use them appropriately. For example, you might only back up data remotely and leave the OS off it. This might speed up backups, as you can always rebuild the OS. Local backups can be made so they are bootable to make recovery very fast.

Reference 7.2
Time Machine

Apple has provided a simple to use and effective backup application in all versions of OS X since v10.5. Time Machine was originally conceived to make it easy to back up computers with little effort. The process of setting up Time Machine is simply to connect an external hard drive and turn on Time Machine.

Time Machine has grown in capability and is a viable choice to back up OS X Server. Time Machine can be considered a form of continuous data protection, and it properly handles the databases OS X Server uses. Time Machine is the supported backup process for OS X Server.

> **NOTE ▶** If you have moved your service data off the startup volume, you need to refer to Apple Support article HT5139, "Restoring OS X Server from a Time Machine backup," for instructions on how to use command-line tools to restore the service data properly.

Backup targets for Time Machine are limited to hard drive volumes visible to the server and Time Machine–enabled network AFP share points.

> **NOTE ▶** For more information regarding Time Machine, refer to Lesson 18 in *Apple Pro Training Series: OS X Support Essentials 10.9.*

For OS X Server, Time Machine can back up service data, including the following:

▶   Contacts

▶   File Sharing

▶   Calendar

▶   Messages

▶   Mail

▶   Open Directory

▶   Profile Manager

▶   Time Machine (the service for providing a backup target across a network)

▶   VPN

▶   Web

▶   Wiki

Time Machine will not back up the following:

▶   /tmp/

▶   /Library/Logs/

▶   /Library/Caches/

▶   /Users/<username>/Library/Caches

Time Machine has the ability to back up to more than one target. This makes it easy to connect a hard drive to the server for continuous protection and connect a second drive that is rotated offsite. With two or more hard drives being rotated offsite, a disaster recovery plan can be implemented while providing instant recovery of data from the local drive as needed.

Time Machine is capable of taking snapshots and backing up onto its own startup volume. The snapshots feature is a convenience designed for laptops but shouldn't be considered for production servers.

Time Machine makes a backup once an hour for 24 hours. Beyond 24 hours it saves a daily backup for a month, and then weekly backups from that point on until the target volume fills up. The oldest backups are deleted at that point. If you don't want to lose your backups, replace the backup targets as they become close to full.

Exercise 7.1
Use Time Machine to Back Up OS X Server

It is important to consider backup when planning your IT environment. With Time Machine, backup and restore becomes very easy. This exercise guides you through the basics of using Time Machine.

Prepare two temporary destinations for the Time Machine backup.

Option 1: Use Two External Disks As Time Machine Destinations

If you have two external HFS+–formatted disks that you can erase before and after you perform the exercises, follow these steps. Otherwise, skip to the next section, "Option 2: Use Internal Volumes As Time Machine Destinations."

1   Physically connect both external disks to your server computer.

2   In the Finder, choose Finder > Finder Preferences.

3   If necessary, click General in the toolbar, and select the checkbox to show Hard disks on the desktop.

4   Select one of your external disks, press Return to change the name, enter Backup1 as the name, and press Return to finish changing the name.

5   Name the other disk Backup2.

Skip the Option 2 section, and continue with the section "Configure Time Machine."

Option 2: Use Internal Volumes As Time Machine Destinations

Alternatively, considering that ACLs prevent you from removing backup files from a Time Machine destination, and that this is a test environment, you can use the following steps to use Disk Utility to create two new temporary volumes on your existing disk. In a production environment, a Time Machine destination should be a volume on a physically separate disk.

NOTE ▸ Using the same disk or partitioning a disk for a Time Machine backup location is really OK only for demonstration and learning. Do not do this on a real production computer. Also, make sure you have a good backup before live-partitioning a disk that already has data on it. For more information regarding disk partitioning, refer to Lesson 18, "Time Machine," in *Apple Pro Training Series: OS X Support Essentials 10.9.*

1   On your server computer, click LaunchPad in the Dock, click Other, and open Disk Utility.

2   In the Disk Utility sidebar, select the disk that contains your server's startup volume. Be sure to select the disk, and not the volume.

3   Click the Partition tab.

4   Click Add (+). If the disk with your startup volume already has multiple partitions, you may need to first select a volume with extra space, like your startup volume, before the Add (+) button becomes available.

5   Select the new volume you just created. In the Name field, enter `Backup1`.

6   Create the second extra volume by clicking Add (+).

7   Select this second new volume, which should be automatically named Backup1 2.

8   To correct the name for Backup1 2, in the Name field for the new partition, enter `Backup2`.

9   Click Apply, and in the dialog to confirm your action, click Partition.

10 Quit Disk Utility.

Configure Time Machine

1   On your server computer, open System Preferences, and select the Time Machine preference pane.

2   In the Time Machine preference pane, click Select Backup Disk.

3 Select Backup1 and click Use Disk. If you have partitioned the startup drive and are asked, "Are you sure you want to back up to the same device your original data is on?" then click "Use Selected Volume." If you are asked to erase the disk, click Erase.

4 In the main Time Machine pane, click Options to review the list of items that you could select to exclude from backups. Review the options, but leave everything as default for this exercise. If you are in an instructor-led class, you may want to exclude all the folders on the disk other than the Users folder. This will make your backups go much faster. If you aren't in an instructor-led class, you may want to back up everything to help you recover to an earlier version if you make a mistake.

5 Click Cancel to close the exclusions sheet.

6 Click Select Disk to add the second destination.

7   Select Backup2 and click Use Disk.

8   When you are asked if you want to replace your existing backup target or use both, click Use Both.

9   From the Time Machine menu, choose Back Up Now. Time Machine prepares for the backups and makes a complete copy of the disk at the first backup. It copies only what has changed from that point on.

Exercise 7.2
Restore from Time Machine Backup (Optional)

> **Prerequisite**
>
> ▶ Exercise 7.1, "Use Time Machine to Back Up OS X Server"

Because it takes a while to complete a backup, consider continuing with another lesson, then returning to this exercise after the backup has completed. Don't worry, you can work while a backup is being made, just be sure to follow the steps of this exercise to initiate one last backup before you restore.

In this exercise, you will restore a file from the Finder (since we know your Downloads folder has a default file named About Downloads, you will use that file as an example), and then you will explore restoring the entire system from OS X Recovery.

1 On your server computer, click the Time Machine menu and confirm that it lists the time the latest backup completed. If the backup is still running, return to this exercise later.

2 Click the Time Machine menu and choose Back Up Now to do one last backup before you perform the restore. If the backup starts on your second backup location, run that backup and do it again on the original backup location. Wait until this backup is complete, which should only take a few moments.

3 On your server computer, from the Go menu, choose Downloads.

4 From the Time Machine menu, choose Enter Time Machine.

5 Navigate to an earlier time by clicking the up arrow. This arrow points back in time.

6 Select the About Downloads file.

7 Click Restore. When asked whether to keep the original file, replace the file, or keep both files, click Keep Both and compare the files.

8   The files in Time Machine's backup volume are also directly available simply by navigating to the backup volume, finding the backup time folder you want, and copying the file you need.

9   Restart your server and hold the Option key. Choose the Recovery volume, and once started from it, choose Restore From Time Machine Backup from the OS X Utilities window. Follow the assistant but do not restore.

   NOTE ► Using Time Machine is a handy way to restore your test server back to a known state. If during your testing you break the server or want to revert to a known good version, Time Machine can make it easy.

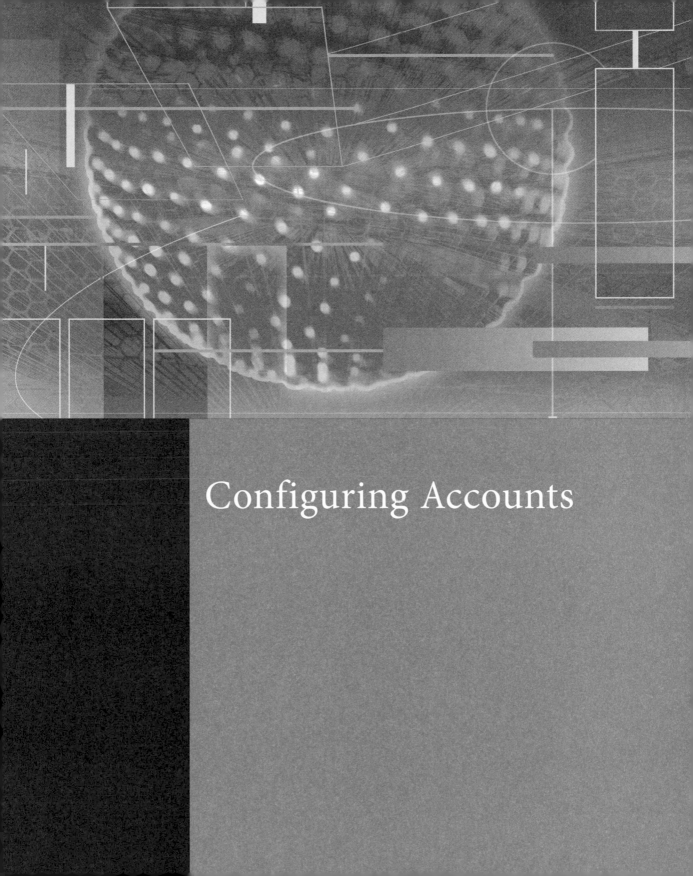

Configuring Accounts

Lesson 8

Managing Local Users

Authentication is the process by which a person identifies which user account she wants to use on the system. This is similar to, but slightly different from, saying that authentication is how a person proves his or her identity to a system. The distinction is useful because multiple people may share the same user name and password, or one person may have multiple user accounts on the same system. In each case, the person supplies user account *credentials* (which usually consist of a name and a password) to identify the user account the person wants to use, and if the supplied credentials are valid, the person successfully authenticates. Although there are other methods of authenticating a user account, such as smart cards or voice print, the combination of name and password is the most common (and is assumed for this lesson).

Authorization is the process that determines what an authenticated user account is allowed to do on the system. OS X Server can disallow authorization to use OS X Server services unless a user is explicitly granted authorization to use the service. In Lesson 13, "Configuring the File Sharing Service," you will learn more about authorization to access a particular file.

In this lesson you will use the Server app to:

▶ Configure local user and group accounts.

▶ Import local accounts.

▶ Configure access to services.

GOALS

▶ Understand authentication and authorization

▶ Create and configure local user accounts

▶ Create and configure local group accounts

▶ Import local accounts

▶ Manage service access authorization

Reference 8.1
Understanding Authentication and Authorization

When configuring any server for access by users, you'll need to determine what services the server will provide and what levels of user access to assign. For many of the services this guide covers, such as File Sharing, you'll need to create specific user accounts on your server.

When considering the creation of user accounts, you'll want to determine how to best set up your users, how to organize them into groups that match the needs of your organization, and how to best maintain this information over time. As with any service or information technology task, the best approach is to thoroughly plan your requirements and approach before starting to implement a solution.

Using Authentication and Authorization

Authentication occurs in many different contexts in OS X and OS X Server, but it most commonly involves using a login window. For example, when you start up an OS X computer, you may have to enter a user name and password in an initial login window before being allowed to use the system at all.

Authentication also occurs when you attempt to connect to a network file service, whether via AFP or SMB; in the following figure, you need to provide a name and a password to authenticate for the AFP service.

A user must authenticate before accessing these services, even if logging in just as a guest user. Depending on what he is trying to access, the user may or may not get feedback on whether he entered the wrong password (authentication) or is not allowed access to the service (authorization). For instance, if you *enter a wrong password* at the login window, the login window will simply shake and return you to the login window; this is the behavior for many authentication dialogs in OS X.

If you *do not have authorization* to log in at a computer, even if the user name and password are correct, the login window will again shake and return to the login window. The user experience is the same, despite the different reasons for the user not being able to access a service.

Reference 8.2
Creating and Administering User and Administrator Server Accounts

A number of tools are available to create and administer user and group accounts. You use the Users & Groups preferences on OS X to define local users and perform very basic administration of local groups. However, System Preferences does not have a remote mode; you have to use tools such as Screen Sharing or Apple Remote Desktop to remotely administer System Preferences on an OS X Server computer.

NOTE ► It is common to drop the word "account" from the term "user account."

This lesson focuses on using the Server app to remotely manage local user and group accounts, and to remotely manage access to the services OS X Server provides.

OS X stores local user and group accounts in the local directory domain (also known as local directory node). You will learn about managing local network accounts in Lesson 10, "Managing Local Network Accounts."

To administer a server with the Server app, you must authenticate as an administrator. This is required whether you use the Server app at the server locally or remotely from another computer.

Using the Server App for Configuring User Accounts

To grant a person specific permissions on OS X Server, you must set up a user account for that person. The Server app is the primary tool you will use in this lesson for creating and configuring user accounts on OS X Server. You'll use the Server app to create network user accounts in Lesson 10.

Standard local user accounts on OS X enable a person to access files and applications local to that computer. After you install OS X Server, local user accounts continue to allow access to files and services, whether you use a local user account to log in on the OS X Server computer, or you use a local user account to access OS X Server services such as Mail and File Sharing. When you use another computer, you can use a server's local user account to remotely access various services offered by that server. But you cannot use that local user account at another computer's login window to log in to that computer, unless that other computer also has a local user account with the same name and password defined in its local directory domain. This is a complication you should avoid by using a centralized directory, which is covered in Lesson 10.

When you use the Server app to create a user, you can specify the following settings:

▶ Full name

▶ Account name

▶ Email address

▶ Password

▶ Whether or not the user can administer the server

▶ Home folder

▶ Disk quota

▶ Keywords

▶ Notes

A user account's full name is also known as a long name or name; it is common practice to use a person's full name, with the first letter of each name capitalized, and a space between each word in the name. The name can contain no more than 255 bytes, so character sets that occupy multiple bytes per character have a lower maximum number of characters.

The account name, also known as a short name, is an abbreviated name, usually consisting of all lowercase characters. A user can authenticate using the full name or account name. OS X uses a user's account name when creating a home folder for that user. Carefully consider the account name before assigning it, because it is not a trivial task to change a user's account name. You are not permitted to use the space character in a user's account name; it must contain at least one letter, and it can contain only the following characters:

▶   a through z

▶   A through Z

▶   0 through 9

▶   _ (underscore)

▶   – (hyphen)

▶   . (period)

Using Keywords and Notes

Keywords and notes are new to OS X Server for Mavericks. They allow you to quickly search and sort accounts, and can help you quickly create groups or edit groups of users. These features are useful for organizing users or searching for particular users based on something other than name or user ID. This provides for a more realistic search pattern should you need to specify a range of users without actually adding them to a specific group.

To add a new keyword, simply enter it in the Keyword field, then press Tab or Return.

> **NOTE** ▶ Local accounts and network accounts (see Lesson 9, "Configuring Open Directory Services") have separate keyword lists.

You can add a note to a user account with information that may be useful later, such as who created the account, the year of graduation, or the purpose of the account.

To search for users with the same keyword or note, enter text in the Filter Users field, then choose the appropriate item from the menu.

You can add more filtering options by entering more search terms.

After filtering the user list, don't forget that you can click the Clear button in the Filter Users field to remove the filter terms and display all users again.

Using Advanced Options

For a little more information about the user, select the user in the Users pane, secondary (or Control-) click, and choose Advanced Options from the shortcut menu.

In the advanced settings pane, you can view and modify several attributes of a user account.

The full list of attributes listed in the advanced settings pane is:

▶ User ID

▶ Group

▶ Account Name

▶ Aliases

▶ Login shell

▶ Home Directory

You should not modify these attributes without completely understanding the ramifications of the change.

NOTE ▶ Invalid settings can prevent the user from logging in or accessing resources.

A full explanation of all of these attributes is outside the scope of this guide, but some are important enough that they are explained in the following sections.

The user ID (UID) is a numerical value that the system uses to differentiate one user from another. Though users gain access to the system with a name or short name, each name is associated with a UID, and the UID is used in making authorization decisions. In the unlikely event that two users are logged in with different names and passwords but with the same UID, when they access documents and folders, the system will consider them to be the same owner. Because of this, the system will provide both users with the same access to documents and folders, a situation you should avoid.

NOTE ▶ The Server app allows you to configure multiple users with the same UID, but this is not recommended.

The group is the primary group the user is associated with, even though you can configure the user to be associated with multiple groups. You do not need to explicitly add a user to its primary group. Note that when you view a group's list of members, a user that is a member of a group because the group is the user's primary group will *not* be listed as a member of the group, even though that user effectively is a member of that group.

It is recommended that you do not change the account name in the advanced settings pane, because this could prevent the user from accessing resources.

You can assign one or more aliases for a user account. An alias allows a user to access services by authenticating with one of her aliases and her password. An alias is sometimes a shorter or otherwise more convenient string of text than the account name.

Creating Templates

You can create user and group templates from an existing account, to cut down on the time it takes you to create new users with the attributes you desire. From the pop-up menu that appears when you secondary (or Control-) click an account, choose either Create Template from User or Create Template from Group. After you've created a template, when you create a new account, a Template pop-up menu appears, and you can choose to use a template or not.

Configuring Local User Accounts

OS X Server maintains a list of local user accounts for managing access to resources. In this section, you will learn how to use the Server app to:

▶ Create local users that can access services and files on your server.

▶ Give a local user the ability to administer your server.

▶ Create local groups.

▶ Assign local users to a local group.

▶ Assign local groups to a local user.

▶ Assign local groups to a local group.

Creating Local Users That Can Access Services and Files on Your Server

In the Users pane in the Server app, simply click the Add (+) button to create a new user.

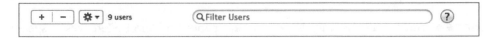

Enter values for the new user's attributes, and then click Create.

Giving a Local User the Ability to Administer Your Server

An administrator account is a special type of user account on OS X Server that enables the user to administer the server. A user with an administrator account can create, edit, and delete user accounts, as well as modify the settings of various running services on the server where the administrator account exists. The administrator uses the Server app to perform basic account and service management.

> **NOTE** ▶ Because an administrator account is so powerful, carefully consider before configuring an account to be able to administer your server.

It is simple to make a local user an administrator. Just select the checkbox "Allow user to administer this server." You can enable this when you create the user, or at any time afterward. You'll create a user and make it an administrator.

John Signal

Full Name: John Signal

Account Name: jsignal

Email Address:

Allow user to: ☑ log in ☑ administer this server

When you make a user account an administrator, the operating system makes that user account a member of the local group that has the full name of Administrators. Any member of the Administrators group can use the Server app and can unlock all the preferences in System Preferences. Any member of the Administrators group can also change file ownership, can make any system-wide change, and can run commands as the root user in the command-line environment, so consider carefully before enabling a user account to be a member of the Administrators group.

> **NOTE ▸** You can also use the Users & Groups pane of System Preferences to specify that any user is an administrator.

> **NOTE ▸** When you select "Allow user to administer this server" for a user, you add him or her to the local group named admin. You can use the credentials for any user in the admin group to access secure system preferences like the Users & Groups and Security panes, among other privileges. Be careful about which users you assign to be part of the local group admin.

In the list of users, there is no indication that any user is an administrator user.

To remove administrator status for a user, simply deselect the checkbox labeled "Allow user to administer this server" and click Done.

Creating Local Groups

Groups allow you to assign privileges to groups of users so you don't have to modify each user individually. In the Server app sidebar, click Groups.

To create a group, click Add (+), enter information in the fields, and click Create.

Assigning Local Users to a Local Group

The most common approach for populating groups with users is to select a group and add one or more users to it. On your server, you will select a group, click Add (+), and then add users to the group. When you use the Server app to add a user to a group, you can't just enter the name; you have to actually choose a user from a list that appears when you start typing.

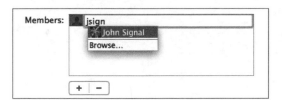

You could also choose Browse, select users and groups from the new window that appears, and then drag them into the list of members.

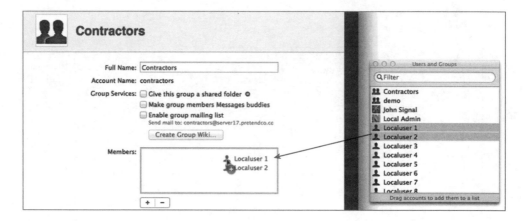

Assigning Local Groups to a Local User

Just as you can assign a user to a group, you can edit a user to add groups to that user. The effect is the same: The user becomes a member of a group.

After you add a group to a user, you can verify your action by looking at that group's list of members.

Assigning Local Groups to a Local Group

You can make a group a member of another group. This way, when you want to allow a group of groups to access the same resource, you can configure the parent group instead of separately configuring each group.

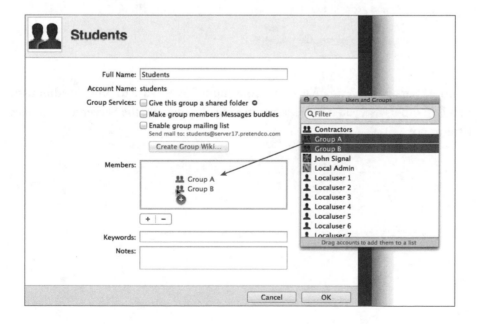

Importing Accounts

You can create accounts individually, or you can import them from a properly formatted file. The file could be created on your own, created with a third-party tool, or created with command-line tools.

Anytime you import users from a file, and that file does not specify a password for a user, you will need to set their passwords after you import the users.

Importing a List of Users with the Server App

The Server app can import a list of users that contains user account data. The first line must be a header line that defines what kind of data is contained in the file and how the text is formatted. The user data must follow the header line.

> **MORE INFO** ▶ If you don't already have a valid header line to copy, you can use an app such as Passenger from macinmind.com to generate a proper header line.

To import accounts, choose Manage > Import Accounts from File.

In the Import Users pane, navigate to select your input file. Be sure to provide administrator credentials; otherwise, you'll get an error message (by default, the Server app supplies administrator credentials).

If the import file does not contain plain text passwords, set the user passwords: Select the users you just imported, secondary (or Control-) click, and choose Reset Password from the shortcut menu.

Of course, you should always use secure passwords in a production environment.

Here's an example of an import file with an appropriate header line that describes the content of the file.

```
● ● ●                    🗋 employees-exported.txt — Edited
0x0A 0x5C 0x3A 0x2C dsRecTypeStandard:Users 15 dsAttrTypeStandard:NFSHomeDirectory
dsAttrTypeStandard:GeneratedUID dsAttrTypeStandard:RecordName
dsAttrTypeStandard:RealName dsAttrTypeStandard:PrimaryGroupID
dsAttrTypeStandard:UniqueID dsAttrTypeStandard:Password dsAttrTypeStandard:UserShell
dsAttrTypeStandard:LastName dsAttrTypeStandard:FirstName
dsAttrTypeStandard:MailAttribute base64:dsAttrTypeStandard:JPEGPhoto
dsAttrTypeStandard:Comment dsAttrTypeStandard:Picture dsAttrTypeStandard:Keywords
/Users/localuser3:7C9D62E3-1A34-4B8B-AA8D-F8B469D2DBBE:localuser3:Localuser
3:20:2027:********:/bin/bash:3:Localuser:::You will eventually delete
these.::demo,imported
/Users/localuser4:3CA0A992-BA49-4A29-947D-568D2E276958:localuser4:Localuser
```

MORE INFO ▶ For information about using Workgroup Manager to generate an appropriate header line for an import file, download and install Workgroup Manager and see Workgroup Manager's Help.

Reference 8.3
Managing Access to Services

By default, if you have not configured your server to be an Open Directory server, it does not check for authorization before granting access to OS X Server services such as Mail, File Sharing, and Calendar. In this state, if a given service is running and someone can connect to it and successfully authenticate, OS X Server grants authorization to use the service.

However, you can choose to manage service access control manually. Once managed, after someone attempts to connect to a given service and successfully authenticates with a user account, OS X Server checks to see if that user is authorized to use the service before granting access to it. As you'll learn in Lesson 10, managing access control is set up automatically after you configure your server as an Open Directory server.

Manually Managing Service Access

When you secondary (or Control-) click a user and choose "Edit Access to Services" from the shortcut menu, you see a list of services and a few buttons. Each service's checkbox is unavailable, because at this point, you are not managing access to service yet; every authenticated user can access the service if the service is running.

When you click the Manage Service Access button, you are asked if you want to manually manage service access. Even after you click Manage, every user you create with the Server app is automatically granted authorization to each of your OS X Server services by default (of course, no user can access a given service if the service isn't running).

When you secondary (or Control-) click a user and choose "Edit Access to Services" from the shortcut menu, you see a list of services, and each service has a checkbox you can select or deselect. When you deselect a checkbox, you remove authorization for that user to access the service.

OS X Server grants authorization to a service for a user if the user, or any group that the user is a member of, has the access checkbox selected for that service. Therefore, when you edit a user's access to services and deselect a checkbox for a service, if the user is in a group for which access to that service is authorized, a message indicates that the user will still have access to the service.

MORE INFO ▶ If you create an account with Workgroup Manager or even the Users & Groups pane of System Preferences, the account does not automatically have access to any services; in fact, Workgroup Manager offers this warning when you create a new user account: "New users may not have access to services. If service access controls are enabled, you need to grant access to desired services for users created in Workgroup Manager." Because you may use Workgroup Manager when importing users, you can later grant access to services with the Server app.

Using Groups to Manage Access to Files and Services

You may find that long-term administration will be easier if you manage access to services based on organizational roles assigned to groups rather than to individual people. This will make it much easier when changes occur within your organization, because you'll need to change only group membership rather than individual file and service permissions for each person.

When you enable File Sharing with the Server app, it automatically enables both the AFP and the SMB file sharing protocols. (You will learn more about these services in Lesson 13, "Configuring the File Sharing Service.")

MORE INFO ▶ Some system groups are normally hidden from view, with names like com.apple.access_afp and com.apple.access_backup. These contain the names of users and groups that have authorization to use a given service. You can view these groups by choosing View > Show System Accounts. You may see this referred to as Service Access Control Lists (SACLs) in other places. In most circumstances, it is best not to directly modify these system group files; instead, use the Server app to configure user or group access to services.

Reference 8.4
Troubleshooting

Keep the concepts of authentication and authorization separate in your head; just because you can authenticate doesn't mean that you're authorized for a given action.

Troubleshooting Importing Users

When you use the Server app to import users or groups, a log file is automatically created in a folder named ImportExport in your home folder's Logs folder (~/Library/Logs/ImportExport). You can use the Console app to view these logs.

Note that this log file shows an example of successfully importing six user records. Some problems associated with importing accounts, if they occur, will appear in these log files.

NOTE ▶ The ImportExport logs are stored on the Mac on which you run the Server app to perform the import.

Troubleshooting Accessing Services

It can be somewhat confusing if a user is trying to connect to a service for which she doesn't have authorization. Despite the fact that she has entered her password correctly, she may believe that she hasn't, because she sees the authentication window shake or sees an error message. It may be useful to have users try to authenticate to a service they do have access to, so you can confirm that their passwords aren't the problem.

Exercise 8.1
Create and Configure Local User Accounts

For any users to access your server, they need to have an account on the server. Use the Server app, the primary tool for creating and managing user accounts for OS X Server, to create users. You will eventually configure Localuser 1 as an administrator, and use Localuser 1 credentials to create a user named Localuser 2.

Create a New User

It is quick and easy to create a new user account. After creating the user, you will edit this user's basic attributes again.

1   Perform these exercises on your administrator computer. If you do not already have a connection to your server computer with Server app on your administrator computer, then connect to it with the following steps: Open the Server app on your administrator computer, choose Manage > Connect to Server, click Other Mac, select your server, click Continue, provide administrator credentials (Administrator Name ladmin and Administrator Password ladminpw), deselect the "Remember this password" checkbox, and then click Connect.

2   In the Server app sidebar, select Users.

3   In the lower left of the Users pane, click the Add (+) button to add a new user.

4   Enter the following information:

▶   Full Name: Localuser 1

▶   Account Name: localuser1

▶   Email Address: Leave blank.

▶   Password: local

▶   Verify: local

5   For now, leave the "Allow user to administer this server" checkbox deselected.

6   Leave the Home Folder pop-up menu set to Local Only.

7   In the Keywords field, enter demo and then press Return so it becomes a distinct keyword.

8   In the Keywords field, enter class and then press Return.

9   In the Notes field, enter Employee #408081.

10   Review the settings for this new user.

11 Click Create to create the user.

Edit a User

Use the Server app to edit the basic attributes for this user: Change the picture for the user, and allow the user to administer the computer. Selecting the checkbox to allow the user to administer the computer automatically adds the user to the system group whose Full Name is Administrators and whose Account Name is admin.

1 In the list of users, double-click Localuser 1 to edit this user's basic attributes.

> **NOTE ▶** Additional methods of editing the user's basic attributes include clicking the Action (gear icon) pop-up menu and choosing Edit User; Control-clicking the user and choosing Edit User from the shortcut menu; and pressing Command-Down Arrow.

2 Click the silhouette for the user, and select a picture from the available pictures.

3 Select the checkbox labeled "Allow user to administer this server."

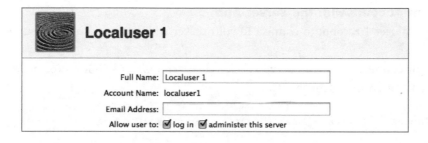

4 Click OK to save the changes you just made.

Use the Server app to inspect and edit additional attributes for this user. Add an alias (you can use an alias instead of your full name or account name for some kinds of authentication, and the Mail service accepts messages addressed using aliases).

5 In the list of users, Control-click Localuser 1 and choose Advanced Options from the shortcut menu.

6 In the Aliases field, enter localuserone.

> **WARNING!** ▶ Even though you have the ability to change various options here, your user may have difficulty logging in or accessing files if you change the value for some attributes. Update only the Aliases field in this exercise.

7 Click OK to close the advanced settings pane.

Use a Different Account with the Server App

Next, use the Localuser 1 account to connect to your server and create another local user.

1   To close your connection to your server, click the Server app's close button (or press Command-W, or choose Manage > Close).

2   Choose Manage > Connect to Server (or press Command-N).

3   Click Other Mac, select your server, and click Continue.

4   For Administrator Name enter localuser1, and for Administrator Password enter local.

5   Deselect the checkbox "Remember this password in my keychain."

NOTE ▶ Be sure to deselect the checkbox "Remember this password in my keychain"; otherwise, the Server app will automatically enter these temporary credentials the next time you connect to the server, until you remove the Keychain entry.

6   Click Connect.

7   Click Users in the Server app sidebar.

8   At the lower left of the Users pane, click the Add (+) button to add a new user.

9   Click the silhouette for this new user, and choose Edit Picture.

10 If your administrator computer has a camera, you can click the Camera tab, take a photo of yourself to use for this user, and click Done to use that photo for this user.

If you do not want to use your photo, or if your administrator computer does not have a camera, click Cancel, and then click the silhouette for the user and select an existing picture.

11 Enter the following information for this new user:

▶ Full Name: **Localuser 2**

▶ Account Name: **localuser2**

▶ Email Address: Leave blank.

▶ Password: **local**

▶ Verify: **local**

12 Leave the checkbox "Allow user to administer this server" deselected.

13 Select the checkbox "Limit disk usage to" and enter **750** in the text field. Leave the unit pop-up menu at MB.

14 In the Keywords field, type **demo** and then press Return.

15 In the Keywords field, type **class** and then press Return.

16 In the Notes field, enter **Another local user.**

17 Click Create to create the user account.

You've proven that you can do something very powerful—create a new user account—by using an account that you configured as an administrator of this server (Localuser 1).

Create a User Template

In the previous exercise, you entered the keywords *demo* and *class*, along with a note. Wouldn't it be nice to be able to create new users with a common set of settings like keywords and notes? You can with the template feature.

Perform the next steps using your original administrator account, to illustrate that it doesn't matter which administrator creates a template; a template is available to any administrator.

1   On your administrator computer, from the Manage menu, choose Close.

2   From the Manage menu, choose Connect to Server.

3   Select your server, and click Continue.

4   For Administrator Name enter ladmin, and for Administrator Password enter ladminpw.

5   Deselect the checkbox to remember this password.

6   Click Connect.

Now that you're connected as a different administrator than the one that created the user account, create a new template from that newly created user account.

1   In the list of users, Control-click the new user you just created, and choose Create Template from User.

2   In the Template Name field, replace the contents with Lesson 8 user template.

3   Confirm that the disk usage quota, Keywords field, and Notes field values are part of the template.

4 Click Done to create the template.

Use a User Template

Now that you have a template, you can use it when creating new accounts.

1 In the Users pane, click Add (+) to create a new user.

2 Click the Template pop-up menu and choose the template you just created and edited.

3 Enter the following information for this new user:

▶ Full Name: Localuser 3

▶ Account Name: localuser3

▶ Email Address: Leave blank.

▶ Password: local

▶ Verify: local

4   Leave the following fields populated from the template:

▶   Home Folder: Local Only

▶   Limit disk usage to: 750 MB

▶   Keywords: demo and class

▶   Notes: Another local user.

5   Leave the checkbox "Allow user to administer this server" deselected.

6   Click Create to create the user account.

Try to Use the Server App as a Nonadministrator User

You were able to create a new local user after you connected as Localuser 1 to your server with the Server app, because earlier you selected the checkbox to allow Localuser 1 to administer the server. Try to use Localuser 2's credentials to connect to your server with the Server app; you won't be able to, which will confirm that only users in the Administrators group have the ability to administer the server.

1   Press Command-W to close your connection to your server.

2   Open a new connection to a server (choose Manage > Connect to Server, or press Command-N).

3   Select your server, and click Continue.

4   For Administrator Name enter localuser2, and for Administrator Password enter local.

5   Deselect the checkbox "Remember this password in my keychain."

6 Click Connect.

Since the user Localuser 2 is not an administrator, you see the message "Server requires administrator login."

7 Click OK to dismiss the alert.

8 Click Cancel to return to the "Choose a Mac" window.

Connect as the regular local administrator account you've been using for most of this guide.

1 At the "Choose a Mac" window, select your server and click Continue.

2 Enter your local administrator credentials (for Administrator Name enter ladmin; for Administrator Password enter ladminpw).

3 Leave the checkbox to remember this password deselected.

4 Click Connect.

You can leave the Server app open while you work on the next exercise.

In this exercise, you used the Server app to create and configure local user accounts, including a local administrator account. You created and used a user template. You demonstrated that you cannot use the Server app with an account that is not an administrator account.

Exercise 8.2
Import Local User Accounts

In this scenario, you have a tab-separated text file that was generated from the employee information database. It includes some information about each employee, including first name, last name, full name, a shortened name to use for the account name, keywords, a note, and a password for the user. This file also has a properly formatted header line.

You also have a text file that was generated from another server (with Workgroup Manager). Because OS X Server cannot export user passwords, the import files do not contain passwords, so you have to reset user passwords after you import them.

Import User Accounts from a Delimited Text File

1   On your administrator computer, if you are not already connected to your server, open the Server app, connect to your server, and authenticate as a local administrator.

2   In the Server app, choose Manage > Import Accounts From File.

3   In the open file dialog, click Documents in the sidebar, open StudentMaterials, and then open Lesson08.

4   Select the employees-tabdelimited.txt file.

5   If necessary, click the Column View button.

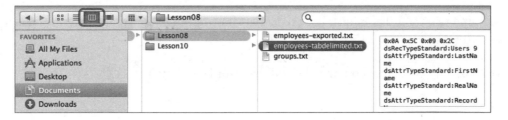

6   Hover the pointer over the right border of the import sheet until the pointer becomes a double-sided arrow, and then drag the border to the right so that you can preview more contents of the file.

    NOTE ▸ Be sure to resize the import sheet instead of the entire Server app window to change the view of the data you are about to import.

The header line (the first line) has the number 9, which indicates that each record contains nine attributes. In the right column of the Import window, you get a preview of the contents of the text file.

In this scenario, the text file contains the following nine attributes:

▶ Last name

▶ First name

▶ Full name

▶ Account name

▶ Password

▶ User Shell

▶ Primary Group ID

▶ Keywords

▶ Comment (Server app displays this field as Notes)

NOTE ▶ Your screen may not allow you to expand the window to be as wide as the following figure, which displays each record as a single line of text.

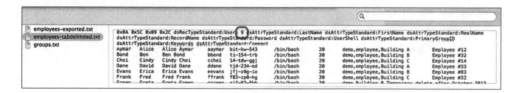

7   Leave the Template for Users checkbox deselected.

8   If necessary, enter your local administrator credentials.

9   Click Import.

    After the import has completed, Server app displays the Users pane.

10 Inspect one of the users to confirm that it was correctly imported. Note that in the following figure, the user does not have a home folder, because there was no home folder specified in the import file. This is fine, because some users do not need a network home location; they just need access to services.

You just imported user accounts.

Import Users from an Exported Formatted File

You'll use the Server app to import users from a properly formatted file, such as one exported on another server with Workgroup Manager. This import file has more users with "Localuser" as the first name, to re-enforce the idea that you are still working in the server's local directory.

1   On your administrator computer, in the Server app choose Manage > Import Accounts From File.

2   Click your Documents icon in the sidebar, open the StudentMaterials folder, and then open the Lesson08 folder.

3   Select the employees-exported.txt file.

   Note that in the right column, you see a preview of the contents of the text file. The first header line is much longer than the previous header line. This header line states that each user record contains 40 attributes (as opposed to the previous file, in which each user record contains nine attributes).

4   If necessary, enter your local administrator credentials.

5   Leave the Template for Users checkbox deselected.

6   Click Import to import the file.

When the Server app displays the list of users, you'll see that an additional five users have been imported (Localuser 4 through Localuser 8).

7   Scroll down to the bottom of the list of users.

Because passwords are not included in this import file, you need to set a password for each of the new accounts. For now, you'll set each account to use the password "local."

8   Select all the newly imported accounts, Localuser 4 through Localuser 8, by selecting Localuser 4, holding down the Shift key, and then selecting Localuser 8.

9   Control-click while your pointer is still over one of the selected users to reveal the shortcut menu. Text indicates how many users are part of your selection.

10 Choose Reset Password.

11 In both the New Password and Verify fields, enter local.

12 Click Change Password.

You've imported users from two different types of files. The first was a simple text file, as if exported from some external list of employees, with attributes separated by the tab character. This file included passwords, so you did not need to reset these user passwords. This file included a header line that specified which characters were used as attribute and value delimiters, as well as which fields in the text file corresponded with which attributes.

The second import file was exported from another server, so it did not include passwords, so you had to set passwords for these users.

You will review the logs related to importing these users in Exercise 8.4, "Troubleshoot Problems with Importing Accounts."

Exercise 8.3
Create and Configure Local Groups

▶ **Prerequisite**

> ▶ Exercise 8.2, "Import Local User Accounts"

You can use the Server app to create and organize groups as well as users. You will create groups with the Server app, and associate users and groups with each other.

1 On your administrator computer, if you are not already connected to your server, open the Server app, connect to your server, and authenticate as a local administrator.

2 In the Server app sidebar, select Groups.

Create a Group

1 In the Groups pane, click the Add (+) button.

2 Enter the following information for the first new group:

▶ Full Name: Engineering

▶ Group Name: engr

3 Click Create to create the group.

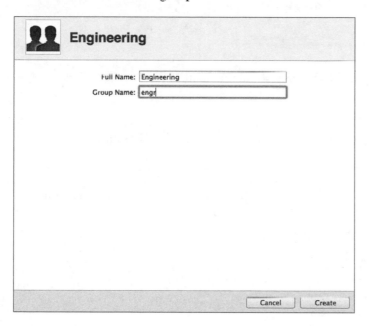

Import Groups

Rather than spend a lot of time creating more groups, import some groups with a group import file. You will use these groups for the rest of the exercise.

1 Choose Manage > Import Accounts from File.

2 If the Lesson08 folder is not already displayed, click your Documents icon in the sidebar, and then open the StudentMaterials/Lesson08 folder.

3 Select the groups.txt file.

Note in the file preview that this text file has a header line that defines the special characters, the account type (Groups), and the names of the attributes included.

4   If necessary, enter your local administrator credentials.

5   Click Import.

The Server app displays the groups you just created and imported.

6   Double-click the Projects group.

The import file included a list of users that are members of the Projects group, so you'll see them listed as members of the group.

7   Click OK to go back to the list of groups.

Add Users to Groups

You'll use the Server app to add users to groups. Even though you used an import file that had a number of groups populated with users, you may need to update group membership at some point later.

In this scenario, a few people in your organization were added to a new Engineering department, so you should add their user accounts to the Engineering group. Add Alice Aymar and Ben Bond to the Engineering group.

1 Double-click the Engineering group.

2 Click the silhouette for the Engineering group, and select a picture for the group.

3 Below the Members field, click the Add (+) button.

4 In the text field, press the Space bar.

5 Choose Browse, which opens a new window that displays the local users and groups.

6 Drag the new window over to one side of the Server app window.

7 Drag Alice Aymar and Ben Bond to the Members list.

8 Click OK to save the changes to the list of groups.

9 Close the window that displays the list of local users and groups.

Add Group Membership to a User Account

While you could easily use the same process you used in the previous section to add users to the newly created groups, this time you'll try an alternate approach by adding groups to a user's account. In this scenario, Cindy Choi joined both the Marketing group and the Engineering group. Add these groups to that user's account.

1 Select Users in the Server app sidebar.

2 Double-click Cindy Choi.

3 Below the Groups list, click the Add (+) button to add a group.

4 Press the Space bar and choose Browse.

5 Drag the window that displays local groups over to the side.

6 Select the Engineering group, hold down the Command key, and then select the Marketing group.

7 Drag the Marketing and Engineering groups to the Groups field.

8 Click OK to save the changes to the user.

9 Close the window that displays the list of local groups.

Add Groups to Groups

Nesting groups, or adding groups to groups, is critical to simplifying user and group management. In this scenario, each Pretendco employee is a member of one of three departments: Marketing, Engineering, or Management. There is a group named Employees, and you plan to use this group to allow all employees access to resources. Although you could populate the Employees group with all the individual Marketing, Engineering, and Management user accounts, the easiest approach is to simply add the three groups to the Employees group. When the structure of your organization changes over time—for example, if a new department is created—you would need to use the Server app to create a new group for this department, and add its group to the Employees group.

When you are finished with this exercise, the Pretendco Employees group will consist of three groups: Marketing, Engineering, and Management.

1   Select Groups in the Server app sidebar.

2   Double-click the Employees group.

3   Click the Add (+) button below the Members list. If the Users & Groups window is not displayed next to the Server app window, enter some text in the text field and then choose Browse.

4   In the Users & Groups window, Command-click the Engineering, Marketing, and Management groups to select these groups.

    You can resize the Users & Groups window to display a larger list of accounts.

5   Drag these three groups to the Members list of the Employees group.

    Note that even though you have three groups selected while holding the Command key, all three groups might not appear in the Members field until you drop the accounts into the field.

6   Click OK to save the changes to the group.

7   Double-click the Employees group to confirm that the new groups are listed in the Members field.

All members of the Marketing, Engineering, and Management groups now have access to the resources the Employees group can access.

You just used the Server app to create and organize groups as well as users. You created groups with the Server app, and associated users and groups with each other.

Exercise 8.4
Troubleshoot Problems with Importing Accounts

▶ **Prerequisites**

- ▶ Exercise 8.2, "Import Local User Accounts"
- ▶ Exercise 8.3, "Create and Configure Local Groups"

When you use the Server app to import users or groups, a log file is automatically created in a folder named ImportExport in the Library/Logs folder of your home folder on the computer you performed the import on. Since you imported users in an earlier exercise, you can use the Console app to inspect the import log.

On your administrator computer, open the Console app.

1   If the Console app is not already running, open Launchpad, open Other, and open Console.

2   If no sidebar is displayed for the Console window, click Show Log List in the toolbar.

The Console app displays logs from several locations on your computer. The tilde character (~) is a symbol for your home folder, so ~/Library/Logs is a folder in your home folder, and is for logs specifically related to your user account. The /var/log and /Library/Logs folders are for system logs. You will look for a log file in the ImportExport folder in your ~/Library/Logs folder.

3   Click the disclosure triangle for ~/Library/Logs to display the contents of that folder, and then click the disclosure triangle for ImportExport to display the contents of that folder.

4   Select a log file under ImportExport.

Note that this log file shows that you imported a number of records without error. Some problems associated with importing accounts, if they occur, will appear in these log files.

You just used the Console app to inspect the logs that were created when you imported accounts. Remember that the import log is stored on the computer that you used to perform the import, not necessarily on the server.

Exercise 8.5
Manage Service Access

> **Prerequisites**
>
> ▶ Exercise 8.1, "Create and Configure Local User Accounts"
>
> ▶ Exercise 8.2, "Import Local User Accounts"
>
> ▶ Exercise 8.3, "Create and Configure Local Groups"

Now that you have experience controlling authentication with users and groups, it's time to move on to authorization. You can limit access to services at the user and group level. Use the Server app to enable specific services from a user's perspective.

You may not want all users with accounts on your server to access all the services your server offers. In this exercise, you will configure access for the two services associated with the File Sharing service: AFP (Apple Filing Protocol, primarily for Mac computers earlier than Mavericks) and SMB (Server Message Block, for both Windows and Mavericks). You will learn more about the File Sharing service in Lesson 13, "Configuring the File Sharing Service."

Use the Server app to disallow a particular user from accessing the File Sharing service.

Start out by restricting access to the File Sharing service.

1   On your administrator computer, if you are not already connected to your server, open the Server app, connect to your server, and authenticate as a local administrator.

2   In the Server app sidebar, select Users.

3   Select Localuser 1 and Localuser 2.

   At this point, Localuser 1 should be an administrator user, and Localuser 2 should be a regular user. If you don't have these users, go ahead and create them now with the Server app.

4   Control-click the selected users and choose "Edit Access to Services" from the shortcut menu.

5   Click Manage Service Access.

6   In the dialog that appears, click Manage.

7   Deselect the File Sharing checkbox.

   NOTE ▶ The Time Machine service relies on the File Sharing service; when you deselect the File Sharing service, you can no longer modify the Time Machine checkbox.

8   Click OK.

You just removed authorization to use the File Sharing service for the two users. Other users are still authorized to use the File Sharing service.

Turn on File Sharing and Verify Authorization

Turn on File Sharing and use it to verify authorization and lack of authorization to use the service.

1   In the Server app sidebar, select File Sharing.

2   Click the On/Off switch to turn on the service.

From your administrator computer, attempt to connect to your server via AFP.

1   On your administrator computer, in the Finder choose Go > Connect to Server.

2   In the Server Address field, enter your server's complete host name (server*n*.pretendco.com, where *n* is your student number), and click Connect.

In the connection dialog, attempt to authenticate with the following user account, which is not authorized to use the File Sharing service.

3   In the Name field enter localuser1, in the Password field enter local, and click Connect.

The window shakes, indicating a problem with either authentication or authorization. In this case, the user is not authorized to use the File Sharing service, even though it is a member of the Administrators group.

4   In the Name field enter localuser2, in the Password field enter local, and click Connect.

The window shakes, indicating a problem with either authentication or authorization. In this case, the user is not authorized to use the File Sharing service.

5 In the Name field enter **localuser3**, in the Password field enter **local**, and click Connect.

A list of available volumes appears.

6 Select the localuser3 volume and click OK.

7 Confirm that you can actually see files; you will see the folders for a network home folder for the user localuser3.

8 In the Finder window sidebar, click the Eject button next to your server's icon to disconnect.

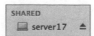

You just verified that when you remove authorization for a user to access a service, the user cannot access the service.

Exercise 8.6
Clean Up

In the next lesson, you will configure your server to manage network accounts. Your server will then have multiple directories: the local directory and the network directory. You'll have network users and groups to work with in the next lesson.

In order to prevent confusion, you will:

- ▶ Delete the local user and local group accounts you were just working with.
- ▶ Stop the File Sharing service.

Make sure that you connect to your server with the local administrator you had been using before you started the exercises in this lesson, rather than with the Localuser 1 account. Start by closing the active Server app window.

1 On your administrator computer, in the Server app, choose Manage > Close (or press Command-W) to close the Server app window.

Open the Server app again and connect with credentials for the local administrator that you had been using before you started the exercises in this lesson. Just to be sure that you do not delete system accounts (accounts that are normally hidden, and which are crucial to the normal operation of the system), confirm that the Server app is not displaying system accounts.

1 Open the Server app, select your server, and authenticate as the local administrator you had been using before you started the exercises in this lesson (for Administrator Name enter ladmin, and for Administrator Password enter ladminpw).

2 Click the View menu, but do not choose any options. Confirm that the second menu choice is Show System Accounts.

NOTE ▶ Do not choose Show System Accounts.

If the second menu choice is Hide System Accounts, choose Hide System Accounts, and then click the View menu again to confirm that Show System Accounts is the second menu choice.

Now that you are sure you will not accidentally delete system accounts, delete the other accounts you created in the exercises for this lesson.

1 For each user (except for the local administrator you had been using before you started the exercises in this lesson), select the user, click the Delete (–) button, and then at the dialog, click Delete.

> **TIP ▶** If you accidentally click Delete after you select the user you are currently using to authenticate to the Server app, you will see a dialog informing you that the Server app will not allow you to delete this user. If you have multiple users selected, it will offer to delete the other selected users.

Delete the groups you created and imported.

1 In the Server app sidebar, select Groups.

2 Select one group, and then press Command-A (or choose Edit > Select All).

3 Click the Delete (–) button.

4 At the confirmation pane, click Delete to delete the groups.

Stop the File Sharing service.

1 In the Server app sidebar, select File Sharing.

2 Click the On/Off switch to turn off the service.

You are ready to continue with the other exercises in this guide.

Lesson 9

Configuring Open Directory Services

This lesson describes how using a directory service can help you manage users and resources on your network. You will learn about the features of Apple Open Directory services and how these services can be integrated with other directory services in a mixed environment. You will also learn how to set up and manage directories and user accounts with the Server app. Finally, you'll become familiar with common Open Directory services issues and learn how to resolve them.

Open Directory is extremely versatile when dealing with a variety of other directory services, such as Active Directory, eDirectory, and OpenLDAP, but mixed platform directory service scenarios are outside the scope of this guide.

If you are performing the exercises independently and do not have an extra server computer, study and review, but do not perform, the tasks that involve the other directory server.

GOALS

▶ Understand the Open Directory service roles you can configure on OS X Server

▶ Configure OS X Server as an Open Directory server

▶ Bind OS X Server to another Open Directory server

▶ Locate and identify Open Directory–related log files

Reference 9.1
Introducing Directory Services Concepts

Giving a user multiple user accounts on different computers can cause problems. For instance, if each computer in a network has its own authentication database, a user might have to remember a different name and password for each computer. Even if you assign the user the same name and password on every computer, the information can become inconsistent over time, because the user may change a password in one location but forget to do so in another. You can solve this problem by using a single source of identification and authentication information.

Directory services provide this central repository for information about the computers, applications, and users in an organization. With directory services, you can maintain consistent information about all the users—such as their names and passwords—as well as about printers and other network resources. You can maintain this information in a single location rather than on individual computers. The result is that you can use directory services to:

▶ Provide a common user experience.

▶ Provide easier access to networked resources such as printers and servers.

▶ Allow users to log in on multiple computers using a single account.

For example, once you *bind* OS X computers to an Open Directory service (to bind is to configure one computer to use the directory services offered by another), users can freely log in to any bound OS X computer. They will have their session managed based on who they are, what group they belong to, what computer they logged in at, and what computer group the computer belongs to. Using a shared directory service also permits a user's home folder to be located on another server and to be mounted automatically on whatever computer the user logs in to, as long as that computer is bound to the shared directory.

What Is Open Directory?

Open Directory is the extensible directory-services architecture that is built into OS X. Open Directory acts as an intermediary between directories (which store information about users and resources) and the applications and system software processes that want to use the information.

In the context of OS X Server, the Open Directory service is actually a set of services that provide identification and authentication.

Many services on OS X require information from the Open Directory service to function. The Open Directory service can securely store and validate the passwords of users who want to log in to client computers on your network or use other network resources that require authentication. You can also use the Open Directory service to enforce global password policies, such as password expiration and minimum length.

You can use the Open Directory service to provide authentication to Windows users for file and print services, as well as other services that OS X Server provides.

Overview of Open Directory Service Components

Open Directory provides a centralized source for identification and authentication. For identification, Open Directory uses OpenLDAP, an open source implementation of the Lightweight Directory Access Protocol (LDAP), a standard protocol used for accessing directory service data. Open Directory uses LDAPv3 to provide read-and-write access to the directory data.

The Open Directory service leverages other open source technologies, such as Kerberos, and combines them with powerful server-administration tools to deliver robust directory and authentication services that are easy to set up and manage. Because there are no per-seat or per-user license fees, Open Directory can scale to the needs of an organization without adding high costs to an IT budget.

After you bind an OS X computer to use an Open Directory server, that bound computer automatically gets access to network resources, including user authentication services, network home folders, and share points.

You can configure OS X Server in four basic Open Directory states:

▶ A standalone server

▶ An Open Directory master

▶ An Open Directory replica

▶ Connected to another directory service or multiple directory services (also referred to as a member server)

> **NOTE ▶** You can configure your server to simultaneously connect to one or more other directory services, at the same time as serving as an Open Directory master or replica.

As you plan directory services for your network, consider the need to share user, resource, and management information among multiple computers and devices. If the need is low, little directory planning is necessary; everything can be accessed from a server's local directory. However, if you want to share information among computers, you need to set up at least one Open Directory server (an Open Directory master). Furthermore, if you want to provide high availability of directory services, you should set up at least one additional server to be an Open Directory replica.

Understanding the Standalone Server Role

The default state is for your server to host its local accounts. People must use accounts that are local users created on your server to access your server's services.

Understanding the Open Directory Master Role

When OS X Server is configured to host network accounts and provide directory services, this is referred to as an Open Directory master (or a master, which is covered in the next section). The action you will select to perform in the Server app is "Create a new Open Directory domain." A domain is an organizational boundary for a directory; you are creating a shared directory domain, also referred to as a node.

When you use the Server app to configure your server as an Open Directory master, it performs the following actions:

▶ Configures OpenLDAP, Kerberos, and Password Server databases

▶ Adds the new directory service to the authentication search path

▶ Creates a local network group named Workgroup

▶ Adds the local group Local Accounts to the network group Workgroup

▶ Creates a new root SSL certification authority (CA) based on the organization name you provide at the time of configuration

▶ Creates a new intermediate SSL certification authority, signed by the CA above

▶ Creates a new SSL certificate with your server's host name, signed by the intermediate CA above (if you don't already have a signed SSL certificate with your server's host name)

▶ Adds the CA, intermediate CA, and SSL certificate to the System keychain of your server

▶ Creates a folder for the intermediate CA and the CA in /var/root/Library/Application Support/Certificate Authority, each with files for Certificate Assistant and a copy of the certificate

▶ Grants local accounts and local network accounts authorization to access OS X Server services

OS X Server for Mountain Lion introduced a new set of terms: local accounts and local network accounts. *Local accounts* are those accounts that are stored in your server's local node. *Local network accounts* are those accounts that are stored in your server's shared Open Directory node (in its OpenLDAP database). The word "local" in the term "local network" differentiates these network accounts from other nodes' directories; local network accounts are from the local network shared OpenLDAP node.

Once you have set up your server to be an Open Directory master, you can configure other computers on your network to access the server's directory services.

To recap, your server has local user and group accounts; after configuring as an Open Directory master, this local database still exists. Creating an Open Directory master creates a secondary, shared LDAP database. The administrator of that database has the default short name of diradmin. Each database is separate, and managing either one requires different credentials. You have also created a Password Server database to store user passwords, as well as a Kerberos Key Distribution Center (KDC). You will learn about those later in this lesson.

Understanding the Open Directory Replica Role

Once you have a server configured as an Open Directory master, you can configure at least one more Mac with OS X Server as a directory replica to provide the same directory information and authentication information as the master. The replica server hosts a copy of the master's LDAP directory, its Password Server authentication database, and its Kerberos KDC. Open Directory servers notify each other whenever there is a change in directory information, so all Open Directory servers have a current store of information.

You can use replicas to scale your directory infrastructure, improve search-and-retrieval time on distributed networks, and provide high availability of Open Directory services. Replication also protects against network outages, because client systems can use any replica in your organization.

When authentication data is transferred from the master to any replica, that data is encrypted as it is copied over.

> **TIP** Because replication and Kerberos use timestamps, it's best to synchronize the clocks on all Open Directory masters, replicas, and member servers. You can use the Date & Time system preference to specify the time server; you can use Apple time servers or an internal time service.

You can create nested replicas—that is, replicas of replicas. One master can have up to 32 replicas, and those replicas can have 32 replicas each; one master plus 32 replicas plus 32 × 32 replicas of those replicas totals 1057 Open Directory servers for a single Open Directory domain. Nesting replicas is accomplished by joining one replica—referred to as a tier one replica—to your Open Directory master, and then joining other replicas to the tier one replica. Any replica created from a tier one replica is referred to as a tier two replica. You cannot have more than two layers of replicas.

The following figure has one Open Directory master and one replica that is also a relay, a replica that in turn has at least one replica.

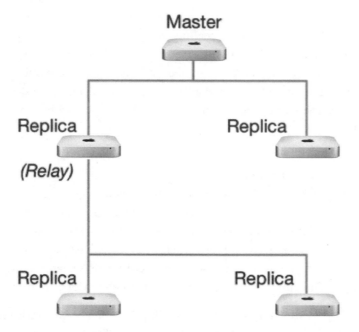

In the case of a disaster, you can promote an Open Directory replica to be the new master, but you must have either a Time Machine backup of your server that's configured as your Open Directory master, or an Open Directory archive. Search for "Archive and restore Open Directory data" in Server Help for more information.

Understanding Open Directory Locales

Open Directory locales is a feature that makes it easy for you to distribute the load among appropriate Open Directory servers. An Open Directory locale is a grouping of one or more Open Directory servers that service a specified subnet; you use the Server app to define a locale, and then associate one or more Open Directory servers and one or more subnets with that locale. When a client computer (OS X v10.7 or later) is bound to any of your Open Directory servers, if that client computer is in a subnet associated with a locale, that client computer will prefer the Open Directory server(s) associated with that locale for identification and authentication.

As soon as you configure your first Open Directory replica, OS X Server creates two additional locales.

▶ The locale named Default Locale is a failsafe, and includes the master and all of the replicas, even if they are not in the same subnet as your master; this is the locale that an OS X client uses if no locale is available for the client's subnet.

▶ The second locale is based on the subnet of the Open Directory master and includes the master and any replicas that are on the same subnet as the master; Open Directory clients on the same subnet use this locale.

▶ As you add more locales, they are displayed in the Locales tab.

To create a new Open Directory locale, click the Locales tab, click Add (+), and specify information for the new locale.

When configuring a new locale, you need to click Add (+) under the Servers field and select one or more of the Open Directory servers listed.

See https://help.apple.com/advancedserveradmin/mac/3.0 for more information on configuring Open Directory locales.

Understanding the Role of Using Another Open Directory Server

If you intend to set up multiple servers, populating each server with the same user accounts would be extremely inefficient. Instead, you can bind your server to another directory system, in which case your server is referred to as a bound server or a member server. In this role, each server gets authentication, user information, and other directory information from some other server's directory service. This way, users can authenticate to your server with an account defined in your server's local directory, or with an account defined in any directory node that your server is bound to. The other directory node is commonly an Open Directory or an Active Directory system, but could include other kinds of directories as well.

The Profile Manager service requires that your server be configured as an Open Directory master. That's fine, because it is possible for your server to both be an Open Directory master and be bound to another directory service. This is particularly useful for providing services to groups within a larger organization. If you are the administrator for a group of users within a larger organization, you can use OS X Server to provide additional services to existing groups defined in your larger organization, or to create additional groups of people for your smaller groups. You can achieve this without bothering the people who administer resources for the larger organization, regardless of what directory service your larger organization uses.

Understanding Access to Services

In the standalone state, your server by default does not check for authorization to access OS X Server services (except the SSH service); see Reference 8.3, "Managing Access to Services," for more information.

If you configure your server as an Open Directory master, the Server app configures your server to start checking for authorization to access OS X Server services. When you create new local accounts and new local network accounts with the Server app, the Server app grants the new accounts authorization to access OS X Server services.

If you configure your server as an Open Directory master and then bind to another directory server, you may need to grant authorization to use your server services to accounts from the other directory node. You may find it convenient to grant authorization to access OS X Server services to the other directory node's groups so you do not need to configure individual user accounts from the other directory node.

Reference 9.2
Configuring Open Directory Services

In order to provide the full range of Open Directory services, each server participating in the Open Directory domain, whether a master, replica, or member server, needs to have consistent access to forward and reverse DNS records for all the other servers in the domain. You should use the Network Utility (or command-line tools) to confirm that DNS records are available.

You use the Server app to configure your server as an Open Directory master or replica, and you use the Users & Groups preferences or Directory Utility to bind to another directory server.

Configuring OS X Server as an Open Directory Master

If your server is not already configured as an Open Directory master or connected to another directory service, you can turn on the Open Directory service, and the Server app walks you through configuring your server to be an Open Directory master or replica.

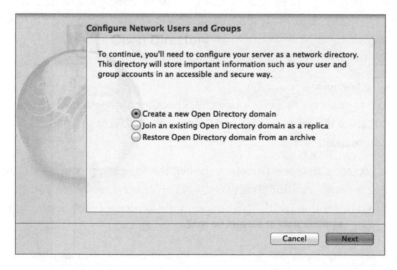

Start by selecting "Create a new Open Directory domain" and clicking Next.

You are prompted to create a new user, with the default name of Directory Administrator and the short name of diradmin.

You are also prompted to provide an organization name and an administrator email address.

Once you confirm these settings, the Server app configures your server as an Open Directory master. Afterward, the Open Directory pane displays your server, listed as master. The Server app displays the IPv4 address of each active network interface for each server in the list of Open Directory servers.

NOTE ▶ Even if a network interface has a self-assigned IPv4 address starting with 169.254, it will be displayed in the list of Open Directory servers. For example, if you find it convenient to use AirDrop on your server, it is possible to configure a Wi-Fi network interface to be active but not connected to any particular Wi-Fi network.

Creating an Open Directory Archive

When you back up your server with Time Machine, you automatically get a periodic archive of all identification and authorization components of your Open Directory server, including:

▶ The OpenLDAP directory database and configuration files, which include authentication information

▶ Kerberos configuration files

▶ Keychain data used by Open Directory

You can also create an Open Directory archive manually. Start by clicking the Action (gear icon) pop-up menu and choosing Archive Open Directory Master.

TIP ▸ You need an Open Directory archive in order to promote an Open Directory replica to an Open Directory master.

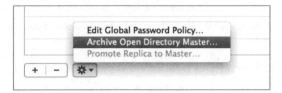

The next step is to specify a location to create the archive file. Because the archive contains sensitive authentication information, be sure to protect the archive with a secure password.

Configuring OS X Server as an Open Directory Replica

If you already have an Open Directory master on another Mac with OS X Server, you use the Server app to configure your server as a replica of another Open Directory master.

You can configure a server to be a replica, using the Server app on an existing master or replica, or using the Server app on a server you want to configure as a replica. The replica server you're adding must have remote administration access enabled before you can add it as a replica.

If you're using the Server app on an existing master or replica, in the Open Directory pane, click the Servers tab and click Add (+). Then:

▶ Enter the host name (you could also enter an IP address or local host name, but this guide recommends using the host name to verify that the crucial DNS host name records are available).

▶ Enter administrator credentials for the server you want to configure as the replica.

▶ Choose the parent server.

▶ Enter the directory administrator's credentials and click Next.

Add a Replica

Replicas provide failover and load balancing for Open Directory clients. Enter the information for the server that you want to make a replica of this Open Directory domain.

Server Address:	
Server Admin Name:	
Password:	
Parent Server:	server17.pretendco.com
Directory Admin Name:	
Password:	

Cancel   Next

If, instead, you're using the Server app on the server you want to configure as an Open Directory replica, select Open Directory in the Server app sidebar. Click the On/Off switch to On, select "Join an existing Open Directory domain as a replica," and click Next.

In the Parent Server field, enter another Open Directory server's host name (enter the master's host name to configure this server as a replica, or enter a replica's host name to configure this server as a replica of the replica), enter directory administrator credentials, and click Next.

Afterward, the Server app displays your server as a replica of the master. In the Open Directory pane's Servers field, you may need to click the disclosure triangle to view the master and its replica(s). In the following figure, server17 is the master, and server18 is the replica.

If you configure a replica of a replica, or a tier two replica, the Servers field looks like the following figure, where server19 is a replica of server18, which is a replica of server17.

Configuring OS X Server to Use Another Open Directory Server

If you want your server to simply take advantage of a centralized directory service, and not offer directory services itself, you can bind your server to another directory service, so users can use credentials hosted by the centralized directory service to access services on your server. This lesson focuses on binding to another Open Directory system.

> **MORE INFO ▶** Just as you can bind your server to another Open Directory service, you can bind your server to an Active Directory domain. This is outside the scope of this guide. See the section for this lesson in the "Additional Resources" appendix which is provided when you download the lesson files.

Use the Users & Groups pane in System Preferences to bind your server to another directory. Open System Preferences, select Users & Groups, select Login Options, and click Join, or if the server is already an Open Directory server, click Edit instead of Join.

Enter the host name of an Open Directory server, or click the pop-up menu to browse for one.

When you see the message "This server provides SSL certificates," click Trust. This adds the Open Directory's CA, intermediate CA, and SSL certificate to the System keychain so your Mac trusts services that use SSL certificates signed by the intermediate CA.

By default, OS X does not always use SSL when it makes an LDAP connection to an Open Directory server; for many organizations this is not a concern, because the information stored in the LDAP directory is not considered sensitive. Configuring OS X to use SSL for LDAP is outside the scope of this guide.

When you see the Client Computer ID window, leave the Client Computer ID, which is generated from your host name, as it is.

You have the option to bind anonymously or set up authenticated binding.

Anonymous binding is appropriate when binding with OS X clients, but you should use authenticated binding, which mutually authenticates the member server and the Open Directory service, when binding a server to an Open Directory server. An authenticated bind creates a computer record in the Open Directory service; this computer record is used to mutually authenticate the bind between the two servers.

NOTE ▶ Provide directory administrator credentials for the authenticated bind.

As an alternative, you can use Directory Utility or the command-line environment, because they offer some advanced binding options, especially if you're binding to an Active Directory node.

Using Directory Utility Remotely

You can still use Directory Utility instead of System Preferences; in fact, Users & Groups preferences offer a shortcut to Directory Utility, which is located in /System/Library/ CoreServices. Directory Utility offers a little more control than the Join button of Users & Groups preferences, and it allows you to control a remote computer from OS X, so you don't need to rely on Screen Sharing being available.

Binding OS X to Your Open Directory Service

Once you have an Open Directory master (and perhaps one or more replicas) set up, you can also configure the client computers to bind to the directory service in order for your client computers to take advantage of Open Directory services. On each client computer, you use the Users & Groups preferences to specify a server that hosts an Open Directory service, or if you need more-advanced binding options, you use Directory Utility to create an LDAP configuration that has the address and search path for an Open Directory server.

Reference 9.3
Troubleshooting

Because Open Directory includes several services, several log files are used for track-ing status and errors. You can use the Server app to view status information and logs for Open Directory services. For example, you can use the password-service logs to monitor failed login attempts for suspicious activity, or use the Open Directory logs to see all failed authentication attempts, including the IP addresses that generated them. Review the logs periodically to determine whether there are numerous failed tries for the same password

ID, which would indicate that somebody might be generating login guesses. It is imperative that you understand where to look first when troubleshooting Open Directory issues.

Accessing Open Directory Log Files

Generally, the first place to look when Open Directory issues arise is the log files. Recall that Open Directory comprises three main components: the LDAP database, the Password Server database, and the Kerberos Key Distribution Center. The Server app allows for easy viewing of many server-related Open Directory log files. The main log files are:

▶ Configuration log—Contains information about setting up and configuring Open Directory services (/Library/Logs/slapconfig.log)

▶ LDAP log—Contains information about providing LDAP services (/var/log/slapd.log)

▶ Open Directory log—Contains information about core Open Directory functionality (/var/log/opendirectoryd.log)

▶ Password Service Server log—Contains information about successes and failures authenticating with local network user credentials (/Library/Logs/PasswordService/ ApplePasswordServer.Service.log)

▶ Password Service Error log—If it exists, contains information about errors in the Password Service (/Library/Logs/PasswordService/ApplePasswordServer.Error.log)

To view these log files, select Logs in the toolbar, click the pop-up menu, scroll to the Open Directory section of the pop-up menu, and choose one of the logs.

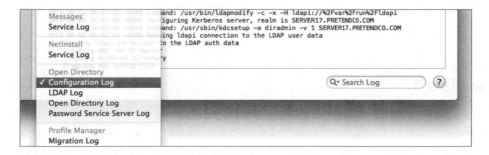

You can use the search field in the lower-right corner of the window. Keep in mind that you can resize the Server app window to view more log information in a single line, which can help you quickly read or skim the log files.

Interpreting log files can be a difficult task, and you may need the help of a more experienced system administrator. You can email the appropriate log file to the administrator.

Troubleshooting Directory Services

If a bound OS X computer experiences a startup delay, or the login window displays a red status indicator with the text "network accounts unavailable," the bound computer could be trying to access a directory node that is not available on your network.

There are several ways to begin troubleshooting when you are unable to connect to a directory service:

▶ Using Network Utility to confirm DNS records

▶ Using Login Options in the Users & Groups preferences to confirm that the network server is available

▶ Using Directory Utility to make sure the LDAP and other configurations are correct

▶ Using the Network preferences to make sure the computer's network location and other network settings are correct

▶ Inspecting the physical network connection for faults

▶ Using the Console app while logged in with a local user account to monitor the Directory Services login /var/log/opendirectoryd.log

> **MORE INFO** ▶ You can increase the level of logging detail for the Open Directory log; see the Apple Support article in the section for this lesson in the "Additional Resources" appendix which is provided when you download the lesson files.

> **TIP** ▶ If you update DNS records but still don't see the results you expect, you can reset (flush) the DNS cache using the method in Apple Support article HT5343, "OS X: How to reset the DNS cache."

Exercise 9.1
Configure Your Server as an Open Directory Master

Now you're ready to configure the Open Directory service to create a shared directory and start authentication services for use by other computers on the network. In particular, three new network services will be running once Open Directory master configuration is complete: an LDAP (Lightweight Directory Access Protocol) service to provide access to shared directory data; and two authentication services, Password Server and Kerberos. In the following steps, you'll configure your server as an Open Directory master and verify the success of the configuration.

At this point, your server should have forward and reverse DNS records for itself, provided by either the classroom DNS service or the DNS service on your server itself. Nevertheless, confirm the records with Network Utility.

You will use your server computer for this exercise.

1   On your administrator computer, quit the Server app if it is open.

2   On your server computer, click the Spotlight icon in the upper-right corner of the screen (or press Command-Space bar) to reveal the Spotlight search field.

3   Enter Network Utility in the Spotlight search field.

4   Press Return to open the "Top Hit" from your Spotlight search, which is Network Utility.

5   Click the Lookup tab.

6   Enter your server's host name in the field, and then click Lookup.

7   Confirm that your server's IPv4 address is returned.

8   Enter your server's primary IPv4 address in the field, and then click Lookup.

9   Confirm that your server's host name is returned.

Once you've confirmed your DNS records, configure your server as an Open Directory master. You can do this from your administrator computer or from your server computer.

1   If the Server app does not display the list of advanced services, hover the pointer above the word Advanced in the sidebar and then click Show.

2   Click Open Directory.

3   Click the On/Off switch to the On position.

4   Select "Create a new Open Directory domain" and click Next.

5   Configure a password.

    If your server is not accessible from the Internet, in the Directory Administrator pane, enter diradminpw in the Password and Verify fields and click Next.

Of course, in a production environment, you should use a secure password.

6 In the Organization Information pane, enter appropriate information.

If the following fields do not already contain the information shown, enter it and click Next.

▶ Organization Name: **Pretendco Project** *n* (where *n* is your student number)

▶ Admin Email Address: **ladmin@server***n***.pretendco.com** (where *n* is your student number)

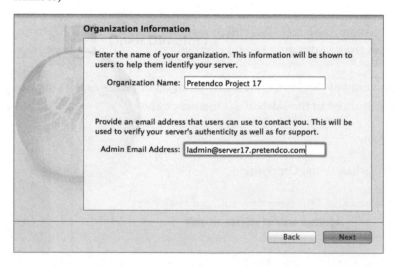

7   View the Confirm Settings pane, and click Set Up.

The Server app displays its progress in the lower-left corner of the Confirm Settings pane.

When it has completed the configuration, the Server app displays the Servers tab of the Open Directory pane, with your server listed as the master.

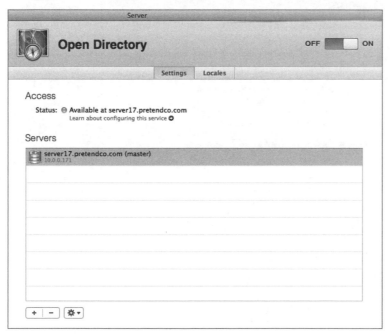

Now that your server is configured as an Open Directory master, it has these three services running: LDAP, Password Server, and Kerberos.

Inspect the Group Workgroup

The Server app automatically created a group named Workgroup. When you create a new user with the Server app, the Server app automatically places the new user in the Workgroup group.

1   In the Server app sidebar, select Groups.

2   If necessary, click the pop-up menu and choose Local Network Groups.

3   Double-click the group Workgroup.

For now, the only entity listed as a member of the group named Workgroup is the group account named Local Accounts. This is a special system group account that doesn't actually have any members listed, but the operating system treats all local accounts as a member of this group, so all local accounts on the server computer are therefore treated as members of the group Workgroup.

4 Click Cancel to return to the list of groups.

5 Quit the Server app.

In this exercise you configured your server to be an Open Directory master, and you inspected the new network group named Workgroup.

Exercise 9.2
Use Logs to Troubleshoot Using Open Directory

▶ **Prerequisite**

  ▶ Exercise 9.1, "Configure Your Server as an Open Directory Master"

The logs on your server relating to being an Open Directory master are located in various folders, but you can access them all quickly with the Server app.

1 On your administrator computer, if you are not already connected to your server, open the Server app, connect to your server, and authenticate as a local administrator.

2 In the Server app sidebar, select Logs.

3 In the Logs pop-up menu, scroll to the Open Directory section, and note the four logs related to Open Directory.

4 Choose Configuration Log.

5 In the search field, enter the word Intermediate, as an example.

Note that the first instance of this word is highlighted. Each time you press Return, the next instance of the search term flashes.

6 Click the pop-up menu that currently displays Configuration Log and choose LDAP Log, as another example.

7 Scroll through the LDAP log, and then inspect the other logs as well.

In this exercise you used the Server app to view logs related to configuring your server as an Open Directory master. Even though the logs are stored on the server, you can use the Server app to view them.

Lesson 10

Managing Local Network Accounts

Once you have created shared LDAP directories, you need to populate them with information. User account information is probably the most important type of information you can store in a directory. User accounts stored in your server's shared directory are accessible to all the computers that search that directory; those accounts are now referred to as *local network user accounts*, though you may also see the terms *network user accounts* or just *network users*.

Reference 10.1
Using the Server App to Manage Network User Accounts

Use the Server app for basic and advanced management of users and services. The Server app automatically adds authorization for OS X Server services to local network users you create, and adds these users to the built-in group called Workgroup.

The Server app gives you the basic options for account management, including the account details, email address, services that a user is authorized to use, groups to which a user belongs, and global password policy.

To create a new user, select Users in the Server app sidebar, and then click the pop-up menu to choose the directory domain Local Network Users.

Click Add (+) to create a new user, and then configure the user. As with creating local user accounts, you can click the Password Assistant button (key icon) for help choosing a more secure password.

After you click Done, the Server app returns you to the list of users. When you double-click the user you just created to edit it, you'll see that when you create a user with the Server app, the user is automatically added to the local network group named Workgroup. You can modify the user's icon, among other attributes.

When you secondary (or Control-) click the user and choose "Edit Access to Services" from the shortcut menu, you'll see that the user has authorization to access each of the listed services.

MORE INFO ▶ When you create network user accounts outside the Server app, such as with Workgroup Manager or with command-line tools, those users are not automatically added to the group named Workgroup, nor are they given authorization to access any service. Therefore, be careful when you use both the Server app and other methods to create network user accounts.

Using the Server App to Allow Access to Services for Accounts from Another Directory Node

If you configure your server to be an Open Directory server, after you bind to another directory service, users from the other directory service are not automatically authorized to use services on your server unless you explicitly give users or groups from the other directory node access to these services.

Simply select one or more external accounts (users or groups), secondary (or Control-) click, choose "Edit Access to Services" from the shortcut menu, and then select the checkboxes for the services you want those accounts to be allowed to access. Of course, adding users to a group and then authorizing services for that group is less tedious than editing access to services for each user.

Importing Local Network Accounts

Just like importing local accounts, you can import local network accounts. The import file must be a properly formatted file containing a header that defines the contents of the file.

> **MORE INFO ▶** For more information on creating a properly formatted file for importing accounts, see the section "Create a file to import users or groups" in Server Help.

Choose Manage > Import Accounts from File, select an import file, make sure the Type pop-up menu is set to Local Network Accounts, provide directory administrator credentials (as opposed to local administrator credentials), and click Import.

If your import file doesn't contain passwords, after you click Import, and after the Server app has completed importing the accounts, select your newly imported users, secondary (or Control-) click, and choose Reset Password.

You can also import local network groups. Note that the only thing that determines whether you are importing users or groups is the header of the import file. In the preceding figure, dsRecTypeStandard:Users specifies that the file contains user accounts. In the following figure, dsRecTypeStandard:Groups specifies that the file contains group accounts. Remember to use the pop-up menu to specify into which directory node the Server app imports the accounts, and to provide appropriate credentials.

Reference 10.2
Configuring Authentication Methods on OS X Server

For authenticating users whose accounts are stored in shared directories on OS X Server, Open Directory offers a variety of options, including Kerberos and the many authentication methods that various network services require. Open Directory can authenticate users by using:

▶ Single sign-on with the Kerberos KDC built in to OS X Server

▶ A password that is stored securely as part of the Open Directory LDAP database, in a way that only the root user (or a process running with root privileges) can access

▶ An older crypt password, for a user record stored in a third-party LDAP directory, for backward compatibility with legacy systems

▶ A shadow password for local (not network) accounts, in which a password is stored in the user record in a way that only the root user (or process running with root privileges) can access

MORE INFO ▸ See the man page for **pwpolicy** and for **mkpassdb** for more information on hashes and authentication methods.

In addition, Open Directory lets you configure the "global password policy" that affects all users (except administrators) in the LDAP domain, such as automatic password expiration and minimum password length.

Disabling a User Account

To prevent a user from logging in or accessing services on your server, you can temporarily disable that user by using the Server app to remove access to his account. Simply edit the user and deselect the "Allow user to log in" checkbox.

Doing so does not delete the user, nor does it change his user ID or any other information. It also doesn't delete any of the user's files. It simply prevents that user from authenticating and gaining access to the server via any method.

When a user account is disabled, you'll see the word "Disabled" next to the user in the list of users.

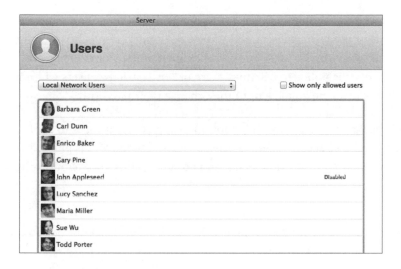

Setting Global Password Policies

Open Directory enforces global password policies. For example, a user's password policy can specify a password expiration interval. If the user is logging in and Open Directory discovers that the user's password has expired, the user must replace the expired password. Open Directory can then authenticate the user.

Password policies can disable a user account on a certain date, after a number of days, after a period of inactivity, or after a number of failed login attempts. Password policies can also require passwords to be a minimum length, contain at least one letter, contain at least one numeral, be mixed case, contain a character that is neither a number nor a letter, differ from the account name, differ from recent passwords, or be changed periodically.

Open Directory applies the same password policy rules to Password Server and Kerberos. Password policies do not affect administrator accounts. Administrators are exempt from password policies because they can change the policies at will; therefore, administrator accounts are not vulnerable to a troublemaker exploiting the "disable login after user makes n failed attempts" policy by performing repeated failed authentication attempts for an administrator account. However, this makes administrator accounts potentially more vulnerable to brute force attacks that attempt to guess the administrator password with repeated guesses of different passwords, so it is crucial that you choose a strong password for each account in the Administrators group.

Kerberos and Open Directory Password Server maintain password policies separately. OS X Server synchronizes the Kerberos password policy rules with Open Directory Password Server password policy rules.

After global password policies are put into effect, they are enforced only for users who change their passwords or users you subsequently create or import. This is because the account's password was established prior to the establishment of the global policy. In other words, if you change the policy to be either more or less restrictive, users will not be bound by the conditions of the new policy until they change their password.

MORE INFO ▶ You can use command-line tools or Workgroup Manager to apply policies for individual user accounts, but this is outside the scope of this guide. User account settings may override global policies, and administrators are exempt from both types of policies.

To configure global password policy, select Users in the Server app sidebar, and confirm that the directory node pop-up menu displays Local Network Users. Click the action pop-up menu, and choose Edit Global Password Policy.

Configure the options to match your organization's policy, and then click OK.

It is important to obtain your organization's password policies prior to setting these options. If you miss certain criteria required by your organization, and all users have been imported and have passwords set, changing these parameters may require users to change their passwords again to conform to the newer standards.

You can use either the Server app's Users pane or the Server app's Open Directory pane to configure global password policy; they have the same options and the same effects (although the Open Directory pane only offers global password policy for the local network users node, not for the local users node).

Remember that the global password policy may not be applied when a user attempts to authenticate; it is applied only when:

▶ You create a new user.

▶ A user (with a password that was established before the password policy was established) changes her password.

Reference 10.3
Using Single Sign-On and Kerberos

Frequently, a user who is logged in on one computer needs to use resources located on another computer on the network. Users typically browse the network in the Finder and click to connect to the other computer. It would be a nuisance for users to have to enter a password for each connection. If you've deployed Open Directory, you've saved them that trouble. Open Directory provides a feature known as single sign-on, which relies on Kerberos. Single sign-on essentially means that when users log in, they automatically have access to other services they may need that day, such as the Mail, File Sharing, Messages, and Calendar services, and VPN connectivity, without again entering their user credentials; in this way, Kerberos provides both identification and authentication services.

Defining Kerberos Basics

A complete Kerberos transaction has three main players:

▶ The user

▶ The service the user is interested in accessing

▶ The KDC (Key Distribution Center), which is responsible for mediating between the user and the service, creating and routing secure tickets, and generally supplying the authentication mechanism

Within Kerberos there are different realms (specific databases or authentication domains). When you configure your server to be an Open Directory master, the realm name is the same as your server's host name, in all capital letters. Each realm contains the authentication information for users and services, called Kerberos principals. For example, for a user with a full name of Barbara Green and an account name of barbara on a KDC with the realm of SERVER17.PRETENDCO.COM, the user principal is barbara@SERVER17.PRETENDCO.COM. By convention, realms use all uppercase characters.

For a service to take advantage of Kerberos, it must be Kerberized (configured to work with Kerberos), which means that it can defer authentication of its users to a KDC. Not only can OS X Server provide a KDC when configured to host a shared LDAP directory, but it can also provide several Kerberized services. An example of a service principal is afpserver/server17.pretendco.com@SERVER17.PRETENDCO.COM.

Finally, Kerberos enables you to keep a list of users in a single database called the KDC, which is configured on OS X Server once an Open Directory master has been created.

The process can be simplified into three major steps, which are illustrated in the following figure.

1. When a network user logs in on a Mac OS X v10.4 or later client computer, that computer negotiates with the KDC. If the user provides the correct user name and password, the KDC provides an initial ticket called a ticket-granting ticket (TGT). The TGT enables the user to subsequently ask for service tickets so she may connect to other servers and services on the network for the duration of the login session.

2. When the user on the client computer wants to access a Kerberized service, her computer presents her TGT to the KDC to obtain a service ticket.

3. The user's computer presents the service ticket to the Kerberized service to provide identification and authentication. The server that provides the Kerberized service grants the user access to the service (as long as the user is authorized to use the service).

When a user with a valid Kerberos TGT tries to access a Kerberized service, she does not need to provide her user name, because the TGT contains her identity. Likewise, she does not need to provide a password, because the TGT provides authentication. In this way, Kerberos provides identification and authentication.

For example, when you have a TGT and attempt to access a Kerberized AFP or SMB service, you immediately see a list of shared folders to which you have access; because the service uses Kerberos to identify and authenticate you, you do not need to provide your user name or password.

Kerberos is one of the components of Open Directory. The reason a user's authentication information is stored in both the Password Server database and the Kerberos principal database is to allow users to authenticate to services that are not Kerberized. Users must enter a password every time they make a new connection to use those non-Kerberized services. Open Directory uses Password Server to provide support for those authentication protocols.

Because Kerberos is an open standard, Open Directory on OS X Server can be easily integrated into an existing Kerberos network. You can set up your OS X computers to use an existing KDC for authentication.

One security aspect to using Kerberos is that the tickets are time sensitive. Kerberos requires that the computers on your network be synchronized to within five minutes by default. Configure your OS X computers and your servers to use NTP, and synchronize to the same time server so this doesn't become an issue that prevents you from getting Kerberos tickets.

In order to obtain Kerberos tickets on a Mac, that Mac must be either of the following:

▶   Bound to a directory node that provides Kerberos services (such as an Active Directory domain or forest, or an Open Directory master or replica)

▶   A Mac running OS X Server that is an Open Directory master or replica

Examining Kerberos Tickets

The Ticket Viewer application allows you to confirm that you're able to obtain Kerberos tickets for a network user (you could also use command-line tools).

To use Ticket Viewer, open it in /System/Library/CoreServices. Unless you've already used Ticket Viewer as the currently logged-in user, Ticket Viewer displays no identity by default; you must provide an identity by clicking Add Identity in the toolbar and entering a network user's principal or account name and password.

TIP ▶ If you're using Ticket Viewer as a troubleshooting tool, deselecting the "Remember password in my keychain" checkbox is probably a good idea so that Ticket Viewer doesn't automatically use your keychain to obtain a ticket for you; leave the checkbox deselected so that you always have to enter an identity and a password.

After you click Continue, Ticket Viewer attempts to obtain a TGT. If Ticket Viewer successfully obtains a TGT, it displays the expiration date and time, which by default is ten hours from the time you obtain the ticket.

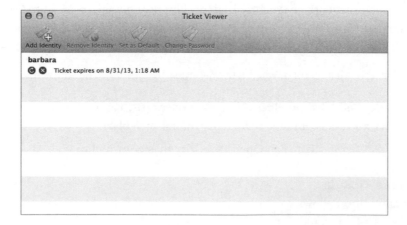

To see detailed information about the tickets associated with your identity, select the entry for your identity and choose Ticket > Diagnostic Information (or press Command-I). In the following figure, the first line includes the user account name (barbara), and the line that starts with "krbtgt" contains information about the TGT.

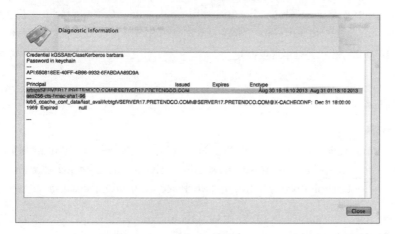

Once you have a TGT, you should be able to seamlessly access Kerberized services, as OS X automatically obtains a service ticket for each Kerberized service. In the following figure, the line that starts with "cifs" represents the service-granting ticket OS X automatically obtained after the user attempted to access an SMB file sharing service.

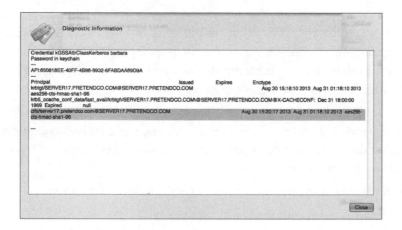

NOTE ▶ Ticket Viewer does not automatically update the diagnostic information pane, so you need to click the Close button in the lower-right corner of the diagnostic information pane and then choose Ticket > Diagnostic Information again to refresh the information.

Once you've confirmed your ability to obtain tickets, you should relinquish the ticket so the ticket will not interfere with further investigation: click the Clear button in your identity entry (next to the Refresh button).

Even though you may be logged in at the login window as a local user, you are able to get a Kerberos ticket as a network user. This is because, although you authenticated *locally* to your administrator computer, you authenticated against the Open Directory service for your network user account with Ticket Viewer.

Reference 10.4
Troubleshooting

See the "Troubleshooting" section of Lesson 8, "Managing Local Users," for troubleshooting importing local accounts and accessing services, and apply the same knowledge and procedures to troubleshoot problems importing network accounts and accessing services.

See the "Troubleshooting" section of Lesson 9, "Configuring Open Directory Services," for general troubleshooting of Open Directory services.

Troubleshooting Kerberos

When a user or service that uses Kerberos experiences authentication failures, try these techniques:

▶ Ensure that the DNS service you use is resolving addresses correctly. This is especially important at the time you are configuring a server to be an Open Directory master. If the DNS doesn't resolve addresses correctly, the incorrect address will be written to the Kerberos configuration files. Kerberos tickets won't be usable.

▶ Kerberos authentication is based on encrypted timestamps. If there's more than a five-minute difference between the KDC, client, and server computers, authentication may fail. Make sure that the clocks for all computers are synchronized using the NTP service of OS X Server or another network time server.

▶ Make sure that Kerberos authentication is enabled for the service in question.

▶ View the user's Kerberos ticket with the Ticket Viewer app.

▶ When you browse for services using the Finder window, OS X may not automatically use the expected Kerberos identity; use Go > Connect to Server and enter a URL instead.

MORE INFO ▶ You can use the **klist** command in the command-line environment to list information about your Kerberos credentials; see the man page for **klist**.

Exercise 10.1
Create and Import Network Accounts

▶ **Prerequisites**

- ▶ Exercise 9.1, "Configure Your Server as an Open Directory Master"
- ▶ You need the text files from the student materials, which you obtained as part of Exercise 2.1 and Exercise 2.3.

You create local network user accounts and local network group accounts just like you create local user accounts and local group accounts, except that you specify the local network node in the pop-up menu.

NOTE ▶ See Lesson 8, "Managing Local Users," for more information about using the new features of OS X Server for Mavericks, including keywords, notes, quotas, and templates.

In this scenario, within the greater Pretendco company, your group is working with some contractors. You need to give them access to your server's services, but these users shouldn't have access to the services outside your group. Therefore, you aren't going to ask the directory administrator of Pretendco's main directory server to create user accounts for these contractors.

Import Users into Your Server's Shared Directory Node

To expedite the exercise, in the student materials is a text file with more contractors your group is working with for the Pretendco scenario. This text file has a properly formatted header line. The import file defines these users with the password of "net." Of course, in a production environment, each user should have his own unique password or passphrase that is secret and secure.

1   Perform these exercises on your administrator computer. If you do not already have a connection to your server computer with Server app on your administrator computer, then connect to it with the following steps: Open the Server app on your administrator computer, choose Manage > Connect to Server, click Other Mac, select your server, click Continue, provide administrator credentials (Administrator Name ladmin and Administrator Password ladminpw), deselect the "Remember this password" checkbox, and then click Connect.

Import the accounts into your server's shared directory node.

1 In the Server app, choose Manage > Import Accounts from File.

2 In the sidebar, click Documents. Open StudentMaterials, and then open the Lesson10 folder.

3 Select the contractors-users.txt file.

4 Click the Column View icon.

5 If necessary, click the Type pop-up menu and choose Local Network Accounts.

6 Provide directory administrator credentials in the Admin Name and Password fields.

The suggested values from Lesson 9, "Configuring Open Directory Services," are Admin Name **diradmin** and Password **diradminpw**.

7 Click Import to start importing the file.

8 At the "Importing these accounts may take a long time. Are you sure you want to continue?" dialog, click Import.

NOTE ▸ If any of the users are listed as "Not Allowed," choose View > Refresh.

9   Select one of the newly imported users, Control-click, and choose "Edit Access to Services" from the shortcut menu.

Note that every service's checkbox is selected, meaning that the Server app has granted each imported local network user account the authorization to use each listed service.

10   Click Cancel to close the Service Access pane without making any changes.

You now have added eight local network user accounts.

On the computer you used to import the users, open the Console app and view the import log.

1   If the Console app is not already running, open Launchpad, open Other, and open Console.

2   If no sidebar is displayed for the Console window, click Show Log List in the toolbar.

The Console app displays logs from several locations on your computer. The tilde character (~) is a symbol for your home folder, so ~/Library/Logs is a folder in your home folder, and it is for logs specifically related to your user account. The /var/log and /Library/Logs folders are for system logs. You will look for a log file in the Import-Export folder in your ~/Library/Logs folder.

3   Click the disclosure triangle for ~/Library/Logs to display the contents of that folder, and then click the disclosure triangle for ImportExport to display its contents.

4   Select a log file under ImportExport.

Note that this log file shows that you imported a number of users without error. Some problems associated with importing accounts, if they occur, will appear in these log files.

Import a Group into Your Server's Shared Directory Node

To expedite the exercise, you have an import file with a properly formatted header line that defines all the imported users as members of the Contractors group (Account Name: contractors). You will confirm that this local network group has no explicit access to your server's services. However, local network user accounts you create with the Server app, or import with the Server app, automatically have access to all the services in this list, so this isn't a big concern.

1 In the Server app, choose Manage > Import Accounts from File.

2 In the sidebar, click Documents. Open StudentMaterials, and then open Lesson10.

3 Select the contractors-group.txt file.

4 Click the Type pop-up menu and choose Local Network Accounts.

5 Provide directory administrator credentials in the Admin Name and Password fields.

6 Click Import to start importing the file.

7   Select the Contractors group, Control-click, and choose "Edit Access to Services" from the shortcut menu.

Note that every service's checkbox is deselected. But remember that if a user has access to a service, it doesn't matter if one of that user's groups doesn't have access to a service.

8   Click Cancel to close the Service Access pane without making any changes.

You now have a new local network group populated with the local network users you previously imported.

Verify That Newly Imported Users Can Connect to Your Server's File Sharing Service

Turn on the File Sharing service if it isn't already on, and then use the Finder on your administrator computer to connect to your server's File Sharing service with a local network user account.

1   In the Server app, if the File Sharing service is not already on, with a green status indicator next to the service name in the sidebar, select File Sharing in the sidebar and click the On/Off switch to turn it on.

2   On your administrator computer, open the Finder.

    If you don't already have a Finder window open, press Command-N to open a new one.

3   If an Eject button appears next to your server in the Finder window sidebar, click the Eject button.

4   In the Finder window sidebar, select your server.

    If your server does not appear in the Finder window sidebar, click All under Shared, and then select your server.

5   Click Connect As.

6   Provide credentials for one of the users you imported:

    ▶   Name: gary

    ▶   Password: net

7 Click Connect.

The Finder window displays the user account you are connected as, and displays the shared folders this user has access to. Note that unless you open a folder, you will not actually mount a network volume.

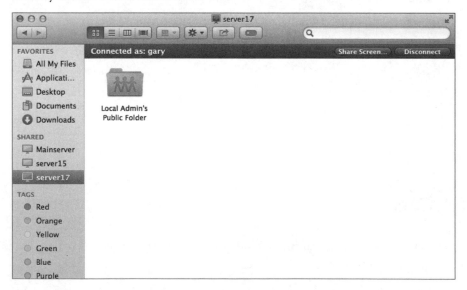

8 In the upper-right corner of the Finder window, click Disconnect.

In this exercise you imported user and group accounts into your server's shared directory domain. You confirmed that when you use the Server app to import user accounts, those users are automatically granted access to all your server's services.

Exercise 10.2
Configure Password Policies

► **Prerequisite**

► Exercise 10.1, "Create and Import Network Accounts"

Configure Global Password Policy

It's easy to set up global password policies using the Server app. The settings you specify affect all network users, except for users in the Administrators group. The settings take effect only when a user changes her password. For this exercise, you'll configure the global password policy such that it requires:

► Users to become disabled after ten failed attempts

► Passwords to contain at least one numeric character

► Passwords to contain at least eight characters

You'll also take advantage of the global password policy that requires newly created users to reset their passwords; you'll create a new local network user account and then use the Change Password feature of making an AFP connection to change the user's password in compliance with global password policy requirements. You'll attempt to change it to something that does not match the policy you just configured, and then change it to a password that does conform to the policy.

1   On your administrator computer, if you are not already connected to your server, open the Server app, connect to your server, and authenticate as a local administrator.

2   In the Server app sidebar, select Users.

3   Click the pop-up menu and choose Local Network Users.

4   From the Action (gear icon) pop-up menu, choose Edit Global Password Policy.

5   Select the checkbox "Disable login after user makes __ failed attempts," and enter 10 in the field.

6   Select the checkbox "Passwords must contain at least one numeric character."

7 Select the checkbox "Passwords must contain at least __ characters," and enter 8 in the field.

Before you click OK, verify your settings against the settings in the following figure.

8 Click OK.

Create a new local network user for this exercise.

1 In the Users pane, set the pop-up menu to Local Network Accounts.

2 Click the Add (+) button.

3 Enter the following values, with a password that matches the above password policy:

▶ Full Name: **Rick Reed**

▶ Account Name: **rick**

▶ Password (and Verify): **rickpw88**

▶ Leave the other fields at their defaults.

4   Click Create to save the changes.

Confirm the Password Policy

Make an AFP connection and use the Change Password feature.

1   In the Server app, if the File Sharing service is not already on, with a green status indicator next to the service name in the sidebar, select File Sharing and click the On/Off switch to turn it on.

2   On your administrator computer, open the Finder.

3   If an Eject button appears next to your server in the Finder window sidebar, click it.

4   Choose Go > Connect to Server.

5   Enter **afp://server*n*.local** (where *n* is your student number).

6   In the Name field, enter rick and click Change Password.

7   Enter the old password as well as a new password, without following the global password policy that it must be at least eight characters and must include at least one number:

▶   Old Password: rickpw88

▶   New Password: net

▶   Verify: net

8   Click Change Password to try to change to the new password.

Because the proposed password does not meet the global password policy, the window shakes, and you see the change password dialog again.

9 Enter the old password as well as a new password, but this time follow the global password policy that it must be at least eight characters and must include at least one number:

▶ Old Password: rickpw88

▶ New Password: rickpw12345

▶ Verify: rickpw12345

Change the password for "rick" on "server17.local".

Old Password: ••••••••

New Password: •••••••••••   🔑

Verify: •••••••••••|

Cancel   Change Password

10 Click Change Password.

Once you've successfully changed the password, you are authenticated and authorized to use the File Sharing service. The Finder displays the user account you are connected as, and displays the shared folders this user has access to.

11 Select the shared folder named rick, and click OK.

Select the volumes you want to mount on "server17.local":

Local Admin's Public Folder
rick

Cancel   OK

12 In the upper-right corner of the Finder window that displays the contents of the shared folder named rick, click Disconnect.

Clean Up Global Password Policy

To prevent confusion in future exercises, remove the Rick Reed user, and remove your global password policy configuration.

1 In the Server app sidebar, select Users.

2 Select Rick Reed.

3 Click the Delete (–) button.

4 When asked to confirm that you want to permanently remove Rick Reed, click Delete.

Remove the global password policy configuration.

1 In the Server app sidebar, select Users.

2 From the Action (gear icon) pop-up menu, choose Edit Global Password Policy.

3 Deselect each checkbox, and then click OK.

In this exercise you used the Server app to set global password policy, and then you confirmed that the policy is in effect when a user attempts to make a password change that does not conform to the policy.

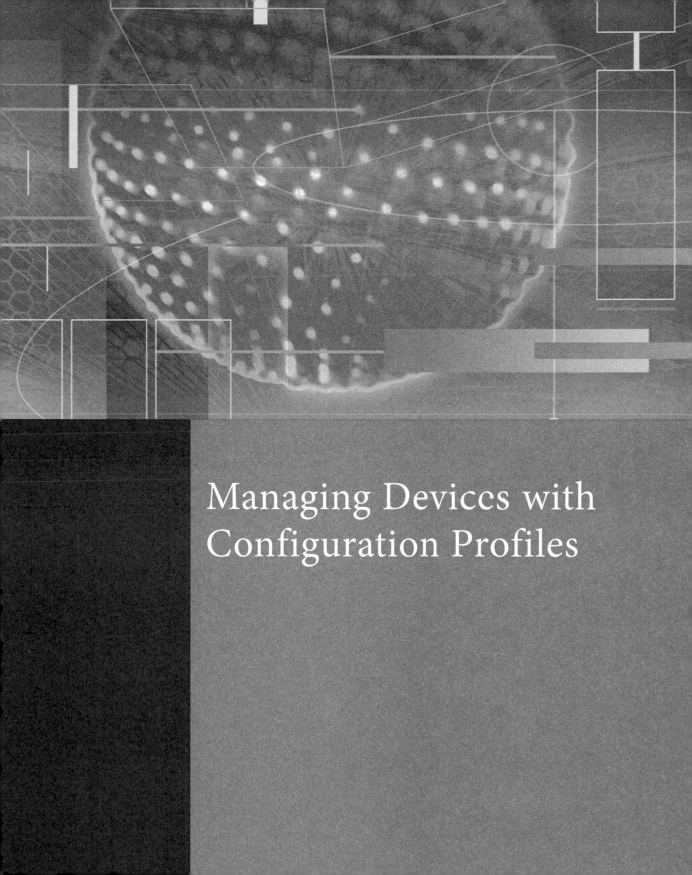

Managing Devices with
Configuration Profiles

Configuring OS X Server to Provide Device Management

OS X Server provides a service called Profile Manager, which allows you, as the administrator, to assign certain behaviors to client devices such as computers and mobile devices. Profile Manager also allows a user to perform basic management of her own devices.

Reference 11.1
Profile Manager

Profile Manager is an account management tool that allows the development and distribution of configurations and settings to control the experience on Lion and later computers and on iOS 4 and later devices. The configurations and settings are contained in XML-based text files called profiles. Profile Manager has three parts:

▶ Profile Manager web tool

▶ User Portal website

▶ Mobile Device Management Server

Profile Manager Web App

The web tool allows easy access to the Profile Manager functionality from any browser that can connect to the OS X Server with the Profile Manager service turned on. An administrator can utilize the web interface to create profiles for use on client machines. It is also used to create and manage device accounts and device group accounts. Users and groups are created in the Server app, but are displayed in the Profile Manager web app. When configured, Profile Manager is reached at https://*server.domain.com*/profilemanager/.

User Portal

The User Portal is a simple way for users to enroll their own devices, obtain profiles, and wipe or lock their devices. When configured, the User Portal is accessed via a web browser at https://*server.domain.com*/mydevices/ and lists the user's enrolled devices and available profiles.

Device Management

You can configure and enable the Mobile Device Management (MDM) functionality to allow you to create profiles for devices. When you or your users enroll Lion or later computers and iOS 4 or later devices, this allows over the air (OTA) management of devices, including remote wipe and lock.

> **NOTE ▶** Profile Manager, the User Portal, and device management will be covered in more detail in Lesson 12, "Managing with Profile Manager."

Reference 11.2
Configuring Profile Manager

To allow assigning profiles, the Profile Manager service must be enabled. Using profiles is significantly different than managing clients in earlier versions of OS X Server.

Terminology

In the context of device management, a profile is a collection of settings that tells a device how to configure itself and what functions to allow or restrict. Configuration profiles define settings such as Wi-Fi settings, email accounts, calendaring accounts, and security policies. Enrollment profiles allow the server to manage your device. A payload is what's inside a profile.

Preparations for Profile Manager

Prior to configuring Profile Manager, you'll need to set up a few items to make the process more streamlined:

▶ Configure your server as a network directory server. This is also referred to as creating an Open Directory master.

▶ Obtain and install an SSL certificate. It is recommended to use one signed by a trusted certificate authority. You could use the certificate that is automatically generated when you configure your server as an Open Directory master, but if you use this certificate, you need to first configure devices to trust that certificate.

▶ Obtain an Apple ID for use when you request a push certificate from Apple through the http://appleid.apple.com website. Prior to using this ID, make sure you log in at that site and verify the email address. Otherwise, you might not have success requesting the push certificate. Use an institutional ID when setting up Profile Manager for an institution. This separates users, who can be transient, from the institution itself. Make sure you record this information and have it available for a later date.

Exercise 11.1
Enable Profile Manager

> **Prerequisite**
>
> ► Exercise 3.1, "Configure DNS Services"

In this section, you'll go through the steps to enable Profile Manager, including the signing of a configuration profile.

1 Perform these exercises on your administrator computer. If you do not already have a connection to your server computer with Server app on your administrator computer, then connect to it with the following steps: Open the Server app on your administrator computer, choose Manage > Connect to Server, click Other Mac, select your server, click Continue, provide administrator credentials (Administrator Name ladmin and Administrator Password ladminpw), deselect the "Remember this password" checkbox, and then click Connect.

2   Select Profile Manager in the services sidebar.

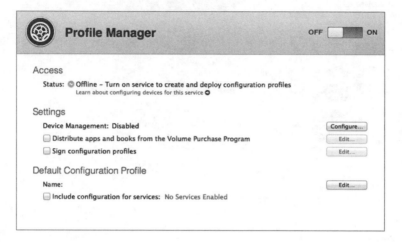

3   Click the Configure button, next to Device Management.

4   The service gathers some data and gives a description of its capabilities.

At the Configure Device Management pane, click Next.

5   If your server is already configured as an Open Directory master, you won't see the following steps. Pick up again at step 9.

6 If your server is not already configured as an Open Directory master, there will be one made for you. Click Next.

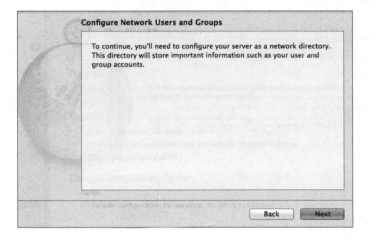

7 At the Directory Administrator pane, leave the Name and Account Name fields at their default settings. Enter diradminpw in the Password and Verify fields (of course, in a production environment, you should always use a strong password).

8 Click Next.

9 At the Organization Information pane, if necessary, in the Organization Name field, enter Pretendco Project *n* (where *n* is your student number), and in the Admin Email Address field, enter ladmin@server*n*.pretendco.com (where *n* is your student number).

10 Click Next.

11 If your server is *not* already configured as an Open Directory master, then at the Confirm Settings pane, review the information and then click Set Up. It may take a few moments while the Server app configures your server as an Open Directory master. You can watch the status of the process in the lower-left corner of the pane.

12 In the Organization Information pane, leave the default information and fill in the additional information with your own phone number and address.

13 At the Configure an SSL Certificate pane, click the Certificate pop-up menu, choose your Open Directory CA–created SSL certificate, and click Next.

14 If you haven't already set up push notifications, you are prompted for an Apple ID, which the Server app uses to request Apple Push Notification certificates.

If you do not already have an Apple ID, click the link under the credential fields to create an Apple ID.

When you create an Apple ID, you need to click the verification link that Apple sends to the email address that you used when you created the new Apple ID.

NOTE ▶ It is possible to have been regularly using an Apple ID for other services, even if you have never verified it. If you have not yet verified your Apple ID, open http://appleid.apple.com in Safari, click "Manage your Apple ID," sign in with your Apple ID, click Send Verification Email to resend a verification email message to your email address, check your email, and finally, click the verification link.

Once you have an Apple ID that you've verified, enter your Apple ID credentials and click Next.

15 A green circle indicates that you've succeeded. Click Finish.

16 Select the "Sign configuration profiles" option, and then in the pop-up menu, choose the code signing certificate that was automatically created and signed by your Open Directory Intermediate CA. Click OK.

By signing profiles with a certificate, you provide a way to validate that the profiles came from where they were supposed to and that they have not been tampered with.

17 Click the On/Off switch to turn on Profile Manager.

18 To configure Profile Manager to distribute apps and books, select the "Distribute apps and books from the Volume Purchase Program" checkbox.

NOTE ▸ This requires you to be a member of the Volume Purchase Program. You can sign up at https://vpp.itunes.apple.com/.

19 When the window opens, click the link to download your VPP service token. This will open Safari and allow you to choose which VPP you signed up for, Business or Education.

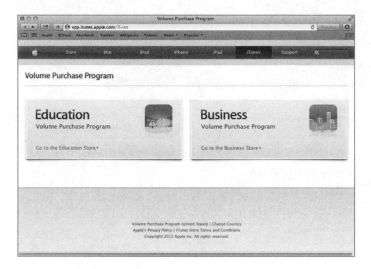

20 Sign in with your VPP credentials.

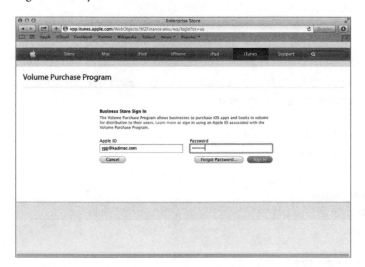

21 Download the VPP service token and then log out of the VPP store.

22 Drag the token into the VPP Managed Distribution window, click Continue, and then click Done.

Clean Up

No changes are required for this lesson, as the work you have just done setting up the Profile Manager service is required for the next lesson.

Lesson 12
Managing with Profile Manager

If you run an organization with several hundred users or even just a handful, how can you manage their experience with OS X and iOS? In previous lessons you learned management techniques involving the user name and password. There are many other aspects to user account management, and it is important to understand how these various aspects interact with each other.

OS X Server provides the Profile Manager service, which allows you, as the administrator, to assign certain behaviors to client devices such as computers and mobile devices.

Reference 12.1
Introducing Account Management

Account management was controlled by Workgroup Manager in Mac OS X 10.6 and earlier, but OS X Lion introduced the concept of profiles that contain configurations and settings. This continues in an expanded fashion with Mavericks. By assigning profiles to users, user groups, devices, or groups of devices you can achieve control over your systems.

With effective account management, you can achieve a range of results including but not limited to:

▶ Providing users with a consistent, controlled interface

▶ Controlling settings on mobile devices and computers

▶ Restricting certain resources for specific groups or individuals

▶ Securing computer use in key areas such as administrative offices, classrooms, or open labs

▶ Customizing the user experience

▶ Customizing Dock settings

GOALS

▶ Configure Profile Manager

▶ Construct management profiles

▶ Deliver profiles

▶ Install and delete profiles

▶ Manage users, groups of users, devices, and groups of devices using profiles

Levels of Management

You can create settings for four different types of accounts:

▶ User—Usually relates to a specific person. This is the account that the person identifies herself with when logging in to the machine. A user's short name or UID number uniquely identifies the user on a system.

▶ Group—Represents a group of users, a group of groups, or a mixture of both.

▶ Device—Similar to a user account, it's the singular entity that represents a given piece of hardware. This can be either a computer or an iOS device. Device accounts are uniquely identified by their Ethernet ID, serial number, IMEI, or MEID.

▶ Device group—Represents a grouping of computers or iOS devices. A device group can include other device groups nested in it, or a mixture of both individuals and nested groups.

Not all management levels make sense for all purposes, so when setting policy you have to decide what is appropriate. For example, you might want to define printers by device groups, because a typical situation has a group of computers located geographically close to a specific printer. You may want to set VPN access via a group of users such as remote salespeople. And individuals might have specific application access rights granted to them.

Each level can have a default group of settings and then custom settings. Mixing and layering profiles with conflicting settings is not recommended. The results may not be what were expected.

If a user or user group has an assigned profile, and the user logs in to the User Portal to enroll an OS X computer, the profiles assigned to that user will be applied to that computer regardless of who logs in to that computer.

Managing Preferences for Users in a Group

Although you can set up preferences individually for users with network accounts, it's more efficient to manage preferences for the groups to which they belong. Using groups allows you to manage users regardless of which devices they use.

Managing Device Group Accounts

A device group account is set up for a group of computers or iOS devices that have the same preference settings and are available to the same set of users and groups. You create and modify these device groups in Profile Manager.

When you set up a device group, make sure you have already determined how the devices are identified. Use descriptions that are logical and easy to remember (for instance, the description might be the computer name). This also makes it easier to find the devices to add them to the correct device group.

Lists of devices can be imported into Profile Manager via a comma-separated value (CSV) file. The file needs to be structured like this:

name, serial number, UDID, IMEI, MEID

Leave a field empty if you're not using that value.

Managing Apps

Apps—both Enterprise and those purchased via Volume Purchase Program (VPP)—can be uploaded to Profile Manager and assigned to users, groups, and device groups.

The first step is to identify the type of app you are uploading and choose the appropriate button. In these images, an Enterprise app is being used.

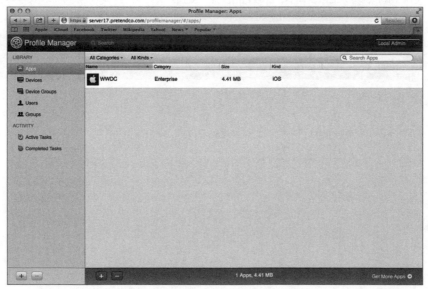

Once uploaded into Profile Manager, it can be assigned via the Edit Apps menu choice in the Action (gear icon) pop-up menu at the bottom of the pane.

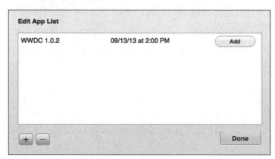

The apps will be assigned to the devices at the next push.

Delivering Profiles

Once created, profiles can be delivered to users and computers or iOS devices in a number of ways:

▶ Via the User Portal—Where users log in to the portal with their account credentials and they are presented with the profiles assigned to them.

▶ Emailed to users—The profile is a simple text file, so it is easily transported.

▶ Web link—The profile can be published on a website for users to visit and download.

▶ Automatic push—The profile gets automatically pushed to the device with no user interaction (the device must be enrolled for this to work).

Automatic push relies on the Apple Push Notification service (APNs). This service is hosted by Apple and is provided to allow secure push notification to client devices. Once a server is configured to utilize APNs, client devices enrolled for management in Profile Manager check in with APNs and wait for notification signals to be sent by the Profile Manager via APNs. No data is included in the notification beyond informing the client that Profile Manager has something for it. This keeps data secure between Profile Manager and the client.

Push notification process:

1. An enrolled device makes contact with the Apple Push Notification service (APNs) and keeps a lightweight communication going between them. This happens any time the enrolled device has a network chance, as would occur when being turned on, changing networks, or switching network interfaces.

2. The Profile Manager service contacts APNs when it needs to notify an enrolled device or group of devices of a new or changed profile. APNs has the ability to send feedback to the Profile Manager service.

3. APNs notifies the device to get in touch with the associated Profile Manager service in which it is enrolled.

4. The device communicates with the Profile Manager service once notified.

5. The Profile Manager service sends the profile to the device.

A list of installed profiles is available in OS X in the Profile preferences. An equivalent list is available in iOS by going to Profiles in Settings.

Remotely Locking or Wiping a Device

Once enrolled, a device or group of devices can be remotely locked or wiped. In this example, a remote lock will be performed. A remote wipe can be attempted, but only do it on a device you don't mind reconfiguring. The device can be locked via Profile Manager by an administrator or via the User Portal by the users themselves.

Upon requesting a lock, a confirmation pane will appear, a passcode will be requested, and the lock command will be sent. On Lion and Mountain Lion computers, the machine is shut down and an EFI passcode is set, so it needs to be entered to use the machine again. For iOS devices, the screen is locked and the passcode enforced.

▶ Profile Manager—Log in to the Profile Manager web app and select the device or group of devices to be locked. In the Action (gear icon) pop-up menu, choose Lock.

▶ User Portal—Once users log in, each device they enrolled will be displayed in the Devices pane.

Which Preferences Can Be Managed?

In addition to various other settings for user, group, device, and device group accounts, Profile Manager provides control over the preferences listed in Table 12.1. Table 12.2 describes the manageable preferences payloads for devices and device groups.

Table 12.1 Manageable Preferences Payloads for Users and Groups

Preference	OS X	iOS	Description
General	✓	✓	Profile distribution type, how the profile can be removed, organization, and description
Passcode	✓	✓	Define passcode requirements such as length, complexity, reuse, and so on
Mail	✓	✓	Configure email settings such as servers, account name, and so on
Exchange	✓	✓	Configure Exchange ActiveSync settings
LDAP	✓	✓	Configure connection to LDAP server
Contacts	✓	✓	Configure access to CardDAV server
Calendar	✓	✓	Configure access to CalDAV server
Network	✓	✓	Configure network setting on the device, including wireless and wired
VPN	✓	✓	Configure VPN settings: L2TP, PPTP, IPSec (Cisco), CiscoAnyConnect, Juniper SSL, F5 SSL, SonicWALL Mobile Connect, and Aruba VIA
Certificate	✓	✓	Allows the installation of PKCS1 and PKCS12 certificates
SCEP	✓	✓	Define connection to Simple Certificate Enrollment Protocol (SCEP) server
Web Clips	✓	✓	Display defined Web Clips as application icons

Table 12.1 Manageable Preferences Payloads for Users and Groups (continued)

Preference	OS X	iOS	Description
Security and Privacy	✓	✓	Control if diagnostic and usage data gets sent to Apple and whether user can override Gatekeeper (OS X only)
Identification	✓		Configures identification information of user
Restrictions	✓	✓	Define application and content restrictions (separate OS X and iOS versions)
Subscribed Calendars		✓	Configure calendar subscriptions
APN		✓	Configure carrier settings such as the Access Point Name (advanced use only)
Messages	✓		Configure connection to Jabber or AIM chat servers
AD Certificate	✓		Specify the settings for retrieving a certificate for your computer from Active Directory
Login Items	✓		Specify applications, items, and network mounts to launch at login
Mobility	✓		Define mobility settings for OS X clients to allow cached credentials and portable home directories
Dock	✓		Configure Dock behavior
Finder	✓		Configure Finder settings
Printing	✓		Configure printing settings and access to printers or print queues
Parental Controls	✓		Define settings for Parental Controls such as contentfiltering and time limits
Universal Access	✓		Manage Universal Access settings

Table 12.1 Manageable Preferences Payloads for Users and Groups (continued)

Preference	OS X	iOS	Description
Single Sign-On		✓	Configure Kerberos settings
Custom Settings	✓		Apply custom preferences for items not defined in other payloads; similar to applying preference manifests in WGM

Table 12.2 Manageable Preferences Payloads for Devices and Device Groups

Preference	OS X	iOS	Description
General	✓	✓	Profile distribution type, how the profile can be removed, organization, and description
Passcode	✓	✓	Define passcode requirements such as length, complexity, reuse, and so on
Mail		✓	Configure email settings such as servers, account name, and so on
Exchange		✓	Configure Exchange ActiveSync settings
LDAP		✓	Configure connection to LDAP server
Contacts		✓	Configure access to CardDAV server
Calendar		✓	Configure access to CalDAV server
Network	✓	✓	Configure network setting on the device, including wireless and wired
VPN	✓	✓	Configure VPN settings: L2TP, PPTP, IPSec (Cisco), CiscoAnyConnect, Juniper SSL, F5 SSL, SonicWALL Mobile Connect, and Aruba VIA
Certificate	✓	✓	Allows the installation of PKCS1 and PKCS12 certificates
SCEP	✓	✓	Define connection to Simple Certificate Enrollment Protocol (SCEP) server

Table 12.2 Manageable Preferences Payloads for Devices and Device Groups (continued)

Preference	OS X	iOS	Description
Web Clips		✓	Display defined Web Clips as application icons
AD Certificate	✓		Specify AD certificate settings
Directory	✓		Specify OD server settings
Restrictions	✓	✓	Define application and content restrictions (separate OS X and iOS versions)
Subscribed Calendars		✓	Configure calendar subscriptions
APN		✓	Configure carrier settings such as the Access Point Name (advanced use only)
Login Items	✓		Specify applications, items, and network mounts to launch at login
Mobility	✓		Define mobility settings for OS X clients to allow cached credentials and portable home directories
Dock	✓		Configure Dock behavior
Printing	✓	✓	Configure printing settings and access to printers or print queues
Parental Controls	✓		Define settings for Parental Controls such as content-filtering and time limits
Security and Privacy	✓		Define whether or not to send diagnostic and usage data to Apple (might change in the future)
Custom Settings	✓		Apply custom preferences for items not defined in other payloads (similar to applying preference manifests in WGM)
Directory	✓		Configure binding to directory services

Table 12.2 Manageable Preferences Payloads for Devices and Device Groups (continued)

Preference	OS X	iOS	Description
Single Sign-On		✓	Configure Kerberos settings
Login Window	✓		Configure Login window options, such as messages, appearance, access, and Login/LogoutHooks
Software Update	✓		Define an Apple Software Update server to be used by the computer
Universal Access	✓		Manage Universal Access settings
Energy Saver	✓		Define Energy Saver policy such as sleeping, timed actions, and wake settings

Layering and Multiple Profiles Considerations

In previous versions of OS X management, different behaviors could be created by layering management techniques reflecting users, groups of users, devices, and groups of devices. While Profile Manager also shows those same four management levels, caution needs to be taken when building profiles.

The general rule is to avoid layering profiles that manage the same preferences, but this is not hard and fast. Some profiles can be additive and others can collide, so you need to be aware of which are which.

Multiple profiles that contain different settings for the same preferences will result in undefined results. There is no order of preference applied to the multiple profiles, so you will not have a predictable outcome.

Payloads that should remain exclusive include:

- ▶ All custom settings
- ▶ APN
- ▶ Directory
- ▶ Dock (preferences)
- ▶ Energy Saver
- ▶ Finder (preferences)
- ▶ General
- ▶ Global HTTP Proxy
- ▶ Identification
- ▶ Login Window
- ▶ Mobility
- ▶ Network (settings)
- ▶ Parental Controls
- ▶ Printing (settings)
- ▶ Security & Privacy
- ▶ Single App Mode
- ▶ Software Update
- ▶ Time Machine

Payloads that can be combined:

- ▶ Accessibility
- ▶ AD Certificate
- ▶ Calendar
- ▶ Certificate
- ▶ Contacts
- ▶ Dock (apps)
- ▶ Finder (commands)
- ▶ Exchange
- ▶ LDAP
- ▶ Login items
- ▶ Mail
- ▶ Messages
- ▶ Network (interfaces)
- ▶ Passcode
- ▶ Printing (printer list)
- ▶ Restrictions
- ▶ SCEP
- ▶ Single Sign-On
- ▶ Subscribed Calendars
- ▶ VPN
- ▶ Web Clips

Reference 12.2
Troubleshooting

Occasionally things won't work the way you expect, and you'll have to troubleshoot the situation. Even a robust service like Profile Manager can have an occasional issue.

Viewing Logs

The Profile Manager–related logs are located at /Library/Logs/ProfileManager/ and can be viewed with Console by double-clicking. Errors may be reported and listed in the logs. Logs can also be viewed in the Server app.

Viewing Profiles

If a device is not behaving as expected, look at the list of installed profiles on the device and see if the proper profiles have been installed. The solution may be as simple as applying the expected profile to the device.

Installing Profiles

If you're having problems installing a profile, you may have improper certificates. Review your SSL certificates for validity and make sure the trust profile has been installed on the device.

Problems Enrolling a Device

A trust profile must be installed prior to enrolling a device, unless you are using a certificate signed by a trusted certificate authority.

Pushing Profiles

If you're having problems pushing a profile, you may not have appropriate outbound ports open. Ports 443, 2195, 2196, and 5223 are APNs related. Also, iOS uses the cellular network whenever possible, even if Wi-Fi is available.

Unexpected Profile Behavior

If the managed device doesn't seem to be acting the way you expect based on the way you set preferences in profiles, you may have multiple overlapping profiles. It is suggested not to have overlapping profiles that try to manage the same preferences; the results can be unpredictable.

Exercise 12.1
Use Profile Manager

▶ **Prerequisites**

- ▶ Exercise 9.1, "Configure Your Server as an Open Directory Master"
- ▶ Exercise 10.1, "Create and Import Network Accounts"; or use the Server app to create network user Carl Dunn with an account name of carl and a password of net.
- ▶ Exercise 11.1, "Enable Profile Manager"

This exercise utilizes Profile Manager to enroll and control devices using the various pieces that it comprises.

User Profile Portal

The User Profile Portal provides simple access for users to log in, apply profiles, and manage their devices. The portal is accessed via a web browser; by simply publishing the website, users anywhere in the world can enroll their devices—whether they be computers, iPhones, or other iOS-based mobile devices. Through the portal, users can lock or wipe their enrolled devices.

NOTE ▶ The following example is for OS X, but the iOS version is conceptually and visually similar. Screenshots show the process in both OS X and iOS.

1 Perform these exercises on your administrator computer. If you do not already have a connection to your server computer with Server app on your administrator computer, then connect to it with the following steps: Open the Server app on your administrator computer, choose Manage > Connect to Server, click Other Mac, select your server, click Continue, provide administrator credentials (Administrator Name **ladmin** and Administrator Password **ladminpw**), deselect the "Remember this password" checkbox, and then click Connect.

2 On your administrator computer, navigate to the site https://server*n*.pretendco.com/mydevices (where *n* is your student number).

3 Through a series of redirects, the user is prompted for credentials to log in. Use Carl Dunn's user name (**carl**) and password (**net**).

The window has two tabs: Devices, where the user can enroll the device; and Profiles, where the various profiles made available will be displayed. Click the Profiles tab.

4 In the Profiles pane, click Install for the trust profile.

The profile downloads, and the Profiles preferences appear.

5 Click the Show Profile button to view the contents of the profile. Review, and then click Continue.

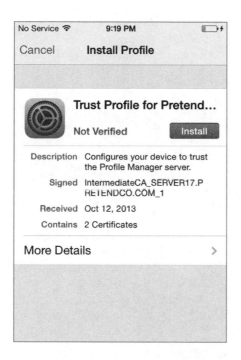

6   In the next window, click Show Details to view more information regarding the certificates involved, and then click Install. Enter an administrator's credentials when prompted.

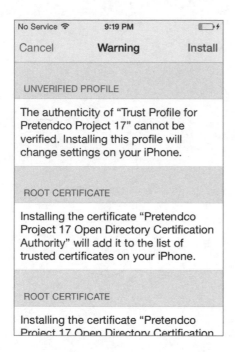

7 Notice that the trust profile is now listed as Verified.

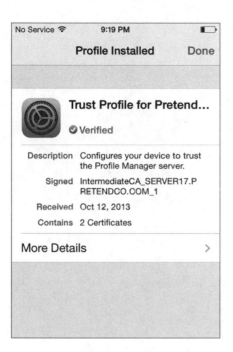

8   Back in the web browser, in the Devices pane, click Enroll.

You are asked if you want to enroll. View the profile and then click Install.

9   In the next screen, you are asked to install Remote Management, which allows the server to manage that machine. View the profile and click Continue. Enter an administrator's credentials when prompted.

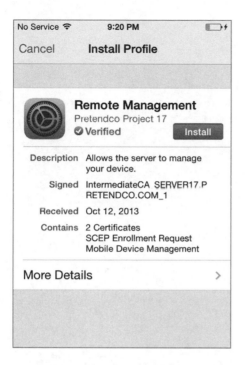

10 You will be given a warning asking if you wish to continue the installation, as it shows that controlling and destructive action commands can now be sent to the device. Click Install.

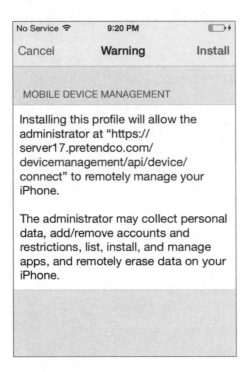

11 Review the installed profiles.

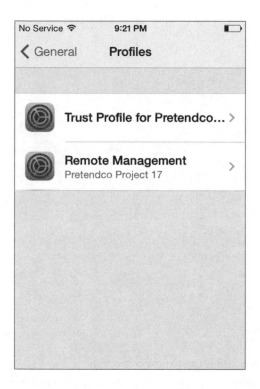

12 Now that the profile has been installed on the computer, refresh the view in the browser and notice that the computer is now listed on the Devices pane.

The user can now utilize any modern web browser to lock or wipe the computer remotely, if the machine were to get lost or stolen.

13 To lock the remote device, navigate to the site https://server*n*.pretendco.com/ mydevices (where *n* is your student number) on a different computer, such as your server, and log in as Carl.

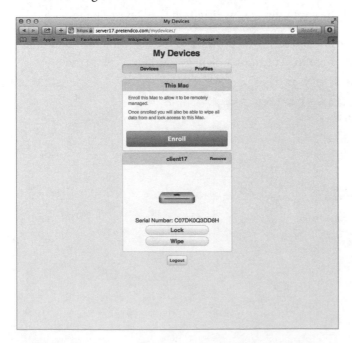

14 Select your administrator computer and lock it by clicking the Lock button and entering a six-digit passcode. For this exercise, use something simple like 123456. Click the Lock button again, and a confirmation box appears.

After confirmation, the remote computer reboots and then offers a dialog to unlock the machine via the passcode. Enter the passcode (123456) and log in as ladmin.

NOTE ▶ Do not lose the passcode you are setting or you will not be able to gain access back on your administrator computer.

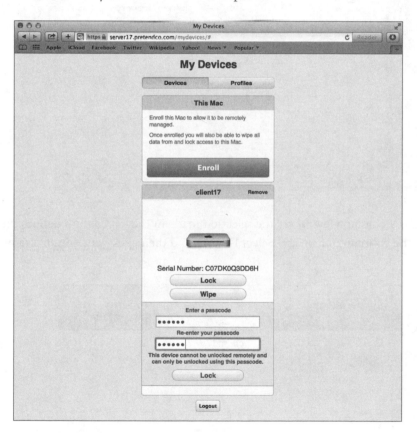

Using Profile Manager

Once Profile Manager has been turned on, you access the actual management interface via a web application. The web application can be reached via web browser on any machine.

1 On your administrator computer, navigate to the site https://server*n*.pretendco.com/profilemanager (where *n* is your student number) from your administrator computer.

2 Log in to the Profile Manager web app as ladmin.

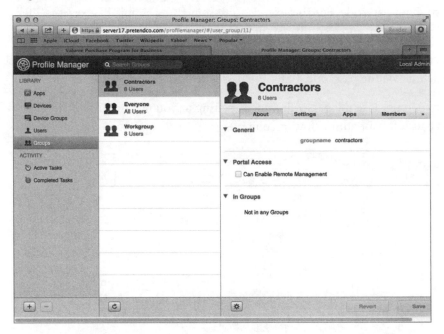

3 The layout is a column view where the selection made in the left column defines the content of the column to the right. Select Devices and then click your administrator computer.

4   In the information pane, click the Settings tab and then click the Edit button.

5   Scroll down the list in the OS X section, noting that there are sections for iOS, OS X, and combined OS X and iOS. Select Dock and then click Configure.

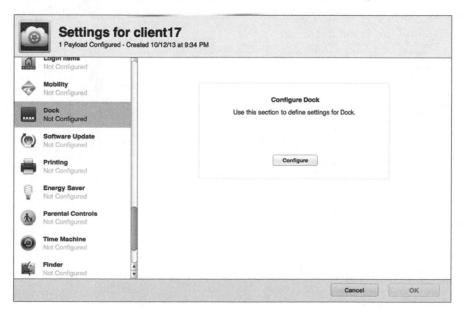

6 Change the Position to Left.

7 Scroll back to the top of the list in the left column and select General. Select Manual Download for the Profile Distribution Type. Click OK.

If Profile Distribution Type had been left on Automatic Push, once the profile was saved, the Apple Push Notification service would have notified the client device and installed the profile automatically. In this example we want to manually download the profile so we can examine it.

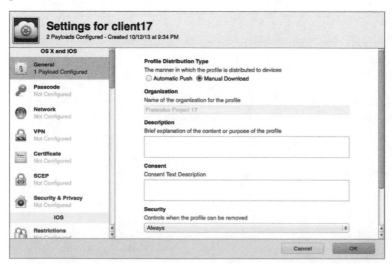

8   Note that the Dock preference is indicated in the settings for the computer.

9   If you had used Automatic Push, there would have been a warning dialog stating that new settings might be pushed to the managed devices, but since you set it for manual download, the warning dialog does not appear. Click Save.

10   Click the Download button. The Profiles preference pane will open, allowing you to install the profile, but just cancel for now.

A copy of the preferences is stored in the profile downloaded to the machine on which Profile Manager is running. It is located in the Downloads folder of the currently running user. Control-click the .mobileconfig file, choose Open With, choose TextEdit, and view the contents. The profile is simply an XML text file with some binary due to it being signed. Quit TextEdit without making any changes to the file.

11   Double-click the profile to install it. Click Show Profile to view the contents of the profile.

12 Click Install and enter the local administrator's password.

13 If the change was not immediate, log out and log back in. Notice that the Dock is now on the left side.

14 Open the Profiles preferences and view the new profile.

15 Remove the Settings profile by highlighting it and clicking the Delete (–) button at the bottom of the left column. Acknowledge the removal and enter a local administrator's credentials. Upon logging out and back in, the original Dock location and behavior will be restored. Log out when done.

16 In Profile Manager, change the Dock preferences by setting the Position to Right and selecting the "Automatically hide and show the Dock" option.

17 In the General payload, change the Profile Distribution Type to Automatic Push.

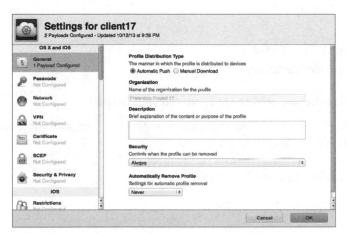

18 Click OK to save the preferences, and then click Save and Save again in the confirmation dialog to push the profile to the managed computer.

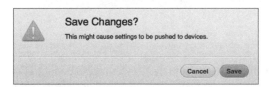

19 Look in the Activity list under Active Tasks to watch the push occur. Once finished, look in the Completed Tasks and find the push.

20 Check that the Dock is now on the right side. You can reverse this by changing the Dock settings in Profile Manager.

Creating a Device Account Placeholder

There are two ways to set up a device account:

▶ During device enrollment the device account is created automatically.

▶ You can create a placeholder in Profile Manager, so when the user logs into the User Portal, predefined profiles are assigned to the device.

To manually create a placeholder in Profile Manager:

1 In the Profile Manager Library, select Devices.

2 Click the Add (+) button below the list of devices, and choose Add Placeholder.

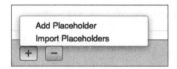

3 Give the placeholder a name, and choose how to identify the device: Ethernet ID, serial number, IMEI, or MEID. Choose Serial Number, and type in the appropriate identifying string. From the Device Type menu, choose iOS/OS X.

4 Click Add.

5 From the placeholder entry, you can add profiles and management that will be applied automatically once the device is enrolled.

Lists of devices can be imported into Profile Manager via a comma-separated value (CSV) file. The file needs to be structured like this:

name, serial number, UDID, IMEI, MEID

Leave a field empty if you're not using that value.

This exercise is optional. To do the exercise you will need to create a CSV file with the appropriate information in it.

1   In the Profile Manager Library, select Devices.

2   Click the Add (+) button below the list of devices, and choose Import Placeholders.

3   Select the import file and upload.

Creating and Populating a Device Group

To create and populate a device group, use Profile Manager:

1   In the Profile Manager Library, select Device Groups.

2   Click the Add (+) button below the list of device groups, which creates a new group that can be populated with the desired name.

3   To add devices to the device group, click the Add (+) button under the device group pane, and choose Add Devices.

4   Click Add next to the placeholder you just made, and then click Done. This simulates how you can prepare management for devices that haven't been enrolled yet.

5   View the placeholder device as a member of the device group.

6   To add device groups to the device group, click the Add (+) button under the device group pane, and choose Add Device Groups. This allows you to nest device groups for management.

7   Click the device group to add to the device group, and then click Done.

8   Click Save.

Managing Profiles Locally

Occasionally a profile will need to be viewed, added, or removed to make way for an updated profile or to simply stop management of the device. Managing the profiles local to a computer is done via the Profiles preferences. You added a profile to the computer in a previous exercise, and now you will remove one.

To remove a profile local to an OS X computer:

1   Open the Profiles preferences.

     The various profiles installed on the computer are listed along with their contents and purposes.

2   Select the Remote Management profile, and click the Remove (–) button.

3 In the confirmation dialog box, click Remove. Enter a local administrator's credentials, if prompted, and click OK.

To remove a profile local to an iOS device:

1 Navigate to Settings/General/Profiles.

2 Tap the profile to show the details.

3 Tap the Remove button.

4 In the confirmation box, confirm the removal by tapping Remove.

5 Exit Settings.

Clean Up

Remove the profiles from your client devices. You learned how to apply profiles to both
OS X and iOS devices. If you need or want to use them for later lessons, you know how to
apply them, and no older management will impact that.

Sharing Files

Lesson 13

Configuring the File Sharing Service

It is quite simple to use OS X Server to share files across a network for your users, whether they are using OS X, Windows, or iOS. The four basic steps are:

▶ Plan.

▶ Configure accounts.

▶ Configure the File Sharing service.

▶ Monitor the server.

In this lesson you will explore the challenges associated with file sharing and the issues to consider when setting up file sharing. The main focus of the lesson is on setting up shared folders, also called share points, with appropriate access settings based on standard POSIX (Portable Operating System Interface) permissions and access control lists (ACLs). This lesson also addresses automatic network mounts, which provide a network destination for home folders for network accounts, and general file sharing troubleshooting issues to consider when enabling File Sharing services on OS X Server.

You will learn how to use the Server app to add and configure individual share points, and you'll use the Console application while logged in to the server to monitor logs.

Reference 13.1
Addressing the Challenges of File Sharing

When planning to offer File Sharing services, there are a number of issues to consider. The obvious questions are:

▶ What content will you share?

▶ What types of clients will be accessing your file server?

▶ What protocols will the client computers or devices use?

▶ What levels of access do your various users and groups require?

At first glance, these questions might seem relatively easy to answer, but in practice, especially in dynamic organizations, requirements can get very complex, and it can be difficult to facilitate your users' access to the things necessary to remain productive, without constant intervention from an administrator.

When accessing a file server, you typically have to authenticate, and then you see a choice of valid share points (also known as shares) available to mount. Here's an example dialog in which you must select one or more share points (which appear as network volumes) to use.

When you navigate inside a mounted share point, folder badges (small icons displayed on the lower-right corner of the folder icon) indicate the access rights for the user account whose credentials you used when you connected to the file service. Folders display a red do-not-enter sign for folders that you are not authorized to access. In the following figure, the connected user does not have access to some of the folders in the shared folder.

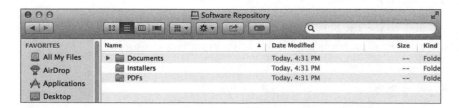

This is a combination of authorization for accessing the file sharing service, as well as authorization for accessing individual files and folders.

Authorization is a constant occurrence; every time a user accesses a file, the computer checks file permissions against the user's account information to see if the user is authorized to use the file.

After completing this lesson, you will be in a good position to carefully consider your file sharing needs before you implement file sharing on your server.

Understanding File Sharing Protocols

OS X Server includes a number of ways to share files. The method you select depends largely on the clients you expect to serve (although security is another factor to consider). You can use the Server app to enable the following file sharing services:

▶ Server Message Block 2 (SMB2)—SMB2 is the new default protocol for file sharing in OS X Mavericks. SMB2 is fast, it increases security over SMB, and it improves Windows compatibility. This guide and the Server app use *SMB* to refer to SMB2.

▶ Apple Filing Protocol (AFP)—This protocol was the native file sharing protocol for Mac up until OS X Mavericks. OS X and OS X Server fall back to AFP for file sharing for Macs running operating systems earlier than OS X Mavericks.

▶ Web-based Distributed Authoring and Versioning (WebDAV)—This protocol is an extension to the web service protocol (HTTP), and it enables various clients, including iOS apps, to access files hosted by your server.

▶ File Transfer Protocol (FTP)—This protocol is compatible with many devices and is still widely used, but in most common uses, it does not protect the authentication traffic. This file sharing protocol is lightweight in the sense that it is simple and does not have all the features available in the other file sharing services. FTP allows you to transfer files back and forth between client and server, but you cannot, for example, open a document over an FTP connection. The primary benefit of FTP is that it is ubiquitous: It is hard to find a Transfer Control Protocol (TCP)–capable computer or device that does not support FTP; some copiers and scanners, for example, place files in a shared folder via FTP.

NOTE ▶ The FTP service is separated from the File Sharing service and has its own pane in the Server app's Advanced services section.

When Windows clients use NetBIOS to browse for network file servers, a computer running OS X Server with file sharing enabled appears just like a Windows server with file sharing enabled.

If you want to share a folder over WebDAV, you must explicitly enable that service for that share point by selecting the "Share over WebDAV" option.

A user with an iOS device can use a share point on your server, but only with apps that support WebDAV, and only to share points for which you enable WebDAV by selecting the appropriate checkbox. A user must specify the URL for the WebDAV shared folder, which consists of the following:

▶ http:// or https://

▶ The server's address

▶ Optionally, the shared folder name

For example, https://server17.pretendco.com/Projects.

If you do not provide a specific share point in the URL, all WebDAV-enabled share points will appear.

In order to access the WebDAV service protected with SSL, users should supply "https://" instead of "http://" as part of the URL. Even without the benefit of SSL, the traffic for authentication is encrypted via WebDAV digest.

Here is an example of using Keynote on an iPhone to open a connection to a WebDAV share point:

MORE INFO ▶ After signing in to your server's WebDAV service with an app like Keynote on iOS, the app displays the share points available via WebDAV; the user can navigate to a folder in which to open or save a document.

You can share a folder over several different protocols simultaneously. When you create a share point in the Server app:

▶   The share point is automatically enabled to be shared over AFP.

▶   The share point is automatically enabled to be shared over SMB.

▶   The share point is not automatically enabled for WebDAV.

▶   The share point is not automatically enabled for guest users.

OS X Server also provides file service via Network File System (NFS). NFS is the traditional method of file sharing for UNIX-based computers. NFS has its heritage in research facilities and academia in the 1980s. Although it can be very convenient and flexible, and can be used with Kerberos to provide robust security, when used with legacy clients it can suffer from some security issues that do not affect the other protocols. The primary use for NFS is to provide files to NetInstall clients and UNIX or Linux computers. Although OS X can use NFS, you should normally use SMB for Mavericks clients, and AFP for clients with earlier versions of OS X.

> **MORE INFO** ▶ The NetInstall service defaults to using HTTP, but when you start the NetInstall service, OS X Server automatically creates the NetBootClients0 share point and makes it available to guest users over NFS. The "Allow guest users to access this share" checkbox for the NetBootClients0 share point has a dash to indicate that the value varies; in this case, guest access is enabled for NFS and AFP but not for SMB.

The configuration and management for NFS are outside the scope of this guide; see the "Additional Resources" Appendix available with the guide's downloadable files for an Apple Support article regarding NFS.

Comparing File Sharing Protocols

This table provides a short comparison of file sharing protocols. There really isn't one best protocol. Instead, think of the protocols as different tools at your disposal to give different types of access.

	SMB	**AFP**	**WebDAV**
Native platform	Multi-platform	OS X versions prior to Mavericks	Multi-platform
Browsable	Bonjour and NetBIOS	Bonjour	Not browsable
Example URL	smb://server17. pretendco.com/Users	afp://server17. pretendco.com/Users	https://server17. pretendco.com/Users

AFP and SMB are both full-featured file sharing protocols with reasonably good security.

> **TIP** ▶ If you use "https://" instead of "http://" in a WebDAV URL, both the authentication transaction and the payload (the files transferred) are protected from snooping. However, your WebDAV client may not allow you to access a WebDAV resource via HTTPS if the SSL certificate that the server uses is not valid or is not signed by a CA that your computer or device trusts,.

> **MORE INFO** ▶ In order to provide WebDAV service to Active Directory accounts, you must configure the WebDAV service to use Basic authentication instead of Digest authentication. In this scenario, it is recommended that you also require SSL for the WebDAV service, in order to protect the authentication. See the Apple Support article in the "Additional Resources" Appendix available with the guide's downloadable files.

When authenticating for FTP access, the user name and password are not encrypted at all.

> **MORE INFO** ▶ SFTP (Secure FTP) uses the SSH service to securely transfer files using the SSH protocol. SFTP does not use the FTP service, and you must enable the SSH service in order for your users to use SFTP.

Planning File Sharing Services

When setting up File Sharing services on OS X Server, proper initial planning can save you time in the long run. Follow these guidelines when you first start planning to implement File Sharing services.

Plan Your File-Server Requirements

Determine your organizational requirements:

▶ How are your users organized?

▶ Is there a logical structure to follow for assigning users to groups that best addresses workflow needs?

- ► What types of computers will be used to access your file server?
- ► What share points and folder structures will be needed?
- ► Who needs what access to various files?
- ► How will users interact with one another when accessing these share points?
- ► How much storage space do you currently have, how much storage space do your users currently need, and at what rate will their need for storage grow?
- ► How will you back up and archive your storage?

These answers will dictate the File Sharing services you configure, as well as how you might organize groups and share points.

Use the Server App to Configure Users and Groups

The main goal is to end up with a group structure that best matches your organizational needs and allows easy maintenance over time. Setting up users and groups at the beginning is trivial. But, setting up users and groups that continue to work as the organization goes through natural changes over time is not as simple as it first appears. Nevertheless, having a logical group structure that can be used to allow and deny access to your server's file system will save you from continually adjusting file-service access later on. OS X Server supports groups within groups and setting access control lists on folders.

> **TIP** ▶ For testing of groups, share points, and ACLs, you do not need to have all users entered. You may decide to test with a skeletal set of users and groups that meet the requirements of your organization. After verifying the groups and share points, you can then enter or import the full set of users.

Use the Server App to Start and Configure the File Sharing Service

The Server app is the main application you use to do the following:

- ► Start and stop the file sharing service.
- ► Add new share points.
- ► Remove share points.

For each share point, you can:

- ► Configure ownership, permissions, and the ACL for the share point.
- ► Enable or disable AFP for the share point.
- ► Enable or disable SMB for the share point.

- ▶ Enable or disable WebDAV for the share point.

- ▶ Allow or disallow guest access to the share point.

- ▶ Make the share point available for network home folders.

Perform Regular Maintenance

After you start the file sharing service, you'll need to perform regular maintenance. You will probably use the Server app to perform the following maintenance tasks as your needs change:

- ▶ Use the Users pane to add users to groups, groups to users, and groups to groups.

- ▶ Use the Users pane to modify the allowed services for each user.

- ▶ Use the File Sharing pane to add and remove share points.

- ▶ Use the File Sharing pane to modify ownership, permissions, and ACLs for share points.

- ▶ Use the Storage pane to modify ownership, permissions, and ACLs for folders and files.

Monitor Your Server for Problems

Monitoring server usage is a valuable method to keep track of workflow. You can view graphs and watch for usual traffic patterns, usage spikes, and low-usage periods that you could use to plan backups or perform server maintenance.

There are several ways to monitor your server:

▶ Use the Server app's Stats pane to monitor processor usage, memory usage, and network traffic.

▶ Use the Server app's Storage pane to check available disk space.

▶ Use the Server app's Connected Users tab in the File Sharing pane to monitor the number of connected users (this displays information about users connected via AFP and via SMB).

Be aware that if your server offers services other than file sharing, those other services could also affect resources such as network throughput, so you need to be careful interpreting the graphs.

Review Logs

If you log in at the server, you can use the Console app to view logs, including the following:

▶ /Library/Logs/AppleFileService/AppleFileServiceError.log

▶ /Library/Logs/AppleFileService/AppleFileServiceAccess.log

▶ /Library/Logs/WebDAVSharing.log

▶ /var/log/apache2/access_log

▶ /var/log/apache2/error_log

From a remote computer (or on the server computer), you can use the Server app Logs pane to view logs related to file sharing, including the AFP Error log, and for WebDAV, the error and access logs associated with the default and secure websites.

The AFP Error log displays events such as the AFP service stopping. In the websites logs, you can use the search term "WebDAV" to separate log entries that relate to WebDAV from the log entries that relate to the Websites service in general.

You might use additional software, such as Terminal or third-party software, to monitor your server.

Reference 13.2
Creating Share Points

After determining server and user requirements and entering at least a sample set of users and groups that represents the organizational structure, the next step in sharing files is to configure your share points. A share point can be any folder or any volume that is mounted on the server. When you create a share point, you make that item and its contents available to network clients via the specified protocols. This includes deciding what items you want to give access to and organizing the items logically. It requires using your initial planning and knowledge of your users and their needs. You might decide that everything belongs in a single share point and use permissions to control access within that share point, or you might set up a more complex workflow. For example, you could have one share point for your copywriters and a separate share point for the copyeditors. Perhaps you would also have a third share point where both groups could access common items or share files. Setting up effective share points requires as much knowledge of your users and how they work together as it does the technology of share points.

The Server app's File Sharing pane does not allow you to create a new shared folder in a location that you don't have write access to; by default the local administrator does not have write access to the root of the startup disk. In a production environment you might share files from an external storage unit connected by Thunderbolt, FireWire, or USB.

> **TIP** ▶ OS X Server for Mountain Lion automatically created a folder named Shared Items at the root of the startup disk; OS X Server for Mavericks does not create this folder. See the section "Create a New Location for Shared Folders" in Exercise 13.1, "Explore the File Sharing Service" for a procedure to create that folder.

Explore File Sharing

The On/Off switch turns the File Sharing service on or off. The lower-right corner of the Server app window indicates the status of starting or stopping the File Sharing service. A service status indicator dot to the left of the service in the Server app sidebar appears when the service is on, and disappears when the service is off.

The Share Points pane is displayed by default, showing the following:

▶ The share points

▶ Buttons to Add (+), Delete (–), and Edit (pencil icon) share points

▶ A text filter field to limit the share points displayed

> **NOTE** ▶ The Server app displays the File Sharing pane slightly differently depending on whether you run the Server app on the server or on a remote Mac.

Understand the Default Share Points

You don't need OS X Server installed in order to offer shared folders. You can open System Preferences, open Sharing preferences, and select the checkbox for File Sharing. But OS X Server gives you much more flexibility in file sharing than OS X itself offers.

Every time you use the Users & Groups preferences in System Preferences to create a new local user account, OS X automatically adds that user's Public folder to the list of folders to share, with a customized folder name (like Local Admin's Public Folder). So when you first install OS X Server and look at the File Sharing pane, you see a list of shared folders that consists of the Public folders for local user accounts.

Although these default share points are convenient, you are free to remove them.

> **MORE INFO** ▶ If you have configured and started the NetInstall service, you will see additional share points named NetBootClients0 and NetBootSP0, which are used for NetInstall. There is more information about NetInstall in Lesson 15, "Leveraging NetInstall."

Add and Remove Share Points

It's pretty simple to add a shared folder that allows your users to access the files in the folder using any combination of AFP, SMB, and WebDAV. You can use the Server app to select an existing folder, or even to create a new folder to share.

To create a new shared folder, click Add (+) to open a pane that contains your startup volume and any other attached volumes. This pane is different depending on whether you run the Server app directly on your server or you run the Server app remotely. The following is an example of the pane when you run the Server app directly on your server. Note that even though it opens to the Documents folder by default, you can click the pop-up menu to access the root of your startup disk.

This is what the pane looks like when you run the Server app on a remote Mac:

You have two options:

▶ Select an existing folder and click Choose.

▶ Create a new folder, select the new folder, and click Choose.

If you click New Folder, you'll be asked for the name of the new folder. Assign the folder a name, and click Create.

After you create a folder, be sure that your newly created folder is selected before you click Choose:

▶ When you use the Server app on a remote Mac, you must remember to select the newly created folder before you click Choose; otherwise, you will share the parent folder.

▶ When you use the Server app while you are logged in directly on server, the Server app automatically selects the folder you just created.

> **TIP** Sometimes, administrators using a remote Mac forget to select the folder they just created, and share the parent folder instead. Don't worry, you can always remove the accidentally shared parent folder and then add the newly created folder.

The newly shared folder appears in a list of shared folders. Each shared folder is listed. Additionally, when you use the Server app from a remote administrator computer, the Server app displays any non-special share point with an icon of a network disk with figures of multiple users (as in the Accounting share point in the following figure).

When you use the Server app while logged in directly on the server computer, the Server app displays any non-special share point with an icon of a simple folder.

Removing a share point is even easier. Select a share point and click Remove (–). When you remove a share point, you don't remove the folder or its contents from the file system, you just stop sharing it.

Configure Individual Share Points

In this section, you will look at what kinds of changes you can make to a share point.

To edit a share point's configuration, you could select a share point and do any of the following:

▶ Double-click the share point.

▶ Click Edit (pencil icon).

▶ Press Command-Down Arrow.

The editing pane includes the following:

▶ An icon for the folder

▶ The full path to the shared folder (like /Volumes/Data/Projects).

▶ The name of the shared folder (which by default is the name of the folder, but you can change it).

► An arrow icon next to "View Files"; when you click the icon, the Server app opens to that folder in the Storage pane of the Server app.

► The Access pane, which includes standard UNIX ownership and permissions, and can also include access control list (ACL) information.

► Checkboxes to enable and disable sharing over various protocols.

► A checkbox to enable or disable guest access.

► A checkbox to "Make available for home directories over" (AFP or SMB).

The guest access checkbox affects both AFP and SMB services, so when you use the Server app to enable guest access for AFP, you also enable guest access for SMB. Users from OS X or Windows client computers can access guest-enabled share points without providing any authentication. When users on OS X select your server's computer name in their Finder window sidebar's Shared section, they automatically connect as Guest. In the following figure, notice that the Finder displays the text "Connected as: Guest" below the toolbar, and displays the folders accessible to the Guest user.

Make Available for Home Directories

The checkbox "Make available for home directories over" (AFP or SMB) is available only after your server is configured as an Open Directory master or replica. This concept is also referred to as a network home directory or a network home folder.

A network home folder makes it easy for a user to move from one shared computer to another shared computer, because when they log in, their computer automatically mounts their network home folder; files they save are stored on the server. Of course, the shared computers must be configured properly (a Mac must be bound to the shared directory) in order for this to work. Keep in mind that a local home folder (a home folder stored on the startup disk of the computer they use) may offer better performance than a network home folder, and may be more appropriate for users who do not share computers.

> **NOTE** ▶ A network home folder is not a backup system; be sure to back up network home folders, as well as local home folders. Keep in mind that OS X Server offers the Time Machine service, and there are plenty of third-party backup services as well.

After you make one or more shared folders "available for home directories," when you create and edit user accounts, you will see these shared folders available in the Home Folder pop-up menu, as shown in the following figure.

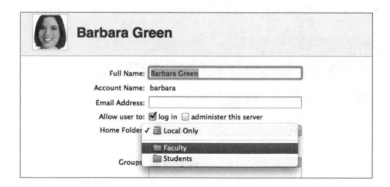

> **NOTE** ▶ When you create a new user account, if there is no Home Folder pop-up menu, this indicates that you do not have any folders configured to be available as network home folders.

Configuring a Group Folder

When you edit a group and select the checkbox "Give this group a shared folder," the Server app performs the following actions:

▶ Creates a Groups shared folder if necessary (creates a folder named Groups at the root of your startup disk if necessary, and configures it as a shared folder)

▶ Creates a folder with that group's account name in the Groups share point

▶ Creates an access control entry (ACE) in the Groups folder ACL that gives the members of the group full access over their group folder so they can use their group folder for collaboration.

NOTE ▶ The behavior of the arrow icon next to the "Give this group a shared folder" checkbox depends on where you are running the server app. If you click the icon while logged in on your server, the Finder will open to the Groups folder. If you click the icon while using the Server app on an administrator computer, it attempts to open an AFP connection for the Groups folder on your server. If the group folder does not yet exist, be sure to select the checkbox "Give this group a shared folder" and then click OK before you click the arrow icon.

Using the Connected Users Pane

The Connected Users pane displays information about the users who are currently connected via AFP or SMB (it does not include WebDAV and FTP connections).

The tab itself displays the number of connected users.

After you click the Connected Users tab, you see a list of connected users, including the following information:

▶ User name

▶ Address

▶ Idle time

▶ Type (AFP or SMB)

You can press Command-R (or choose View > Refresh) to refresh the list of currently connected users.

If you select a user currently connected via AFP, you can click the Disconnect button to forcibly disconnect that client's file sharing connection, without any warning to the client.

If you click Disconnect for a user currently connected via SMB, you see a message that you can only disconnect AFP users.

Reference 13.3
Troubleshooting File Sharing Services

Whether you're using AFP, SMB, or WebDAV, troubleshooting File Sharing services on OS X Server typically involves the following considerations:

▶ Service availability—Is the service turned on? For Time Machine, the File Sharing service must be turned on.

▶ User access—What users or groups should have access to the specific files and folders on the server, and are their appropriate permissions set correctly?

▶ Platform and protocol access—From which clients, such as Mac computers, Windows computers, or iOS devices, are users trying to access the server? What protocols are they using when accessing the server?

▶ Special needs—Are there any special circumstances, such as users needing access to files in a format not native to the system they are using?

▶ Concurrent access—Is there a possibility that in your users' workflow, there could be multiple clients simultaneously accessing the same files, regardless of the file sharing protocol(s) being used?

While the different sharing protocols (AFP, SMB, WebDAV) support multiple platforms, it can be tricky to provide concurrent access to the same files, especially with the Auto Save and Versions document management features in OS X. Concurrent access means that multiple users are trying to access or modify the same files at the same time. Many times this is dependent on the specific cross-platform applications knowing how to allow multiple users to access the same file. Because OS X Server includes support for ACLs, and these ACLs are compatible with those from the Windows platform, permissions mapping between Windows clients will be in line with what Windows users expect to see.

Reference 13.4
Providing FTP Service

You use the File Sharing service to serve files via AFP, SMB, and WebDAV (and NFS, but you don't use the Server app to configure NFS), and you use the FTP service to serve files via FTP. As stated earlier, in most cases, the FTP service leaves everything in clear text: user name, password, and the data in the files being transferred, so the FTP service might not be appropriate except for certain circumstances.

The FTP pane offers the On/Off switch, the Share pop-up menu to choose the parent folder (the folder that contains the files you make available via FTP), a basic access pane, and a View Files link to open the parent folder in the Storage pane.

By default, if you simply turn on the FTP service, users who successfully authenticate see contents of the default Websites folder (see Lesson 21, "Hosting Websites," for more information).

However, you can click the Share pop-up menu to change the parent folder.

You can choose any share point configured on your server, or configure another folder to be the parent folder and then choose it. If you configure a custom parent folder, the FTP pane offers the View Files link to open the folder in the Storage pane, and the Server app displays the Access section (you'll learn more about controlling access to files in Lesson 14, "Understanding File Access").

In the following figure, the parent folder is a folder named FTPStuff, which is not otherwise a shared folder.

If, instead, you choose a parent folder that's configured as a File Sharing share point (regardless of whether or not your File Sharing service is started), the FTP pane offers the Edit Share Point link to open the share point in the File Sharing pane.

You can use the OS X command-line environment or third-party software to access the FTP service with read and write capabilities. In the Finder, you can connect to the FTP service by choosing Go > Connect to Server, entering ftp://*<your server's host name>*, providing credentials, and clicking Connect, but the Finder is a read-only FTP client.

MORE INFO ▶ If someone attempts to connect anonymously, he will appear to make a successful connection but will see no files or folders available.

Because the FTP service normally does not encrypt the user name or password, it's recommended to leave the FTP service off unless there is no other alternative to meet your organization's needs to provide file service.

Exercise 13.1
Explore the File Sharing Service

▶ **Prerequisites**

▶ Exercise 9.1, "Configure Your Server as an Open Directory Master"

▶ Exercise 10.1, "Create and Import Network Accounts"; or use the Server app to create users Barbara Green and Todd Porter, each with an account name that is the same as their first name in lowercase, and a password of net, and each a member of a group named Contractors.

If you don't already have a Contractors group and the user accounts mentioned in this exercise, you can use the Users pane to create the users, use the Groups pane to create the Contractors group, and add the Barbara Green and Todd Porter users to the group.

You'll use the Server app to view the default shared folders, their respective protocols, and the available free space on your server's storage devices. Then you will create a new folder and make it available for file sharing.

1   Perform these exercises on your administrator computer. If you do not already have a connection to your server computer with Server app on your administrator computer, then connect to it with the following steps: Open the Server app on your administrator computer, choose Manage > Connect to Server, click Other Mac, select your server, click Continue, provide administrator credentials (Administrator Name **ladmin** and Administrator Password **ladminpw**), deselect the "Remember this password" checkbox, and then click Connect.

2   In the Server app sidebar, select your server, and then click the Storage tab.

The Storage pane displays your server's storage devices, including the startup volume. Using the disclosure triangles, you can navigate the hierarchy of the storage devices. The lower portion of the pane has a Column View button and a List View button.

3   Click the List View button, and then click the Column View button. Note the change.

4   Click the Action (gear icon) pop-up menu, but do not choose any item in the menu at this time.

Note that you can use this menu to create a new folder, edit permissions, and propagate permissions. You will explore permissions in Exercise 14.1, "Configure Access Control."

5   In the Server app sidebar, click File Sharing.

6   In the Shared Folders field, double-click Local Admin's Public Folder to edit that share point.

7   If it is not already selected, select the "Allow guest users to access this share" option.

NOTE ▶ When you enable guest access, you enable it for both the AFP and SMB protocols. Of course, in order for guests to access the share point using a given protocol, that protocol must be enabled for that share point; in other words, enabling guest access does not automatically enable any specific protocol.

8 Click OK to return from the Local Admin's Public Folder detail view to the File Sharing overview.

Stop and Start the File Sharing Service

Use the Server app to stop and start the File Sharing service and to verify that it is working properly. Regardless of how your File Sharing service is currently configured, start this exercise by making sure that "Enable screen sharing and remote management" is enabled and that the File Sharing service is off.

1 In the Server app, select your server in the sidebar, and then click Settings.

2 Ensure that the checkbox "Enable screen sharing and remote management" is selected.

3 In the Server app sidebar, select the File Sharing service.

4 Click the On/Off switch to turn off the service.

On your administrator computer, observe how browsing for services with the Finder behaves before and after File Sharing services are started.

1 On your administrator computer, in the Finder, press Command-N to open a new Finder window.

2 If your server appears in the Finder window sidebar, select your server.

Otherwise, if there are enough computers on your network that your server does not appear in the Shared section of the Finder sidebar, click All and then select your server.

Because your server's File Sharing service is off, the Finder displays only the Share Screen button, and not the Connect As button.

3 Close the Finder window.

NOTE ► Be sure to close the Finder window, otherwise the rest of this section will not work as expected.

4 In the Server app, in the File Sharing pane, click the On/Off switch to turn on the service.

Once the File Sharing service has started, its service status indicator dot in the Server app sidebar reappears.

5 In the Finder, press Command-N to open a new Finder window.

6 If your server appears in the Finder window sidebar, select your server; otherwise, click All and then select your server.

7 In the Finder, observe the change in your administrator computer's Finder: You are automatically connected as the Guest user, a Connect As button appears, and the shared folders identified as "guest accessible" in the Server app list of share points are listed in the Finder window (in this case, it is just Local Admin's Public Folder).

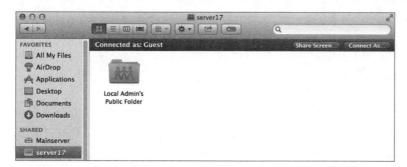

When you turned on File Sharing, OS X Server used Bonjour to broadcast the availability of file sharing service to the local subnet. Your administrator computer's Finder received the broadcast and updated the Finder window sidebar accordingly.

Create a New Location for Shared Folders

For the purposes of the exercises, you will create a folder at the root of your startup disk and change the ownership of that folder in order use the File Sharing pane to create new shared folders in that folder (you will learn more about permissions in the next lesson, "Understanding File Access").

1 On your administrator computer, in the File Sharing pane, double-click the default shared folder, Local Admin's Public Folder.

2 Click the View Files link to open the folder in the Storage pane.

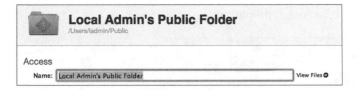

3 In the Storage pane, click the List View button, then click the disclosure triangle to reveal the contents of your startup disk.

4 Select your server computer's startup disk.

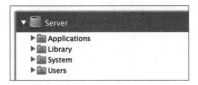

5 Click the Action (gear icon) pop-up menu and choose New Folder.

6 Enter Shared Items in the "Name of new folder" field, then click Create.

7 Select the Shared Items folder.

8 Click the Action (gear icon) pop-up menu and choose Edit Permissions.

9   Double-click the name "root" in the User or Group column to edit it.

10   Enter ladmin, then choose Local Admin (ladmin).

11   Click OK to save the change.

Create a New Shared Folder

A folder has to exist on the server to be used as a file share. One way to create a new folder is to log in on the server and create a new folder with the Finder. However, you can also use the Server app to make new folders on your server.

1   In the Server app, click the File Sharing pane, then click the Add (+) button to add a new shared folder.

The Server app displays a list of volumes on the left, and a column view of folders for the selected volume on the right.

NOTE ▶ If you create the new shared folder using your server computer rather than your administrator computer, the Server app displays files similar to what you would see in the Finder. Be sure to perform these steps from your administrator computer so your experience matches the steps in this exercise.

While the contents look similar to that of the Finder, there is a significant difference: You are looking at the file system of the server, not the local file system of your administrator computer. Any folders you create or choose are ones that exist on your server's storage devices.

2   Select your server's startup volume, and then select the Shared Items folder.

3   Click the New Folder button to create a new folder on the server.

The Server app prompts you for the folder name.

4   Enter the name Software Repository and click Create.

In this example, Software Repository could be a folder in which you place installation images of software you make available to individuals at your organization.

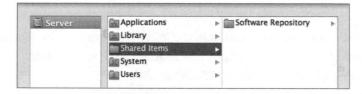

5   Select the new Software Repository folder.

6   Click Choose.

The new shared folder appears in the list of shared folders and is immediately avail-able for file sharing clients to use.

On your administrator computer, you're currently connected via AFP as the Guest user. Connect to the new folder as the user Barbara Green.

1   On your administrator computer, in the Finder, press Command-N to open a new Finder window if necessary, and select your server in the Finder window sidebar (or click All and select your server).

2   Click Connect As in the upper-right corner of the Finder window.

3   Provide Barbara Green's credentials (Name barbara and Password net), and click Connect.

You see a list of shared folders you can access.

4   Open the Software Repository folder.

5 Choose View > Show Status Bar.

Note the icon of a pencil with a slash through it in the lower-left corner of the Finder window, indicating that you do not have write access to this folder. You will learn more about this in Lesson 14, "Understanding File Access."

It is easy to use the Server app to create a new shared folder, but you need to update the permissions in order to allow users to create files and folders in that folder. One big timesaver is the feature in the Server app to create a shared folder for a group, which you will use next.

Give a Group a Shared Folder

Use the Server app to give the Contractors group a shared folder. One of the great things about this feature is that you do not need to perform any additional configuration to give users shared read and write access to the resources they create in this shared folder.

You'll give the Contractors group a shared folder, and then confirm that members of the group have read and write access to resources in the folder.

1 In the Server app sidebar, select Groups.

2 Double-click the Contractors group to edit that group.

3 Select the checkbox labeled "Give this group a shared folder."

4 Click OK to create the shared folder in the Groups folder.

Note that this creates a folder named Groups at the root of your startup disk if it did not previously exist, and configures it as a shared folder.

5   In the Server app sidebar, select File Sharing to return to that pane.

Use the following steps to confirm that a member of the Contractors group can edit files in the Contractors group folder. You should still be connected to the server as the user Barbara Green, who is a member of the Contractors group.

Confirm that you are still connected as Barbara Green.

1   On your administrator computer, in the Finder, press Command-N to open a new Finder window.

2   In the Finder window sidebar, select your server, or click All and select your server.

3   If you do not see "Connected as: barbara" under the Finder window toolbar, click Connect As, and then provide barbara's credentials (Name **barbara** and Password **net**) and click Connect.

4   Open the Groups folder.

5   Open the contractors folder.

Note that the folder's name is based on the short name of the group.

6   Create a new folder by pressing Command-Shift-N, enter **Barbara Created This** as the folder name, and press Return to save the name change.

Note that when you view the contractors folder in the Finder, no icon appears in the lower-left corner of the Finder window. This means that you have read and write access to this folder (because the Server app automatically configures read and write access for members of the group).

Connect as Todd Porter, another member of the Contractors group, and confirm that you can edit the resources Barbara Green placed into the folder.

1 In the Finder window, click the Eject icon next to your server sidebar to eject the volume.

2 Click Connect As, provide user credentials for a different user in the group (such as Name **todd** and Password **net**), and click Connect.

3 Open the Groups folder, and then open the contractors folder.

4 Press Command-Shift-N to create a new folder, enter **Todd Created This** as the folder name, and press Return to save the name change.

5 While you are still connected as Todd Porter, drag the folder the other user created (named Barbara Created This) to the Trash, to demonstrate that you can modify a resource a different user created.

When you are asked if you are sure, click Delete.

6 Next to your server in the Finder window sidebar, click the Eject icon to eject the volume.

Clean Up

Remove the Software Repository folder, since you will not use it for any other exercise. Eject any network volumes if you still have them mounted.

1 On your administrator computer, in the Server app sidebar, select File Sharing.

2 Select the Software Repository share point.

3 Click Remove (–), and at the confirmation dialog, click Remove.

Note that the contents of the share point will not be deleted.

4   Select the Local Admin's Public Folder share point.

5   Click Remove (–), and at the confirmation dialog, click Remove.

You used the Server app to view the default shared folders, their respective protocols, and the available free space on your server's storage devices. Then you created a folder at the root of your startup disk as a location for new shared folders, created a new folder there, and made it available for file sharing. You created a group folder and saw that you do not need to take any extra steps to grant write access to this folder for members of the group.

You will learn more about how OS X Server controls access to files, so you have the ability to modify resources other users create, in Lesson 14, "Understanding File Access."

Exercise 13.2
Use Logs to Troubleshoot Problems with File Sharing Services

> **Prerequisite**
>
> ▶   Exercise 13.1, "Explore the File Sharing Service"

Inspect the AFP Access Log
The AFP Access Log keeps track of AFP activity.

1   On your administrator computer, if you are not already connected to your server, open the Server app, connect to your server, and authenticate as a local administrator.

2   In the Server app sidebar, select Logs.

3   Click the pop-up menu and choose AFP Access Log.

4   Note that you see activity that includes connecting to, disconnecting from, and creating files in shared folders.

Note that SMB2 is the default file sharing protocol for OS X Mavericks, so the folders you created were created via SMB and are not included in the AFP Access Log.

Inspect the AFP Error Log

Given the classroom nature of the course, there may be few or no error messages within the logs. However, you should practice locating the logs and viewing their contents when you are experiencing no issues.

1 In the Server app sidebar, select Logs.

2 Click the pop-up menu and choose AFP Error Log.

There shouldn't be much here under normal operation.

3 Click the pop-up menu and choose one of the logs in the Websites section.

If you haven't accessed the File Sharing service via WebDAV, there will not be any WebDAV information in any of the Websites logs.

You used the Server app to inspect various logs. Remember that even though the logs are stored on the server, you can use the Server app from any Mac running Mavericks to inspect the logs.

Lesson 14

Understanding File Access

Now that Lesson 13 has familiarized you with the file sharing protocols you can enable, and the basics of creating, removing, and editing share points, it's time to configure access to files. For access to files and folders, OS X Server uses basic file permissions in addition to optional access control lists (ACLs) to make authorization decisions about access to files and folders. In OS X, every file and every folder has a single user account assigned as its "owner," a single group associated with it, and an optional ACL. Access permissions are assigned for the owner, for the group, and for everyone else, and the optional ACL adds additional permissions information.

When a file sharing client uses the File Sharing service, she must authenticate as a user (or as a guest if you enabled guest access for the share point). A remote user has the same access to files over file sharing that she would have if she logged in locally with the same user credentials she provided to mount the share point.

This lesson covers how to use the Server app to configure access to files.

GOALS

▶ Use the Server app to configure shared folders

▶ Understand the POSIX (Portable Operating System Interface) ownership and permissions model

▶ Understand access control lists (ACLs) and access control entries (ACEs)

▶ Configure OS X Server to control access to files based on user and group accounts, standard POSIX permissions, and ACLs

Reference 14.1
Configuring Access to Share Points and Folders

Once you've created a share point and determined the protocols you will use, you can begin to address levels of access within that share point. You need to consider POSIX privileges (UNIX-based ownership and permissions) as well as file system ACLs. Using this very flexible system, you can apply complex access settings to any folder or file.

You can configure access for your *shared folders* with the Server app *File Sharing pane*, and you can configure access for *any folder or file* with the Server app *Storage pane*. Be aware that these two panes behave differently, and they display information differently. This guide first addresses the File Sharing pane; then it addresses the Storage pane.

Configuring Basic Access with the Server App File Sharing Pane

To configure access settings for a share point, use the Access pane when viewing that share point. The standard POSIX settings are listed with the owner's full name, followed by the word "owner" in parentheses; the full name of the group associated with the folder, followed by the words "primary group" in parentheses; and Everyone Else.

In the following figure, the local user Local Admin is the owner, and the local group named System Group is the primary group associated with this sample share point.

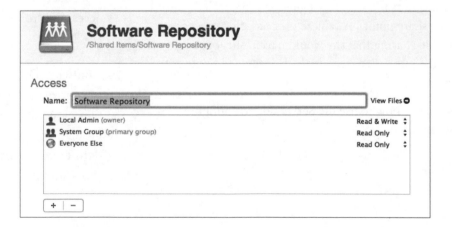

If there are any access control entries (ACEs) in that folder's ACL, these ACEs will appear above the POSIX entries. In the following figure, the first entry in the Access field is an ACE for the local network group ProjectZ, and the second is an ACE for the local network group Vice Presidents.

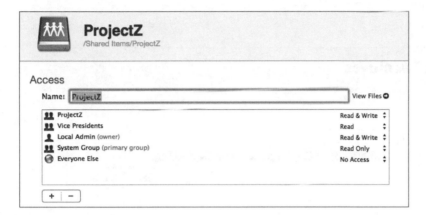

To change the standard POSIX owner of a share point, double-click the name of the current owner; to change the group, double-click the name of the current primary group. Once you start typing, a menu with names that match what you have typed appears. The following figure illustrates the process of changing the POSIX owner.

From there, you can either choose a name or click Browse. If you click Browse, a dialog window of accounts appears; choose an account and then click OK. The Server app then displays the account's full name in the owner or primary group field.

To change permissions, click the pop-up menu on the right and choose any of the four options:

► Read & Write

► Read Only

► Write Only

► No Access

After making permissions changes, be sure to click OK to save your changes. If you select a different pane in the Server app, or quit the Server app, your changes might not get saved.

Once the user is authenticated, file permissions control access to the files and folders on your server. One setting should be called out with respect to permissions: the Others permissions, which is displayed as Everyone Else when editing permissions with the File Sharing pane. When you set Others permissions, those permissions apply to everyone who can see the item (either a file or folder) who is neither the owner nor a member of the group assigned to the item.

Allowing Guest Access

You enable guest access for a share point by selecting the checkbox "Allow guest users to access this share."

Guest access can be very useful, but before you enable it, be sure you understand its implications in your permissions scheme. As the name implies, guest access lets anyone who can connect to your server use its share points. A user who authenticates as Guest is given Others permissions for file and folder access. If you give read-only access to Others on a share point that allows guest access, everyone on your network (and, if your server has a public IP address and is not protected by a firewall, the entire Internet) can see and mount that share point, a situation you might not intend to allow.

If a user creates an item on an AFP share point while connected as Guest, the AFP client sets the owner of that item to "nobody."

If a folder is buried deep within a file hierarchy where guests can't go (because the enclosing folders don't grant access to Others), guests can't browse to that folder.

> **TIP** The best way to validate permissions is by connecting to the file sharing service from a client computer, providing valid credentials (or connecting as Guest), and testing access.

Configure Access with the Server App Storage Pane

In contrast to the File Sharing pane, where you can configure access to share points, you can use the Server app Storage pane to configure permissions for individual files and folders; additionally, you have more granular control.

One way to get to the Storage pane is by selecting your server in the Server app sidebar and then clicking the Storage pane. You can then navigate to a specific file or folder.

The other way to get to the Storage pane is via this shortcut: In the File Sharing pane, when you edit a share point and click the arrow next to the words "View Files," the Server app opens the share point's folder in the Storage pane.

In the Storage pane, when you select a file or folder and click the Action (gear icon) pop-up menu, you see three choices:

▶ New Folder

▶ Edit Permissions

▶ Propagate Permissions

You'll learn more about Propagate Permissions later in this lesson. If you choose Edit Permissions, the Server app opens a permissions dialog that's similar to the File Sharing pane's permissions field, but the Storage pane's permissions dialog offers you more configuration options.

Using the Storage Pane's Permissions Dialog

In the Storage pane's permissions dialog in the following figure, each ACE has a disclosure triangle to hide or reveal more information about the ACE; additionally, some information, like the Spotlight ACE, which is hidden in the File Sharing pane, is displayed in the permissions dialog.

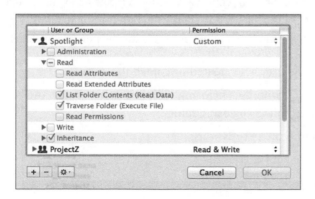

NOTE ▶ The inherited ACE for Spotlight allows Spotlight to maintain an index of the files on your server. Do not modify or remove this ACE or you may experience unexpected behavior.

You'll learn more about modifying an item's ACL in the next section.

Reference 14.2
Understanding POSIX Permissions vs. ACL Settings

The Server app is a powerful tool with many options to configure file access. It is important to understand how the POSIX (Portable Operating System Interface) permissions model and the file system ACLs behave, and how they behave together, in order to accurately configure share points to behave as you intend. This section starts out with a quick review of POSIX ownership and permissions, and then considers ACLs.

Understanding POSIX Ownership and Permissions

The OS X standard file system permissions structure is based on decades-old UNIX-style permissions. This system is also sometimes referred to as POSIX-style permissions. In the POSIX permissions model, which OS X and OS X Server use, every file and every folder is associated with exactly one "owner" and exactly one "group." As an administrator, you can change the POSIX owner and the POSIX group, but keep in mind that every file must have one and only one owner, and one and only one group as part of the POSIX ownership. This limits your flexibility, so you may choose to use ACLs to add flexibility in managing access to files, but it is important for you to understand the basics of POSIX ownership and permissions. For more information, see "File System Permissions" in Lesson 12, "Permissions and Sharing" in the guide *Apple Pro Training Series: OS X Support Essentials 10.9*.

When you move an item from one folder to another *within* a single volume, that item always retains its original ownership and permissions. In contrast, when you create a new item on a network volume via AFP, SMB, or WebDAV, or copy an item from one volume to another volume, OS X uses the following rules for ownership and permissions for the new file or folder:

▶ The owner of the new item is the user who created or copied the item.

▶ The group is the group associated with the enclosing folder; in other words, the newly copied item inherits its group from the enclosing folder.

▶ The owner is assigned read and write permissions.

▶ The group is assigned read-only permissions.

▶ Others (also displayed as Everyone Else) is assigned read-only permissions.

Under this model, if you create an item in a folder in which the group has read/write permission, the new item will not inherit that group permission, so other users are not able to edit that item (but because they have read/write permission to the folder, they can remove the item from the folder).

Without using ACLs, if a user wants to grant other group members write access to the new item, she must modify its permissions manually, using the Finder's Get Info command, chmod in the command line, or some third-party tool. This would be required for every new item; instead, you can use ACLs to prevent the need for users to add this step of manually modifying permissions to their workflow.

> **MORE INFO ▶** The variable that controls the POSIX permissions for newly created files is called the umask. Changing the umask from the default value is not recommended, and is outside the scope of this guide. When a user creates files on the server via AFP or SMB, the user's umask on the client computer affects the permissions for the newly created items; however, the umask on the server computer affects the permissions for files created via WebDAV.

Understanding Access Control Lists

Because of the limitations of the POSIX permissions model, consider using ACLs to help control access to folders and files. The Apple ACL model maps to the Windows ACL model, so Windows users experience the same permissions for folders and files that OS X users do.

In this section you'll learn about applying ACLs with the Server app, with the File Sharing pane—which presents a simplified interface—and also with the Storage pane's permissions dialog, which offers more flexibility. You'll learn how ACL inheritance works, and why it is so powerful.

> **NOTE ▶** You can apply ACLs only on Mac OS Extended (Journaled or not) volumes.

In OS X Server, you use the Server app to configure ACLs. An ACL is made up of one or more ACEs. Each ACE includes the following:

▶   The globally unique ID (GUID) of the one user or group for which this ACE applies.

▶   Whether the ACE allows access or denies access (you can use the Server app only to create Allow entries; and though you cannot use the Server app to create Deny entries, it displays a selected Deny checkbox in order to indicate that a rule specifies *either* Allow or Deny—as further explained in the text at the end of this list).

▶ The permission the ACE allows or denies (see the section "Configuring Complex Permissions for an ACE").

▶ The inheritance rules for the ACE (see the section "Understanding ACL Inheritance").

▶ The folder or file to which the ACE applies.

The Server app does not visually distinguish between Allow and Deny. You simply see a checkbox. When you assign a new ACE, it is assumed that you are assigning an Allow rule. However, when you use the Server app to inspect an ACE that has a Deny rule, there is no indication whether this rule is an Allow rule or a Deny rule. For example, OS X automatically applies a Deny ACE to some items in each user's home folder to prevent accidental removal, as shown in the following figure.

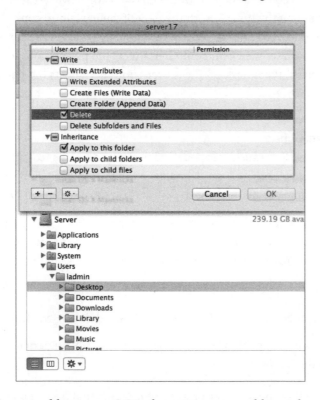

You can add as many ACEs for an item as you like, and you have a much larger range of permission types available than with standard POSIX permissions, which you'll learn about in the section "Configuring Complex Permissions for an ACE."

Understanding How File System ACLs Work

When you use the Server app to define ACLs, you are creating individual ACEs.

The order of entries is important because lists are evaluated top to bottom by OS X.

Allow and deny matches work differently for ACLs. When evaluating ACLs, the operating system starts with the first ACE and moves downward, stopping at the ACE that applies to the user, and matches the operation, such as reading, being performed. The permission (either to allow or to deny) for the ACE is then applied. Any ACEs farther down in the list are then ignored. Any matching Allow or Deny ACE overrides standard POSIX permissions.

Configuring ACLs with the Server App File Sharing Pane

In the Server app File Sharing pane, when editing a share point, you add a new ACE for a share point with the following general steps:

> **NOTE** ▶ This is an example workflow, and not part of this lesson's exercise.

1   Click Add (+).

2   Specify the user or group. You must choose the account from the list, or choose Browse and choose the account from the list.

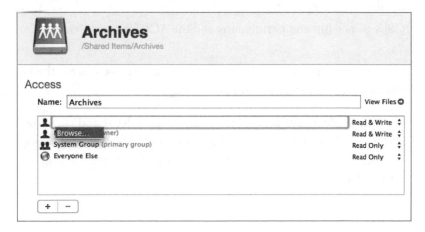

3   Specify the access to allow. Note that you can specify Read & Write, Read, or Write.

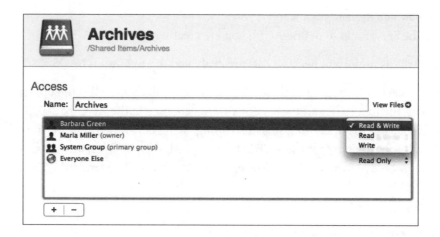

4   Repeat steps 1 through 3 for additional ACEs, and then click OK to save the changes.

Configuring ACLs with the Server App Storage Pane

The Storage pane of the Server app offers a little more flexibility than the File Sharing pane for configuring ACLs, particularly the ability to:

▶   Configure complex permissions for an ACE, more than just Read & Write, Read, or Write.

▶   Configure the inheritance for ACLs.

▶   Configure POSIX ownership and permissions and the ACL for an individual file, not just for folders.

▶   Configure POSIX ownership and permissions for files that are not shared (the File Sharing pane allows you to configure share points only).

To access the Storage pane, select your server in the Server app sidebar and click the Storage tab. You can select an existing folder or create a new folder. To access the permissions dialog for a file or folder, select a file or folder, click the Action (gear icon) pop-up menu, and choose Edit Permissions.

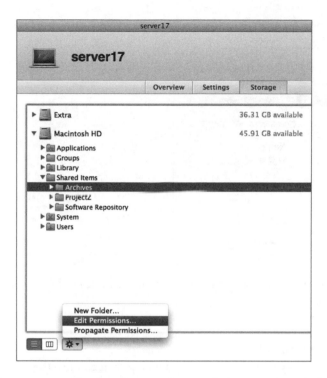

Once you are viewing the permissions dialog, you can click Add (+) to create a new ACE. Unlike in the File Sharing pane, there is no Browse option; you need to start typing and choose a user or group that matches what you have entered from the list.

After you specify the user or group for the ACE, you can click the permissions pop-up menu and choose Full Control, Read & Write, Read, or Write.

Of course, your permissions choice is just a starting point; you can fine-tune the permissions, as you'll see in the next section.

Configuring Complex Permissions for an ACE

When you edit an ACE with the Storage pane's permissions dialog, you can use the disclosure triangles to show the details for the ACE. You have four broad categories for which you can apply Allow rules:

- ▶ Administration
- ▶ Read
- ▶ Write
- ▶ Inheritance

For the first three (Administration, Read, and Write), selecting a checkbox allows access for the user or group in the ACE. Deselecting a checkbox does not deny access; it just doesn't explicitly allow access.

For the Administration set of permissions, you can select or deselect to allow permissions for:

▶ Change Permissions—User can change standard permissions.

▶ Change Owner—User can change the item's ownership to him- or herself.

For the Read set of permissions, you can select or deselect to allow permissions for:

▶ Read Attributes—User can view the item's attributes, such as name, size, and date modified.

▶ Read Extended Attributes—User can view additional attributes, including ACL and attributes added by third-party software.

▶ List Folder Contents (Read Data)—User can read files and see the contents of a folder.

▶ Traverse Folder (Execute File)—User can open files, or traverse a folder.

▶ Read Permissions—User can read the POSIX permissions.

For the Write set of permissions, you can select or deselect to allow permissions for:

▶ Write Attributes—User can change POSIX permissions.

▶ Write Extended Attributes—User can change ACL or other extended attributes.

▶ Create Files (Write Data)—User can create files, including changing files for most applications.

▶ Create Folder (Append Data)—User can create new folders and append data to files.

▶ Delete—User can delete files or folders.

▶ Delete Subfolders and Files—User can delete subfolders and files.

With just these 13 checkboxes, you have a large amount of flexibility to allow additional permissions beyond what you can configure with just POSIX permissions.

Because the Server app does not allow you to create Deny rules, the best strategy is to set the standard POSIX permissions for Others to No Access, and then configure an ACL to build up rules to allow appropriate access for various groups.

Understanding ACL Inheritance

One powerful feature of ACLs is inheritance: When you create an ACE for a folder, from that point on, when a user creates a new item in that folder, the operating system assigns that same ACE to the new item. In other words, the ACE is inherited. For each ACE in the folder's ACL, you can control how that ACE is inherited; when you edit an ACE, you can select or deselect each of the following checkboxes (by default, all four "Apply to" checkboxes are selected):

▶ Apply to this folder—This ACE applies to this folder.

▶ Apply to child folders—This ACE will be assigned to new folders inside this folder, but not necessarily to new folders that are created inside the child folders of this folder, unless "Apply to all descendants" is also selected.

▶ Apply to child files—This ACE will be assigned to new files inside this folder, but not necessarily to files that are inside the child folders of this folder, unless "Apply to all descendants" is also selected.

▶ Apply to all descendants—This makes the two preceding options apply to items in an infinite level of nested folders and files in this folder.

When an ACE is inherited from a folder, it appears dimmed, as in the following figure (you can remove or inspect an inherited ACE, but you cannot otherwise change it as long as it is inherited).

If an inherited ACL doesn't meet your needs, first consider why the ACL model didn't work in this case: Do you need a different share point, a different group, or maybe a different set of ACEs in the ACL? In any event, you can click the Action (gear icon) pop-up menu and choose one of these two actions to change the inherited entries:

► Remove Inherited Entries

► Make Inherited Entries Explicit

Remove Inherited Entries removes all the inherited ACEs, not just one ACE that you might have selected. The inherited ACL could be an aggregation of inherited ACEs from more than one parent folder.

Make Inherited Entries Explicit applies all the inherited ACEs as if they were applied directly to the ACL on the current file or folder. Once you perform this action, you can edit the ACEs, including editing or removing individual ACEs that were previously dimmed. The following figure illustrates what happens if you choose Make Inherited Entries Explicit: The ACEs are no longer dimmed, and you can remove them or modify them. The ACE for Spotlight is automatically created—do not modify that ACE.

When you use the Server app's File Sharing pane to update a folder's ACL that has inheritance rules, the Server app automatically updates the ACL for items in the folder that have already inherited the ACL (this is not the case if you update the ACL using the Storage pane).

Understanding Sorting ACLs Canonically

The order in which each ACE is listed in an ACL is important, and can possibly change the behavior of an ACL, especially if a Deny rule is involved. Although the Server app does *not* allow you to create ACEs to deny access, some ACLs do contain one or more Deny ACEs. In the Storage pane's permissions dialog, you can click the Action (gear icon) pop-up menu and choose Sort Access Control List Canonically. This reorders the ACEs into a standard order for applying ACLs. If you don't have Deny rules in your ACL, it isn't crucial to use this command.

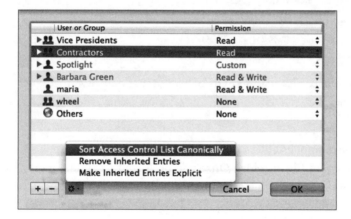

Understanding ACL Portability

Because ACLs are applied when a file or folder is created:

▸ If you move an item from one location to another on the same volume, the ACL for that item (if one exists) does not change, and is still associated with the item.

▸ If you copy an item from one location to another, the item's ACL does not get copied; the copied item will inherit, from its enclosing folder, any ACEs that are appropriately configured to be inherited.

However, what happens if you update an existing ACL, or create a new ACL, *after* files have already been created? You'll need to propagate the ACL.

Understanding Propagating Permissions

When you use the File Sharing pane to update a share point's ACL or POSIX permissions, the Server app automatically propagates the ACL. When you propagate the ACL, the Server app adds each ACE of the current folder to the ACL of each child object (folders and files inside the parent folder) as an inherited ACE. Don't worry about overwriting explicitly defined ACEs for child objects, because propagating an ACL does not remove any explicitly defined ACEs.

In contrast, when you use the Storage pane's permissions dialog to create or update an ACL for an item, your actions affect only that item and do not affect existing child objects. In the Storage permissions dialog, to propagate the ACL changes to existing child objects, you must do so manually. Click the Action (gear icon) pop-up menu and choose Propagate Permissions. The following figure illustrates that by default, the Access Control List checkbox is selected, but you can select additional checkboxes to also update different combinations of standard POSIX ownership and permissions to existing child objects.

Understanding Features Common to POSIX and ACLs

Now that you have a better understanding of POSIX ownership and permissions, as well as ACLs and ACEs, this section covers how the two models work together to affect access to files.

Distinguishing Between the Uses of UID, GID, and GUID

You have learned that POSIX owners and groups are determined by user and group IDs (UIDs and GIDs). Because UIDs and GIDs are simple integers, it is possible (but not recommended) for users to have duplicate user IDs. Usually this is an error, but sometimes an administrator will want the POSIX UID to be identical on two separate users. From a permissions perspective, this will grant these users identical access rights.

ACLs are much more complex and require a unique identification of a user or group. For this purpose, every user and group has a globally unique ID, or GUID (in the Accounts system preferences, when you secondary [or Control-] click a user account and choose Advanced Options, the GUID is labeled UUID; it is also referred to as a generated UID).

An account's GUID is not exposed in the Server app, because there should be no reason to change it. Every time a user or group is created, a new 128-bit string (as shown in the following figure) is randomly generated for that user or group. In this way, users and groups are virtually guaranteed unique identification in ACLs.

When you create an ACE for a user or group, the ACE uses the GUID of that user or group, rather than the user name, user ID, group name, or group ID. When displaying an ACL, if the server computer cannot match an ACE's GUID to an account, the Server app displays the GUID instead of the account name in the ACL. Some reasons for this include that the account associated with the ACE

▶   Has been deleted

▶   Belongs to a directory node that the server is bound to but is unavailable

▶   Belongs to a directory node that is unavailable, because the volume was connected to a different server when the ACE was created

Here's an example of an exposed GUID in the Server app. In the following figure, an ACE was created for a local network user, and then an administrator deleted the local network user with the Server app; the ACE was not automatically removed.

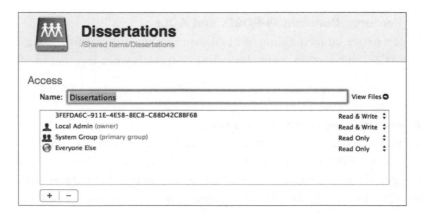

If you see this, without knowing what account corresponds to the GUID, you could either leave the entry in place or remove the entry. If you happen to import the account in a way that also imports its GUID, that entry will be associated with the user or group again.

However, if the account associated with the GUID is truly gone forever, you can remove the ACE; highlight the ACE and click the Delete (–) button.

Understanding Group Membership and ACLs

When working with ACLs, it is important that you plan your setup properly to avoid conflicting permissions settings, such as having a user be a member of two groups, one with read permissions on a folder and one with no access permissions on the same folder. These types of conflicts can occur if you do not plan your ACL permissions models well.

Using ACLs to control access to server resources can be extremely valuable, as long as you take care up front to organize your user and group accounts appropriately. The recommended way to approach this management is to take advantage of using smaller groups to correctly reflect the needs of your organization, including nesting groups within groups. Use these group accounts to manage access on a more granular basis.

Understanding Multiple Groups

The standard POSIX permissions work well in a single desktop model such as OS X. Yet when the system becomes more complex, the standard POSIX permissions model does not scale well.

Complex workflows might require more than just the User, Group, and Others classes available with the standard POSIX permissions model. In particular, having a single group is very limiting. The POSIX owner must be an individual user account (it can't be a group), and granting permission to Others (Everyone Else) usually opens up the files to a wider audience than you want. Adding an ACL permits you to assign multiple groups to a folder, and assign each a unique permissions setting. Because ACLs can assign different permissions to multiple groups, you must carefully plan what your group structure is going to look like to avoid any confusion. This is a common requirement in any environment that has multiple groups collaborating on a single project.

Understanding Nested Groups

In addition to assigning multiple groups to a single folder, OS X Server allows groups to contain other groups. Breaking groups down into subgroups can make your access easier to understand as an administrator. You can use nested groups to reflect the structure of your organization.

While nested groups are powerful, they should be used with care. If you build a deep, complex hierarchy, you may find that access is harder—rather than easier—to understand.

Mirroring your organizational structure is usually safe and useful. However, be wary of ad hoc groups that don't relate to any external structure. They may be a quick way to give access to some users, but later on may make it more difficult to understand your access.

Understanding POSIX and ACL Rules of Precedence

When a user attempts to perform an action that requires authorization (read a file, or create a folder), OS X will allow this action only if the user has permission for that action. Here is how OS X combines POSIX and ACLs when there is a request for a specific action:

1. If there is no ACL, POSIX rules apply.

2. If there is an ACL, the order of the ACEs matters. You can sort the ACEs in an ACL in a consistent and predictable way: In the Server app Storage pane, select an ACL, and then from the Action (gear icon) pop-up menu choose Sort Access Control List Canonically. This is especially important if you add an ACE to an ACL containing an ACE that denies access.

3. When evaluating an ACL, OS X evaluates the first ACE in the list and continues on to the next ACE until it finds an ACE that matches the permission required for the requested action, whether that permission is Allow or Deny. Even if a Deny ACE exists in an ACL, if a similar Allow ACE is listed first, the Allow ACE is the one that is used, because it is listed first. This is why it is so important to use the Sort Access Control List Canonically command.

4. A POSIX permission that is restrictive does not override an ACE that specifically allows a permission.

5. If no ACE applies to the permission required for the requested action, the POSIX permissions apply.

For example, if Barbara Green attempts to create a folder, the requested permission is Create Folder. Each ACE is evaluated until there is an ACE that either allows or denies Create Folder for Barbara Green or a group that Barbara Green belongs to.

Even though this is an unlikely scenario, it illustrates the combination of an ACL and POSIX permissions: If a folder has an ACE that allows Barbara Green (short name: barbara) full control, but the POSIX permission defines Barbara Green as the owner with access set to None, Barbara Green effectively has full control. The ACE is evaluated before the POSIX permissions.

As another example, consider a folder with an ACL that has a single ACE that allows Carl Dunn to have Read permission, and the folder's POSIX permission defines Carl Dunn as the owner with Read & Write permission. When Carl Dunn attempts to create a file in that folder, there is no ACE that specifically addresses the Create Files (Write Data) request, so no ACE applies to that request. Therefore, the POSIX permissions apply, and Carl Dunn can create the file.

In this lesson you learned about POSIX ownership and permissions, file ACLs, and how you can configure share points and files to control access to files.

Exercise 14.1
Configure Access Control

▶ **Prerequisite**

- ▶ You must have File Sharing turned on.

- ▶ Exercise 9.1, "Configure Your Server as an Open Directory Master," and Exercise 10.1, "Create and Import Network Accounts"; or use the Server app to create users Maria Miller, Gary Pine, Lucy Sanchez, Enrico Baker, and Todd Porter, each with an account name that is the same as their first name in lowercase, and a password of net.

- ▶ Exercise 13.1, "Explore the File Sharing Service"; or use the Storage pane to create at the root of the startup disk a folder that is named Shared Items and that is owned by the user Local Admin.

In this exercise you will create a folder hierarchy and a means of controlling access to facilitate the workflow of the users and groups on your server, using standard POSIX permissions and file system ACLs. You will discover that the ability to manipulate a file can be determined by where the file is located in the system, rather than by who created or owns the specific file.

To properly configure your server, you will need to understand the intended workflow of your users. Here is the scenario: Your group needs a share point for a secret project, ProjectZ. The two people in the project, Maria Miller and Gary Pine, need to be able to read and write documents in the share point, including documents that the other person created. It is expected that more people will be added to the project later. No one else in the organization should see the folder for the project, except the Vice President (VP) of Sales, Lucy Sanchez, who needs only Read access to the files.

You can't just use the Server app to create the folder for the group in the Groups folder, because this folder would be visible to other people, and even though other people would not be able to browse the contents of the folder, other people would start asking questions about it.

You could start out by creating a group, configuring that group as the primary group for a folder, and assigning read-write permissions for the group to the folder, but that's not enough, because any new items created will automatically have a permission of read-only for the primary group. In addition, you need to create an ACE for the ProjectZ group to allow them read-write access. You will also need to create an ACE for Lucy Sanchez, the VP of Sales, to allow read access.

As part of this scenario, after you get the users, groups, and share points configured, be prepared for management to assign another request, which you will cheerfully fulfill.

Create the ProjectZ group and add the two users to the group.

1   Perform these exercises on your administrator computer. If you do not already have a connection to your server computer with Server app on your administrator computer, then connect to it with the following steps: Open the Server app on your administrator computer, choose Manage > Connect to Server, click Other Mac, select your server, click Continue, provide administrator credentials (Administrator Name ladmin and Administrator Password ladminpw), deselect the "Remember this password" checkbox, and then click Connect.

2   In the Server app sidebar, select Groups.

3   If a pop-up menu is visible, set the pop-up menu to Local Network Groups.

4   Click Add (+) to create a new group, and enter the following information:

▶ Full Name: ProjectZ

▶ Group Name: projectz

5   Click Create to create the group.

6   Double-click the ProjectZ group and click Add (+). Press the Space bar, choose Browse, and drag Maria Miller and Gary Pine to the Members list.

7   Click OK to save the changes.

8   If necessary, close the Users & Groups window.

Next, create a shared folder for the ProjectZ group, and configure its permissions so that:

▶ No one else can see the share point or its contents.

▶ Members of the ProjectZ group have Read & Write access to all items.

▶ Lucy Sanchez, the Sales VP, has Read-Only access to all items.

Start by creating the share point.

1   In the Server app sidebar, select File Sharing.

2   Click Add (+).

3   Navigate to the Shared Items folder on your server's startup volume.

4   Click New Folder.

5   Name the folder ProjectZ, and then click Create.

6   Select the new ProjectZ folder you just created, and then click Choose.

Configure access to the share point.

1   In the File Sharing pane, double-click the ProjectZ share point.

2   Make sure the "Allow guest users to access this share" checkbox is unselected.

3   Click the pop-up menu for permissions for the Everyone Else entry, and choose No Access.

Note that the owner and primary group are inherited from the enclosing folder (Shared Items). Don't worry about that; the owner of new items will be the user that creates the item, and remember that over AFP and SMB, newly created items will get read-only access applied to the primary group, so you need to use an ACL to provide Read & Write access to the ProjectZ group.

4   Click Add (+).

5   Start typing ProjectZ, and then choose ProjectZ.

Confirm that the permission is automatically set to Read & Write for the ProjectZ group.

Create an ACE that allows Lucy Sanchez, the Sales VP, read-only access.

1   Click Add (+), start typing Lucy, and choose Lucy Sanchez.

2   Set the permissions for Lucy Sanchez to Read.

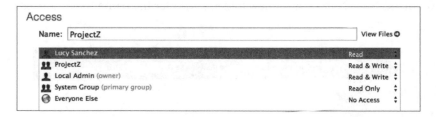

3   Click OK to save these settings.

Confirm that Maria Miller and Gary Pine can create and edit items in the ProjectZ share point, and that the Sales VP (Lucy Sanchez) cannot create, edit, or remove items.

1   On your administrator computer, in the Finder, choose File > New Finder Window.

2   If there is an Eject button next to your server in the Finder sidebar, click it to eject any mounted volumes from that server.

3   If your server appears in the Finder sidebar, select your server.

Otherwise, if there are so many computers on your network that your server does not appear in the Shared section of the Finder sidebar, click All and then select your server.

If Guest access is enabled for any share point, you are automatically connected as Guest.

4   In the Finder window, click Connect As.

5   At the authentication window, provide credentials for Maria Miller (Name maria; Password net).

> **NOTE ▶** Do not select the checkbox to remember the password; otherwise, you will need to use Keychain Access to remove the password before you can connect as a different user.

6   Click Connect.

After you successfully authenticate, you see all the share points that the user Maria Miler has access to read.

7   Open the ProjectZ folder.

8   Press Command-Shift-N to create a new folder, and enter the name Folder created by Maria.

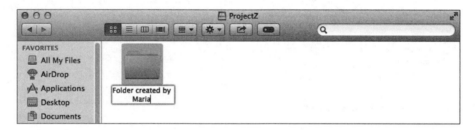

9   Press Return to stop editing the folder name.

You won't do anything else with this folder in the exercise, but you confirmed that Maria Miller has permission to create a folder.

Create a text file as Maria Miller; you will eventually confirm the following:

▶   Gary Pine can also edit that document.

▶   Lucy Sanchez can read, but cannot change, that document.

▶   Other users cannot see that the ProjectZ share point exists.

1   In the Dock, click Launchpad, and then open TextEdit.

2   If you do not see a new blank document, create a new blank document by pressing Command-N or choosing File > New.

3   Enter the following text: This is a file started by Maria.

4 Save the TextEdit document by pressing Command-S or choosing File > Save.

5 If necessary, click the triangle next to the Save As field to reveal more options.

6 In the Shared section of the Save As window sidebar, select your server, and then open the folder ProjectZ.

7 In the Save As field, name the file Maria Text File.

8 Click Save.

9 Close the TextEdit document by pressing Command-W or choosing File > Close.

10 If no Finder window is still open, in the Finder press Command-N to open one.

11 In the Finder sidebar, click the Eject button next to your server (if your Finder window is configured with the Icon view, click Disconnect).

Connect as the other project member, Gary Pine, and confirm that you can edit files with his credentials.

1   If your server appears in the Finder sidebar, select your server.

   Otherwise, if there are so many computers on your network that your server does not appear in the Shared section of the Finder sidebar, click All and then select your server.

2   In the Finder window, click Connect As.

3   At the authentication window, provide credentials for Gary Pine (Name gary; Password net).

   Leave the checkbox to remember the password unselected.

4   Click Connect.

5   Open the ProjectZ folder.

6   Open the file named Maria Text File.

7   Add another line at the end of the text file: This was added by Gary.

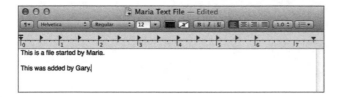

8   Close the TextEdit document by pressing Command-W or choosing File > Close. This automatically saves the change you just made to the file.

   If you see a dialog that the document is on a volume that does not support permanent version storage and that you will not be able to access older versions of the document once you close it, click OK.

   NOTE ▶ For more information about version storage, see Reference 20.3, "Auto Save and Versions," in Lesson 20, "Document Management," of *OS X Support Essentials 10.9*.

9   In the Finder window sidebar, click the Eject button next to your server.

Confirm that you can see, but not edit, a file in the ProjectZ folder when connected as the Sales VP, Lucy Sanchez.

1   If your server appears in the Finder sidebar, select your server.

Otherwise, if there are so many computers on your network that your server does not appear in the Shared section of the Finder sidebar, click All and then select your server.

2   In the Finder window, click Connect As.

3   At the authentication window, provide credentials for Lucy Sanchez (Name lucy; Password net).

Do not select the checkbox to remember the password.

4   Click Connect.

5   Open the ProjectZ folder.

6   Open the file named Maria Text File.

7   Confirm that you can read the text, and that the toolbar contains the text "Locked," indicating that you cannot save changes to this file.

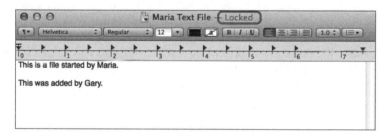

8   Attempt to edit the file by appending text, and note that you see a dialog stating that the file is locked.

9   Click Cancel.

10   Close the TextEdit document by pressing Command-W or choosing File > Close.

Confirm that you cannot create a new folder in the ProjectZ folder as the Lucy Sanchez user.

1 In the Finder window, confirm that you are viewing the ProjectZ folder.

2 Click the File menu and confirm that New Folder is dimmed.

You are not able to create a new folder on the network volume, because the user Lucy Sanchez has only read permissions.

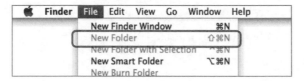

Confirm that you cannot delete an item in the ProjectZ folder as the Lucy Sanchez user.

1 Select Maria Text File, and choose File > Move to Trash.

2 At the "Are you sure" dialog, click Delete.

3 Because you effectively have read-only permission, you see a dialog that you don't have permission. Click OK to close the dialog.

Confirm that a different user (Todd Porter, who isn't a member of the ProjectZ group) cannot view items in the ProjectZ folder.

1 In the Finder sidebar, click the Eject button next to your server.

2 If your server appears in the Finder sidebar, select your server.

Otherwise, if there are so many computers on your network that your server does not appear in the Shared section of the Finder sidebar, click All and then select your server.

3 In the Finder window, click Connect As.

4 At the authentication window, provide credentials for Todd Porter (Name todd; Password net).

Do not select the checkbox to remember the password.

5 Click Connect.

6 Confirm that the ProjectZ folder is not visible.

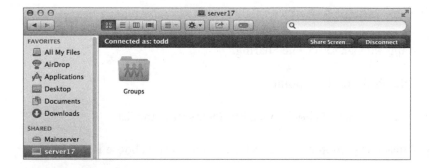

7   In the upper-right corner of the Finder window, click Disconnect, or if you selected a shared folder, click the Eject button next to your server in the Finder sidebar.

You have successfully managed users and groups, created a share point, and managed the POSIX permissions and ACL for the share point to provide the access that management requested.

However, the company just promoted a new Marketing Vice President, Enrico Baker, who also wants read access to the files.

Rather than adding another individual user to the ACL, at this point in the scenario it makes more sense to create a group for vice presidents, add appropriate users to that group, and then add an ACE to allow read access for that group. To prevent confusion in the future, you will also remove the original ACE for Lucy Sanchez; her ACE is unnecessary because her user account is part of a group that has an ACE.

Create the Vice Presidents group and add the two users to the group.

1   In the Server app sidebar, select Groups.

2   If there's a pop-up menu visible, set the pop-up menu to Local Network Groups.

3   Click Add (+) to create the following group:

▶   Full Name: Vice Presidents

▶   Group Name: vps

4   Click Create to create the group.

5   Double-click the Vice Presidents group and click Add (+). Press the Space bar, click Browse, and drag Lucy Sanchez and Enrico Baker to the Members list.

6   Click OK to finish editing the group.

Update the ACL for the ProjectZ folder using the File Sharing pane.

1   In the Server app sidebar, select File Sharing.

2   Double-click the ProjectZ share point.

3   Click Add (+), enter vps, and choose Vice Presidents from the list.

4   Click the permissions pop-up menu for Vice Presidents and choose Read.

5   Select the ACE for Lucy Sanchez and click Delete (–).

The Access section of the Server app should appear like the following figure (the positions of the Vice Presidents ACE and the ProjectZ ACE relative to each other do not matter for the purposes of this exercise).

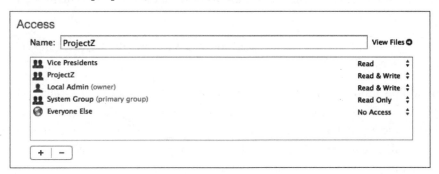

6   Click OK to save the changes to the ACL.

The Server app automatically propagates the updated ACL to items in the share point.

Confirm that Enrico Baker, a member of the Vice Presidents group, can read files in the ProjectZ folder.

1   On your administrator computer, in the Finder, if there is no Finder window visible, choose New > New Finder Window.

2   If your server appears in the Finder sidebar, select your server.

Otherwise, if there are so many computers on your network that your server does not appear in the Shared section of the Finder sidebar, click All and then select your server.

3   In the Finder window, click Connect As.

4   Enter credentials for Enrico Baker (Name enrico; Password net).

5   Do not select the checkbox to remember the password.

6   Click Connect.

After you authenticate, you see a list of share points you can access.

1   Open the ProjectZ folder, and open Maria Text File.

2   Confirm that the toolbar contains the text "Locked" to indicate that you cannot make changes to the file.

3   Press Command-W to close the file.

Use the Server app Storage pane's permissions dialog to inspect the ACL for the share point.

1   In the Server app sidebar, select File Sharing.

2   Double-click the ProjectZ share point.

3   Click the arrow next to View Files.

4   Select the ProjectZ folder.

5   From the Action (gear icon) pop-up menu, choose Edit Permissions.

6   Click the disclosure triangle for ProjectZ to reveal the permissions allowed for the ProjectZ group.

7   Click the disclosure triangle for the Write set of permissions.

The permissions dialog should look like the following figure.

The ProjectZ group has full Read access and partial Write access (the ACE does not specify to allow Delete permission, but "Delete Subfolders and Files" is selected, so anyone in the ProjectZ group can effectively delete any item except the ProjectZ share point itself).

Inspect the permissions for the Vice Presidents group.

1   Click the disclosure triangle to hide the detail for the ProjectZ group.

2   Click the disclosure triangle to reveal the permissions for the Vice Presidents group.

3   Click the disclosure triangle for the Read permissions allowed for the Vice Presidents group.

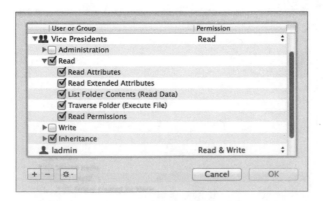

The Vice Presidents group has full read access, and this ACE gets inherited to all new items created in this folder.

4   Click the disclosure triangle to hide the detail for the Vice Presidents group.

5   View the standard POSIX permissions.

6   Click Cancel to close the permissions dialog.

The POSIX permissions for Others is None (Others appears as Everyone Else in the File Sharing pane of the Server app), so a user will not be able to access or examine files in this share point unless the user is one of the following:

▶   The local user account whose account name is ladmin (Full Name: Local Admin)

▶   In the local group whose group name is wheel (a legacy group)

▶   A member of the ProjectZ group or the Vice Presidents group

As long as you don't share any of the shared folder's ancestor folders (in this case, /Shared Items, or the root of the startup volume), no other users will see the existence of the ProjectZ folder (although skilled users could inspect the attributes for a user and see that they are a member of the ProjectZ group).

Inspect the ACL for a folder inside the ProjectZ folder, to show that when you updated the ACL for ProjectZ, the Server app automatically propagated the change. For the ProjectZ folder, you started out with an ACE for Lucy Sanchez, but after you created the "Folder created by Maria" folder, you removed that ACE for Lucy Sanchez and added an ACE for the Vice Presidents group.

1   Select the "Folder created by Maria" folder.

2   Click the Action (gear icon) pop-up menu and choose Edit Permissions.

Note in the following figure that there is no ACE for Lucy Sanchez, but there is an inherited ACE for Vice Presidents. It was automatically inherited from the ProjectZ folder's ACL when you used the Server app's File Sharing pane to update the share point's ACL.

3   Click Cancel to close the permissions dialog for the folder.

View the permissions to see the contrasting ways in which the File Sharing pane and the Storage pane's permissions dialog display permissions information for this share point.

1 In the Server app sidebar, select File Sharing.

2 Double-click the ProjectZ share point.

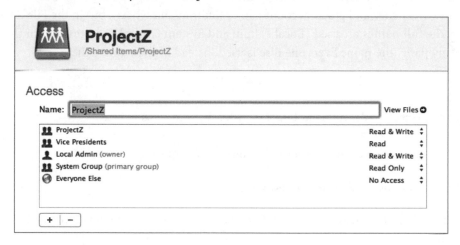

3 Click the View Files link.

The Storage pane opens and the ProjectZ folder is automatically selected.

4 Click the Action menu (gear icon) and choose Edit Permissions.

Note that in the Storage pane's permission dialog, you see there is an ACE for Spotlight, but the File Sharing pane simplifies your view and hides that particular ACE. In the

Storage pane's permission dialog, you can use the disclosure triangles to configure a custom set of access settings, as well as configure that ACE's inheritance rules; the File Sharing pane offers a pop-up menu with Read & Write, Read, and Write options for an ACE. The File Sharing pane can also display "Custom" for an ACE, but you cannot modify the custom access in the File Sharing pane. Both panes offer Read & Write, Read Only, Write Only, and No Access options for POSIX permissions. The Storage pane permissions dialog lists the POSIX owner and group account names (ladmin and wheel), but in the File Sharing pane, the full names are used (Local Admin and System Group). Additionally, in the File Sharing pane, the name Everyone Else is used instead of the name Others.

Clean Up

Remove the ProjectZ folder; it is not necessary for any other exercises.

1   In the Finder sidebar, click the Eject button next to your server.

2   In the Server app sidebar, select File Sharing.

3   Select the ProjectZ share point, click Remove (–), and at the confirmation dialog, click Remove.

Remove the Vice Presidents group; the group is not necessary for any other exercises.

1   In the Server app sidebar, select Groups.

2   Select the Vice Presidents group.

3   Click Remove (–), and at the confirmation dialog, click Remove.

In this exercise, you used POSIX permissions and an ACL to control access to a shared folder and a text file. You assigned No Access for Everyone Else to prevent all users from accessing the shared folder, and then added an ACE to grant read and write access to a group. You also created an ACE for a particular user, but as the situation evolved, you replaced that ACE with an ACE for yet another group, and noted that this change you made with the File Sharing pane was automatically propagated to existing items. You saw that the File Sharing and Storage panes offer different views of POSIX ownership and permissions and an item's ACL; the File Sharing pane offers a simple summary and options, and the Storage pane offers more advanced information and options. Finally, the Server app automatically propagates the share point's ACL whenever you use the File Sharing pane to make a change to the share point's ACL or POSIX permissions.

Implementing
Deployment Solutions

Lesson 15

Leveraging NetInstall

One significant challenge for OS X administrators today is the deployment of software to multiple computers. Whether it is operating system (OS) releases and updates or commercial applications, installing the software manually is a labor-intensive process. OS X Server provides services and technologies to aid in this deployment. The NetInstall service simplifies OS rollout and upgrades.

Knowing how to use time efficiently is a very important aspect of an administrator's job. When managing several hundred OS X computers, an administrator needs a solution that is both speedy and flexible for performing day-to-day management of computers. When computers need to be set up for the first time, what software should be installed? Should they have the latest software updates? Should they have a full complement of non-Apple software, such as Adobe Creative Cloud or Microsoft Office? What about shareware programs and the necessary work-related files? Safety videos? Mandatory PDFs?

Before you can push out data to a computer, you must decide *how* to push out that data and in what state. Though there are several third-party tools that complete the tasks of image creation and deployment, Apple has several applications to assist you with this process. These helpful applications include System Image Utility, Apple Software Restore (ASR), Apple Remote Desktop (ARD), and NetInstall.

With the advantage of these deployment software tools, you can build an automated system that needs very little user interaction to function. This lesson focuses primarily on the NetInstall service provided by OS X Server.

> ## GOALS
>
> ► Understand the concepts of NetBoot, NetInstall, and NetRestore
>
> ► Create an image for deployment
>
> ► Configure the NetInstall service
>
> ► Configure clients to use NetInstall
>
> ► Learn to troubleshoot NetInstall

Creating NetInstall images can be a lengthy process, but most of the time is spent waiting for the image to be processed. Because this lesson includes the creation of two images, you may want to split this lesson over a couple of days, or over a dinner break, at either of the two image-creation steps.

Reference 15.1
Managing Computers with NetInstall

Think about the ways in which you start up your computer. Most often, your computer starts up from system software located on the local hard disk. This local startup provides you with a typical computer experience of running applications, accessing information, and accomplishing tasks. When you perform an OS installation for versions of OS X prior to Lion, you could start up from a CD-ROM or DVD-ROM disc.

Managing a single standalone computer isn't much of an inconvenience. However, imagine managing a lab of computers. Every time you need to upgrade the operating system or install a clean version of OS X, you would need to boot each computer in the lab from Mavericks Recovery. That isn't very practical.

OS X Server provides the NetInstall service, which simplifies the management of operating systems on multiple computers. With NetInstall, client computers start up using system software they access from a server instead of from the client's local hard disk. With NetInstall, the client obtains information from a remote location on the network. With other startup methods, the client boots off a local source, such as the internal hard disk or other device.

NetInstall is most effective in situations in which there is a high frequency of user turn-over and in which a large number of computers are being deployed with a common configuration. The ability to deploy standard configurations across multiple computers makes NetInstall ideal for computing environments such as:

▶ Classrooms and computer labs—The NetInstall service makes it easy to configure multiple identical desktop systems and repurpose them quickly. With the NetInstall service, you can reconfigure systems for a different class simply by restarting from a different image.

▶ Corporate workstations—Using NetInstall to install system software allows you to reimage, deploy, and update workstations very quickly. Also, because installation is done over the network, it can even be done in place at the user's desk. A creative way to take advantage of this technology is to create a NetInstall service image with various computer diagnosis and disk recovery software. Booting into a rescue image at a user's desk could save a lot of time for a frustrated user.

▶ Kiosks and libraries—With the NetInstall service, you can set up protected computing environments for customers or visitors. For example, you can configure an information station with an Internet browser that connects only to your company's website, or set up a visitor kiosk that runs only a database for collecting feedback. If a system is altered, a simple restart restores it to its original condition.

▶ Computational clusters—The NetInstall service is a powerful solution for data centers and computational clusters with identically configured web or application servers. Similarly purposed systems can boot from a single network-hosted image maintained on a network-based storage device.

▶ Emergency boot disk—The NetInstall service can be used to troubleshoot, restore, and maintain client computers. The NetInstall service can also help access computers whose boot drives have failed and whose recovery partition is not available.

Hardware Requirements
For NetInstall to function properly, certain minimum hardware requirements must be met:

▶ 512 MB RAM on the client computer
▶ 100Base-T switched Ethernet (up to 50 clients)
▶ 1000Base-T switched Ethernet (beyond 50 clients)

Apple has no official test results for configurations beyond 50 clients. Although there are some Mac computers that can use NetInstall over Wi-Fi, it is best to use Ethernet for NetInstall when possible. NetInstall over Wi-Fi is neither supported by Apple nor recommended. For computers shipped without an Ethernet port, such as the MacBook Air, using a USB or Thunderbolt to Ethernet adapter is recommended.

Understanding NetInstall Image Types

There are three different NetInstall image types:

▶ A NetBoot startup (using a NetBoot boot image) provides a fairly typical user experience, because clients start up using an operating system they access from a server. Most users won't even know they aren't booted from their computer's hard disk.

▶ A Network Install, also known as NetInstall, startup sequence (using a NetInstall image) enables you to quickly perform fresh installations of your operating system. It also allows you to install applications or updates, or install configured disk images. The terms Network Install and NetInstall are used interchangeably in this lesson.

▶ NetRestore is aimed at deploying full system images. Another defining choice is the ability to define a restore image source other than the disk image embedded in the NetInstall set. This allows you to host the image on other servers.

Keep these three types of NetInstall images in mind while you work through the remainder of this lesson.

With NetBoot, you create disk images on the server that contain OS X system software. Multiple network clients can use each disk image at once. Because you are setting up a centralized source of system software, you need to configure, test, and deploy only once. This dramatically reduces the maintenance required for network computers.

When you start up from a NetBoot image, the startup volume is read-only. When a client needs to write anything back to its startup volume, NetBoot automatically redirects the written data to the client's shadow files (which are discussed later in this lesson, in the section "Understanding Shadow Files"). Data in shadow files is kept for the duration of a NetBoot session. Because the startup volume is read-only, you always start from a clean image. This is ideal in lab and kiosk situations in which you want to ensure that users never alter the startup volume.

Stepping Through the NetInstall Client Startup Process

When a client computer boots from a NetInstall image, it performs a number of steps to start up successfully:

1. The client places a request for an IP address.

    When a NetInstall client is turned on or restarted, it requests an IP address from a DHCP server. While the server providing the address can be the same server providing the NetInstall service, the two services do not have to be provided by the same computer.

    NOTE ▶ DHCP is a requirement for NetInstall to work.

2. After receiving an IP address, the NetInstall client sends out a request via the Boot Service Discovery Protocol (BSDP) for startup software. The NetInstall server then delivers the core system files (booter and kernel files) to the client using Trivial File Transfer Protocol (TFTP) via its default port, 69.

3. Once the client has the core system files, it initiates a mount and loads the images for the NetBoot network disk image.

    The images can be served using Hypertext Transfer Protocol (HTTP) or Network File System (NFS).

4. After booting from the NetInstall image, the NetInstall client requests an IP address from the DHCP server.

    Depending on the type of DHCP server used, the NetInstall client might receive an IP address different from the one received in step 1.

Using Home Folders with NetBoot

When you restart a client computer from a NetBoot image, the client computer receives a fresh copy of the system software and the startup volume. Users cannot store documents or preserve preferences on this startup volume, because it is a read-only image. If the administrator denies access to the local hard disk or removes the hard disk, users might not have any place to store documents. However, if you configure network user accounts to use network home folders, users can store documents and preserve preferences in their network home folders.

When a user logs in to a NetBoot client computer using a network user account, he retrieves his home folder from a share point. Typically, this share point resides on a server other than the NetBoot server, although with a small number of clients, one could perform both duties from the same server.

> **TIP** ▶ Using NetInstall places high demands on a server. To prevent performance degradation, store home folders on a different, preferably dedicated, home folder server.

Reference 15.2
Creating Images with System Image Utility

System Image Utility is the tool you use to create all three types of NetInstall images. Available from the Tools menu in the Server app, System Image Utility uses files from a mounted volume, disk image, or the "Install OS X Mavericks" application to create a NetInstall image. The actual application is located in /System/Library/Core Services.

Each image requires an image ID, or index, which client computers use to identify similar images. If, when a client lists the available NetInstall images in the Startup Disk pane of System Preferences, two images have the same index, the client assumes that the images are identical and displays only one entry. If only one server will serve an image, assign it a value between 1 and 4095. If multiple servers will serve the same image, assign it a value between 4096 and 65535. System Image Utility generates a semi-random index between 1 and 4095, but you can change it if you customize the image during creation or after using the Server app.

When creating an image, you specify where to store it. For the NetInstall service to recognize the image, it must be stored in /<volume>/Library/NetBoot/NetBootSP*n*/*imagename*.nbi, where *n* is the volume number and *imagename* is the image name you entered when you created the image. If you have already configured the NetInstall service, the Save dialog includes a pop-up menu listing the available volumes. If you choose a volume from that pop-up menu, the save location changes to the NetBootSP*n* share point on that volume.

TIP In a NetInstall environment, many clients booting from the same NetInstall server can place high demands on the server and slow down performance. To improve performance, you can set up additional NetInstall servers to serve the same images.

System Image Utility also enables you to customize your NetBoot, NetRestore, or Network Install configurations by adding any of the following Automator workflow items:

▶ Add Configuration Profiles.

▶ Add Packages and Post-Install Scripts—Allows you to add third-party software or make virtually any customization you desire automatically.

▶ Add User Account—Will include additional users in your image. These users could include system administrator accounts or user accounts.

▶ Apply System Configuration Settings—Allows you to automatically bind computers to LDAP Directory servers, along with applying basic preferences such as the computer's host name.

▶ Create Image—The basis for all image building.

▶ Customize Package Selection—Defines which packages are usable and visible.

▶ Define Image Source—Allows the user to pick the source for the image.

▶ Define Multi-Volume NetRestore—Allows restoration of multi-boot systems.

▶ Define NetRestore Source—Defines the network location of the NetRestore image.

▶ Automated Installation—Can assist in doing speedy deployments in which you're dealing with identical configurations and want to do hands-off installation.

▶ Filter Client by MAC Address—Restricts which clients can use the network-based images.

▶ Filter Computer Models—Restricts which model computers can use the network-based images.

▶ Disk partition support—Built in to System Image Utility so you can add a partition automatically in your deployments.

Using Network Install

Network Install is a convenient way to reinstall the OS, applications, or other software onto local hard disks. For system administrators deploying large numbers of computers with the same version of OS X, Network Install can prove very useful. All startup and installation information is delivered over the network. You can perform software installations with Network Install using a collection of packages or an entire disk image (depending on the source used to create the image).

> **TIP** ▶ For installing small packages rather than entire disks, it might be easier to use ARD, because not all packages require a restart. If NetInstall is used to deploy a package, the client will need to be rebooted whether or not the package requires it.

When creating an install image with System Image Utility, you have the option to automate the installation process to limit the amount of interaction from anyone at the client computer. Keep in mind that responsibility comes with this automation. Because an automatic network installation can be configured to erase the contents of the local hard disk before installation, data loss can occur. You must control access to this type of Network Install disk image, and you must communicate to users the implications of using these images. Always instruct users to back up critical data before using automatic network installations. When configuring your NetInstall server, you will be warned about this even if you aren't doing automated installs.

> **NOTE** ▶ Set the default NetInstall image on every server. Images that normal users can select should probably be NetBoot images, not Network Install images. You may also turn off the NetInstall service when you don't need it.

When creating NetInstall images, specify a source for the image in System Image Utility. System Image Utility should only be used to build images of like versions of OS X. You can use OS X Server to serve images of any version of OS X, but if you want to make images of earlier OS X versions, you should use the respective version of OS X and its version of System Image Utility to build the image. You can create images from the following sources:

▶ "Install OS X Mavericks," as downloaded from the Mac App Store.

▶ Disk images—Instead of using a configured hard disk as a source, you can use Disk Utility to create a disk image of a configured hard disk, and then use the disk image as a source for creating NetBoot images.

▶ Mounted volumes—When a mounted volume is selected as a source, the entire contents of the volume—including the operating system, configuration files, and applications—are copied to the image. When a client computer starts up from an image created from a mounted volume, the boot experience is similar to that of starting up from the original source volume. A copy of the source volume is written to the client computer's hard disk. A benefit of using volumes for image sources is that the image creation is much faster than when using discs. In addition, installations that use images created from volumes are faster than installations that use disc-created images.

There are additional features available, including external image sources such as a network share or ASR multicast streams available by choosing Customize and the Define NetRestore Source Automator action. This is where you can define that a network share with a disk image made from an existing volume is available.

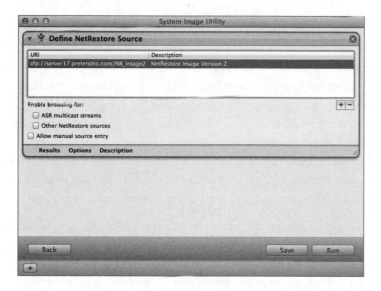

Use the latest version of the operating system when creating NetBoot images. If you are creating OS X 10.8 images, use the imaging tools from OS X 10.8. If you are creating OS X 10.9 images, use the imaging tools on OS X 10.9 or OS X Server 10.9.

When adding new computers to the NetInstall environment, you may need to update the NetInstall image to support them. Check the OS software version that accompanied the new computer.

Reference 15.3
Understanding Shadow Files

Many clients can read from the same NetBoot image, but when a client needs to write anything (such as print jobs and other temporary files) back to its startup volume, NetBoot automatically redirects the written data to the client's shadow files, which are separate from regular system and application software files. These shadow files preserve the unique identity of each client during the entire time the client is running off a NetBoot image. NetBoot also transparently maintains changed user data in the shadow files, while reading unchanged data from the shared system image. The shadow files are re-created at boot time, so any changes that the user makes to the startup volume are lost at restart.

This behavior has important implications. For example, if a user saves a document to the startup volume, the document will be gone after restart. This preserves the condition of the environment the administrator set up, but it also means that you should configure each network user account to have a network home folder if you want them to be able to save their documents.

For each image, you can specify where the shadow file is stored using the Diskless checkbox in the NetBoot image configuration in the Server app. When the Diskless option for an image is disabled, the shadow file is stored on the client computer's local hard disk at /private/var/netboot/.com.apple.NetBootX/Shadow. When the Diskless option is enabled, the shadow file is stored in a share point on the server named NetBootClients$n$ in /<volume>/Library/NetBoot, where n is the number of the volume that stores the shadow file. With the Diskless option enabled, a NetBoot image enables you to operate client computers that are literally diskless.

> **TIP** Make sure you consider the storage need for shadow files when configuring your server. When running diskless, users may experience delays, since writes to the shadow files take place via the network and not locally.

Diskless enabled   Diskless disabled

Reference 15.4
Troubleshooting NetInstall

NetInstall is a fairly straightforward process. If a client does not successfully start up from a NetInstall server, you can troubleshoot the issue by looking into the following areas:

▶ Check the network. The client must have an IP address obtained through DHCP.

▶ Check the server logs for `bootpd` messages, since the underlying process that serves NetInstall is bootpd. These logs can also identify if you mistyped an Ethernet hardware address or selected the wrong type of hardware for a filter.

▶ Press and hold the Option key as you boot the client, which will indicate whether you have a firmware password configured for the computer. A firmware password requires that a password be entered before any alternate boot sources are used, such as a NetInstall image. A firmware password is applied if a lock command was ever sent to an OS X computer.

▶ Check the disk space on the server. Shadow files and disk images may be filling the server's disk space. You may want to add disks with larger capacity or more of them to accommodate these files.

▶ Check for server filters. Do you have filters enabled for IP address, hardware address, and model type? If so, you should disable the filters to allow all computers on the network to start up using the NetInstall service.

▶ Check firewall configurations. NetInstall requires that a combination of DHCP/ BOOTP, TFTP, NFS, AFP, and HTTP ports be open. Temporarily disabling the firewall or adding a rule to allow all traffic from the subnet you're starting up with NetInstall will indicate if you have a firewall configuration problem.

Exercise 15.1
Create NetInstall Images

To create a Network Install image from the "Install OS X Mavericks" application as downloaded from the Mac App Store, follow these steps:

NOTE ▶ This exercise can be done on either the administrator or server computer. It can even be done on a different computer altogether as long as you access the System Image Utility. In this exercise we will be using the server computer to limit how much file copying needs to be done.

1   On your server computer, copy the "Install OS X Mavericks" application into the /Applications folder of the server if it isn't already there.

NOTE ▶ The installer will be available in the Student Materials folder for instructor-led classes or available from the Mac App Store for those who aren't in a classroom situation.

2   Open System Image Utility from the Tools menu in the Server app. The application resides in /System/Library/CoreServices.

3   From the menu, select "Install OS X Mavericks."

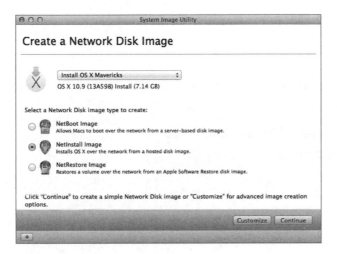

4 Select NetInstall Image.

5 Click Continue.

6 Change the Image Name to **My NetInstall Client** *n* **v1** (where *n* is your student number).

7 Change the Description to **NetInstall of OS X 10.9 v1**.

> **TIP** ▶ Give your images unique identifiers to help you keep track of which image is which. This process often involves multiple attempts and updates, which you'll want to be able to track.

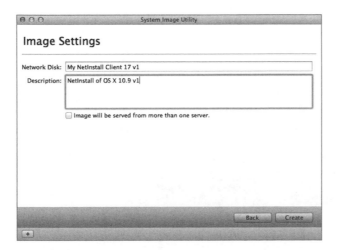

8 Click Create.

9 Agree to the software license agreement.

10 When prompted where to save the image, select your desktop and click Save. Authenticate as ladmin if asked.

Creating an image can take from 15 minutes to a few hours, depending on the size of the source image and the speed of the computer.

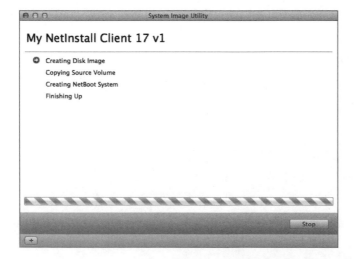

Exercise 15.2
Create NetBoot and NetRestore Images

▶ **Prerequisite**

▶ FireWire or Thunderbolt cable as appropriate for the computers.

The NetInstall image you created is a very basic image used for the same purpose as the OS X installation app. In most NetInstall situations in which people are working off the network image, you'll probably want to create a customized environment for them.

NetBoot Image Creation

In this example, you'll take the OS X administrator computer you've been working on and use it as your template computer for creating a NetBoot image that hundreds of computers could boot and operate from.

1 If you haven't already, rename the administrator computer startup disk to make it distinguishable from your server computer's startup disk and then shut down the computer.

2 Hold down the T key on your administrator computer and power it on. Release the T key once you see a FireWire or Thunderbolt logo on the screen.

 This boots your administrator computer into target disk mode, effectively turning the computer into an external FireWire or Thunderbolt disk enclosure.

3 Connect a FireWire or Thunderbolt cable between your administrator and server computers.

 You should see your administrator computer's hard disk appear on your server's desktop. If you don't, in the Finder, choose Finder > Preferences, click General in the toolbar, and select the option to show hard disks on the desktop.

4 On your server, open System Image Utility and select NetBoot Image.

5   Click Customize, and then click Agree when the license agreement appears.

This opens a window containing Automator Library actions related to System Image Utility. This is a feature that allows you to create complex workflows for creating NetInstall images and save them for later repeated use if desired.

6   In the Define Image Source action in the window, identify the Source as your client computer's hard disk.

7   Drag the Add User Account action to the workflow.

8   Configure the Add User Account action as follows:

▶   Name: NetBoot Admin

▶   Short Name: nbadmin

▶   Password: nbadminpw

▶   Allow user to administer this computer.

If desired, you could add additional local accounts by adding more Add User Account actions to the workflow.

9   Drag the Apply System Configuration Settings action item to the workflow and configure it as follows:

▶   Generate unique Computer Names starting with Mav_Client.

▶   Select "Change ByHost preferences to match client after install."

This last setting may or may not be desired in your environment. Certain settings are saved in preference list (plist) files that include a MAC (Media Access Control) or UUID (universally unique) identifier in the filename. You should use this option so these files are correctly applied to target computers.

10 Drag the Create Image action to the bottom of the workflow and make sure NetBoot is selected. Fill in:

▶ Image Name: **NetBoot of Mav_Client**

▶ Installed Volume: Will already be filled in.

▶ Description: This is the boot image made from a target mode computer.

▶ Index: Pick a number below 4095 that is different from the index of your first image, such as 2796.

▶ Save to: Desktop

11 Click Run. Enter the administrator account credentials to create the image.

If you'd like to see more information about what's happening, you can choose View > Show Log. You can also save this workflow for use later.

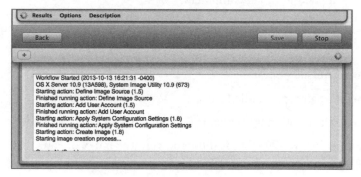

12 When the image has completed, eject the administrator computer from the desktop, disconnect the Thunderbolt or FireWire cable, and then shut it down using the power button. Wait a moment and then restart it.

NetRestore Image Creation (Optional)

NetRestore image building is much the same as making a NetBoot or NetInstall image. The main difference is that the image you create will be restored to the hard disk of the target computer. This is a great way to deploy preconfigured images.

To create a NetRestore image, follow the instructions for NetBoot, but choose NetRestore Image in Step 4. Follow the rest of the exercise as written, changing the word NetBoot to NetRestore in the image's name and description as appropriate.

Exercise 15.3
Configure a NetInstall Server

▶ **Prerequisite**

▶ Exercise 15.1, "Create NetInstall Images"

You need to configure your server to offer NetInstall images to your client computers. This, like many other services, is done through the Server app.

1   On your server, open the Server app and connect.

2   In the left column, select the NetInstall service under Advanced.

3   Select the Settings tab.

4   In Access, enable the Ethernet port, if it isn't already enabled.

5   In Edit Storage Settings, select your server's storage volume to serve both Images & Client Data. Click OK.

Configure NetInstall to Serve an Image

Before you can start the NetInstall service, it has to have an image it can serve, and be configured to use it.

1   After the image is created, on your server copy your NetBoot image (NBI) to the NetBootSP0 folder, if it isn't already there. Do so by dragging the entire My NetInstall Client *n* v1.nbi folder to the NetBootSP0 folder (in the Finder, choose Go > Go To Folder, enter **/Library/NetBoot/NetBootSP0** and click Go to open that folder). Provide local administrator credentials when prompted.

2   After it has copied over, return to the Server app.

3   In the left column, select the NetInstall service.

4   Double-click your My NetInstall Client *n* v1 image.

5   Enable the image by selecting the "Make available over" checkbox and choosing NFS from the pop-up menu.

For each image, you can also specify which protocol, NFS or HTTP, is used to serve the image. NFS is no longer the default and can offer some performance advantages. HTTP is now the default and enables you to serve disk images without having to reconfigure your firewall to allow NFS traffic. It does not require the Websites service to be turned on to work.

6   Click OK.

7   Click the On/Off switch to turn the NetInstall service on.

Verify the Share Points

Your NetInstall service is now configured. The action of selecting a volume to serve the images automatically configured two share points for you. You should verify this now. Running AFP is only needed if you will host diskless NetBoot images.

1   Open the Server app.

2   Select File Sharing.

3   Review the Share Points list. There will be a NetBootClients*n* share point in addition to any other configured share points. Because HTTP is being used to share the images, no share point for NetBootSP*n* appears.

4   Back in NetInstall, change the protocol for sharing from HTTP to NFS and click Save. Look back in File Sharing and notice the addition of NetBootSP*n*. Return the protocol to HTTP in NetInstall.

These share points are used for the shadow files and NetInstall images, respectively. However, only the NetBootClients*n* share is available over AFP by default. Additionally, this process may not start the File Sharing service, so you should do that now.

Specify a Default Image

Within the Server app, the Images pane lists the available NetInstall images on the server, which can host up to 25 different disk images. Each image can be enabled, allowing client computers to use the image to boot, or each image can be disabled, preventing client computers from accessing the image. While you can have several images, you must specify one of the NetInstall images as the default image. When you hold down the N key on a client computer at startup, if the client has never started up from that NetInstall server before, the server will provide the default image to start up the client; hold down Option-N to use the current default.

1   In the Images pane of the NetInstall service, select the image you want to be the default image.

2 From the Action (gear icon) menu, choose Use as Default Boot Image.

The image is now noted as "(default)" on the right side of the pane.

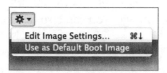

TIP ▶ Remember that image files can be very large and can take up a significant amount of disk space on the server. Consider using a second volume to hold the images and keep them off the boot volume.

Exercise 15.4
Filter NetInstall Clients

▶ **Prerequisite**

▶ Exercise 15.3, "Configure a NetInstall Server"

The NetInstall Settings pane permits you to allow or deny access to NetInstall services globally or per image based on the client computer's hardware, or MAC, address. Filtering removes the risk of allowing non-NetInstall clients to access unlicensed applications or to accidentally perform a network installation. By maintaining accurate Filters settings, you can seamlessly integrate NetInstall into traditional network configurations.

You also have the ability to set NetInstall filters on a per-image basis in addition to the per-server filters. This could be particularly useful if you have one server for multiple Mac classrooms. Each classroom could be configured with its own NetBoot image, and use per-image filters to limit which classrooms can access which image. You can also filter by Mac model.

> **NOTE ▶** You can find the model of computer by searching for the System Information app in Spotlight. Once open, it will report the model of computer it is being run on.

1   Open the Server app on your server computer and select the NetInstall service.

2   In the Images pane, double-click the image My NetInstall Client *n* v1.

This pane allows you to perform per-image filters based on hardware type, specific Ethernet hardware addresses, or both. It's important to differentiate between the per-image filters and the NetInstall service-wide filters.

3   Select the "Image is visible to" pop-up menu, choose "only some Mac models," and select Allow for your client computer hardware type in the list.

4   Click OK to close the Mac Model Filter pane.

5   Click Done to return to the NetInstall pane.

6   Boot your client computer normally and log in.

7   Open System Preferences.

8   Click Startup Disk.

9   Select the NetInstall image with the filters.

10   Restart your client computer.

It boots from the NetInstall image you just defined. It will look like the start of an OS installation since the image was made from an installation source.

Exercise 15.5
Configure a NetInstall Client

▶ **Prerequisites**

- ▶   DHCP must be available on your network
- ▶   Exercise 15.3, "Configure a NetInstall Server"

As long as your client computer has the latest version of its firmware and is a supported client computer, you don't need to install any other special software. The Extensible Firmware Interface (EFI) (Intel) boot code contains the software used to boot a computer using a NetInstall image.

There are at least three ways to cause a computer to use NetInstall at startup:

- ▶   Hold down the N key until the blinking NetInstall globe appears in the center of the screen. This method allows you to use NetInstall for a single startup. Subsequent reboots return the computer to the previous startup state. Your client computer will then boot from the default NetInstall image hosted by the NetInstall server.

- ▶   Select the desired network disk image from the Startup Disk pane in System Preferences. The version of the Startup Disk pane included with OS X v10.2 and later presents all available network disk images on the local network. Notice that each type of NetInstall image maintains a unique icon to help users differentiate between the types of images. With the desired network disk image selected, you can reboot the computer. The computer then attempts to use the NetInstall service on every subsequent startup.

► Hold down the Option key during startup. This invokes the Startup Manager, which presents a list of available system folders as well as a globe icon for NetInstall. Click the globe icon and click the advance arrow to begin the NetInstall process. This option doesn't allow you to pick which image you want to boot from. As when holding down the N key, you will get the default image.

It is important to note a couple of things that can upset the NetInstall process:

► If no network connection exists, a NetInstall client will eventually time out and look to a local drive to start up. You can prevent this by keeping local hard disks free of system software and denying users physical access to the Ethernet ports on a computer.

► Resetting the parameter random-access memory (PRAM) resets the configured startup disk, requiring you to reselect the NetInstall volume in the Startup Disk pane of System Preferences.

You'll try starting up your client computer with NetInstall now.

1 Shut down your client computer.

2 Turn on the computer while holding down the N key until the blinking NetBoot globe appears.

It boots into the OS X Installer from the NetInstall image you just created and enabled. Because you don't actually want to reinstall your computer, just shut down the computer.

Exercise 15.6
Monitor NetInstall Clients

You can monitor NetInstall usage with Server Admin. The Connections pane provides a list of client computers that are booted from the server. It will report the computer's host name and IP address, its progress in percentage, and its status.

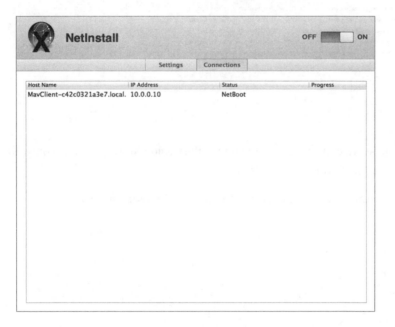

Additionally, the NetInstall logs can be useful when monitoring the progress of a NetInstall in action. You can access your NetInstall server logs using these steps:

1   Open the Server app and connect to your server.

2 In the Server app sidebar, under Status, select Logs.

3 In the pop-up menu, choose NetInstall – Service Log.

Clean Up

Disable the NetInstall service on your server, and set the default startup volume on your administrator computer to be the internal drive.

You learned how to configure NetInstall and leverage it for imaging and startup.

Lesson 16
Caching Content from Apple

The Caching service speeds up the download and distribution of software and other content distributed by Apple. It caches the first download of various items distributed by Apple, then makes these items available to devices and computers on your local network. This means you can offer fast downloads of items distributed by Apple to clients on your network.

This allows you to save time as well as Internet use.

> **MORE INFO** ► One big new feature in the Caching service for OS X Server for Mavericks is that it serves iOS 7 devices. Apple gave this service a new name: Caching Server 2.

Reference 16.1
Understanding the Caching Service

For eligible computers and devices, the Caching service transparently caches many items, including:

- Software updates
- App Store purchases and downloads
- Mac App Store purchases and downloads
- iBooks Store purchases and downloads
- iTunes U items
- Internet Recovery

The Caching service supports Macs with OS X 10.8.2 or later and iOS 7 or later. It also supports iTunes content for Macs and Windows computers with iTunes 11.0.2 or later.

The network requirements to use the Caching service include the requirements to:

▶   Be on a network with a network device that performs Network Address Translation (NAT) to and from the Internet

▶   Have the same public IPv4 source address on the Internet side of the NAT device as on the Caching server for outgoing traffic (in simpler terms, have the same public IP address as the server behind NAT)

In order to use the Caching service with the Mac App Store, a Mac must:

▶   Have OS X version 10.8.2 or later

▶   Not be configured to use the OS X Server Software Update service

The key is that your clients and the Caching server(s) must share the same Internet connection behind a NAT device, and their traffic from your network to the Internet must have the same source IPv4 address. (This applies even if the client and the Caching server are on different subnets, as long as they have the same public IPv4 source address.) Fortunately, this is a common configuration.

Eligible clients will automatically use the appropriate Caching server. Otherwise, the client will use servers operated by Apple or a content distribution network partner (just like they did before the Caching service was introduced as a feature).

In the following figure, a network device performs NAT, and the organization has two subnets. The clients and the Caching servers in both subnets have the same public IPv4 source address on the public Internet side of the NAT device, even though they are in different subnets. The clients in both subnets automatically use one of the Caching servers in their organization's network (in the figure, one subnet has two servers to illustrate that you don't need a Caching service for each subnet behind NAT). Once the clients leave the local network, they automatically use servers controlled by Apple.

The Caching server automatically registers its public IPv4 address and local network information with Apple servers. When a client communicates with Apple servers to download an item, if the client's public IPv4 address matches your Caching server's public IPv4 address, the Apple servers instruct the client to get the content from the local Caching server. If the client cannot communicate with its local Caching server, it automatically downloads the content from servers controlled by Apple on the Internet.

The Caching service caches only items distributed by servers that are under Apple's control (including items from a content distribution network partner); it does not cache content from random third parties.

Be sure to read the "Provide a Caching server" topic in the Help Center for the Server app, as it is an informative and up-to-date reference. Click the link on the Caching server pane; or in the Server app, from the Help menu, enter Provide a Caching server in the search field.

Reference 16.2
Configuring and Maintaining the Caching Service

It's really simple to configure the Caching service. You could click the On/Off switch to turn the service on and be done configuring.

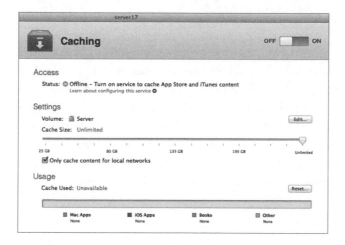

The Server app allows a few configuration features. You can:

▶ Click the link next to Status to learn more about configuring this service.

▶ Click Edit to select a volume for caching.

▶ Use the slider to set the cache size.

▶ Deselect the checkbox "Only cache content for local networks" to serve only clients on subnets that your server is not directly connected to (for complex networks).

▶ Click Reset to erase the existing cached content.

The volume you select to use for the Caching service must have at least 50 GB free (even if you set the Cache Size slider to 25 GB). If you select a volume that doesn't have enough space, the Server app alerts you, and the Choose button becomes unavailable. Simply select a different volume.

By default, the Caching service uses the startup volume for the cached content. Even though the slider is labeled "Unlimited," the Caching service is smart enough to not fill up the entire volume; when only 25 GB is left on the volume you're using for the Caching service, your server deletes the least recently used cached content (not necessarily the oldest content) to make space for new content. If your users download a large variety of different content, consider using a volume large enough to cache as much content as you can, otherwise the Caching service may constantly delete items that it will end up downloading again, after deleting yet more items in order to make room for the newly requested items.

If you change the volume used for the Caching service, the existing cached content will be copied to the newly selected volume.

> **MORE INFO** ▶ See the "Configure advanced cache settings" section of the OS X Server: Advanced Administration guide (https://help.apple.com/advancedserveradmin/mac/3.0/) for more advanced options, such as limiting the network interfaces on which the service listens and limiting the number of concurrent client connections.

Because of the nature of the Caching service, it will not start unless your server has a wired Ethernet connection.

If your organization has a number of subnets that are all behind the same network device that performs NAT, and they all have the same public IPv4 address, but the internal subnets have slow links between them, you may want to select the checkbox "Only cache content for local networks" so that each subnet has its own local copy of items. This way, clients on each subnet can download cached content quickly from a local Caching server, as opposed to using up the slow link between subnets. Caching servers will download content from their peers, if available, rather than from the Internet.

The Usage section shows you at a glance the kind of content your Caching server has downloaded.

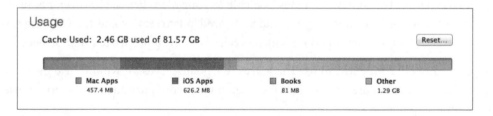

The Stats pane of the Server app has one graph dedicated to the Caching service. Start by selecting the Stats pane in the Server app sidebar. Use the pop-up menus to choose Bytes Served as the type of activity, then choose a time period. The graph shows how much data the Caching service has downloaded from the Internet and from other peer servers, and how much it has served to clients from its cache.

Reference 16.3
Comparing Software Update and Caching Services

The current and several previous versions of OS X Server have offered the Software Update service (see Lesson 17, "Implementing Software Update Service"). This service allows you to limit the software updates available to your Mac clients. However, because OS X clients cannot simultaneously use the Software Update service and the Caching service of OS X Server, you must choose which service is more appropriate for your needs.

If a Mac is already configured to use the Software Update service, it will not use the Caching service; in order to use a Caching server, you must reconfigure such a Mac to *not* use the Software Update service.

Here are the main differences between the two services:

▶ The Caching service caches many different kinds of content but the Software Update service caches software updates only.

▶ The Caching service caches an item only after the first client requests it, but the Software Update service allows you to automatically download software updates before the first Mac client needs them.

▶ The Caching service makes all appropriate items available to clients automatically, but with the Software Update service, you can allow clients to download only the updates you have approved (for instance, if you are required to confirm that each software update is compatible with your other software and workflows).

▶ Eligible computers with OS X automatically use an appropriate Caching server, but you must configure a computer with OS X to use a specific Software Update server.

▶ The Caching service provides no ability to manage what clients can download, but the Software Update service does.

▶ The Caching service is great for mobile clients whether or not they are inside your local network. In contrast, if a client that is configured to use your server's Software Update server cannot contact it once the client leaves your local network, then the client could not use Software Update or the Mac App Store to install software updates until it returns to your local network.

▶ The Software Update service does not provide any service at all to iOS devices.

Table 16.1 summarizes the differences between the Caching service and the Software Update service.

Table 16.1: Caching Service vs. Software Update Service

Category	Caching Service	Software Update Service
Type of content cached	OS X and iOS software updates; App Store, Mac App Store and iBooks Store items; iTunes U items; Internet Recovery	OS X software updates only
Specify content to serve	Not Applicable	Automatic or Manual
Download trigger	Client requests item from Apple	Immediate or Manual
Client configuration	None	defaults command, managed preferences, or configuration profile

Even though it is possible to use the same server to provide Software Update and Caching services, be aware that this may require a large amount of storage space, and a single client cannot use both services.

Unless you need to prevent Mac clients from installing specific software updates via Software Update or the Mac App Store, it is recommended that you use the Caching service instead of the Software Update service.

Reference 16.4
Troubleshooting the Caching Service

The Caching service is transparent, so there isn't much troubleshooting necessary. The first time a client downloads an item that isn't already cached, that initial download isn't any faster. However, subsequent downloads of the same item, whether from the same client or from a different client, are limited only by the speed of the disks of the client and the server, or the bandwidth of the local network.

Deleting Items to Test the Caching Service

To test downloading items, you can use a computer that's an eligible client of the Caching server to download an item from iTunes (11.0.2 or later), the Mac App Store, or the App Store, then delete it, and download it again (or download the same item from multiple eligible clients) and confirm that the subsequent download speeds are appropriate for downloading items locally as opposed to across the Internet.

> **TIP** ▶ You can use your server that's running the Caching service to perform the first download of an item; it is automatically a Caching service client as well as a server.

Confirming the Basics

If you suspect problems with the Caching service:

▶ For iTunes, confirm that iTunes is version 11.0.2 or later. On a Mac, choose iTunes > About iTunes. On a PC with Windows and iTunes, on the Help menu, click About iTunes.

▶ Confirm that the Caching service is turned on in the Server app. The Caching service status indicator in the Server app sidebar list of services is green when the service is turned on.

▶ Confirm that the client and the server have the same public IPv4 source address on the Internet side of a NAT device.

▶ Confirm that the Mac clients are not configured to use a Software Update server.

▶ Confirm that iOS devices are using the same network as your Caching service. In other words, confirm that the iOS device is using Wi-Fi, and is not using *only* a cellular network.

▶ Check the Cache Used field. If the value is "None," perhaps no eligible client has downloaded any eligible content.

Use Activity Monitor to confirm that your server is downloading items from the Internet and then serving items to clients. On your server, open Activity Monitor, choose View > All Processes, click the Network tab, set the pop-up menu to Data, and monitor the graph. When the Caching service downloads an item from the Internet to cache it, this is reflected in a purple "Data received/sec" line. When the Caching service sends a cached item to a local client, this is reflected in a red "Data sent/sec" line.

Using the Caching Service Logs

You can use the Logs pane of the Server app to check the service log for the basics. In the Logs pop-up menu, choose Service Log under the Caching menu item. If the system log has been automatically rotated as part of daily system maintenance tasks, the Logs field may simply contain "No contents to display." This view filters out any line in the generic system log that does not contain the "AssetCache" string.

For more detailed information, use the Console app on your server. Choose File > Open, navigate to /Library/Server/Caching/Logs, select Debug.log, and click Open. You can click Hide Log List in the Console app toolbar to devote more room to displaying the log contents.

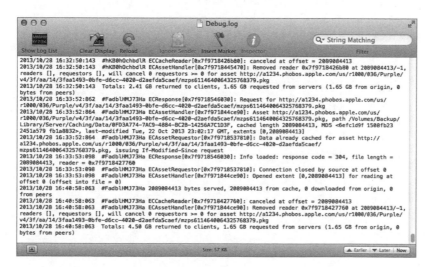

Some strings in Debug.log that might help you understand what is happening include:

▶ "Issuing outgoing full request" when the Caching service downloads an item from public servers

▶ "Data already cached for asset" when the Caching service already has an item cached locally

Some items have human-recognizable names, but other items have names that might seem random.

Understanding Performance Bottlenecks

A single Caching server can handle hundreds of clients simultaneously and can saturate a Gigabit Ethernet network interface. To determine if your server (as opposed to local network capacity) is the bottleneck, open Activity Monitor on your server, click the CPU tab, and monitor the CPU Usage graph. If your server's CPU usage is near its maximum, consider additional servers for the Caching service.

Moving the Caching Service Data Volume

If you attach a new volume to your server after you've started the Server app and connected to your server, choose View > Refresh (or press Command-R) in order to select the newly attached volume as the destination for the Caching service. After you choose a new location, the Server app automatically moves the cached content to the new volume.

Lesson 17

Implementing Software Update Service

Once you have deployed computers, the question of how to keep the software on them up to date will arise. Built into OS X Server is the ability to mirror the Apple software updates that exist on the Apple Software Update servers onto your local server.

Reference 17.1
Managing Software Updates

With OS X Server, you have the option of mirroring the Apple Software Update servers on your local server. This has two distinct advantages. The first is that you can save Internet bandwidth, and the second is that you can control the updates available to your users.

Only software updates to Apple-supplied software can be served by the update services. Third-party software or modified Apple updates can't be added to the service.

When using a Software Update server, all of your client computers will retrieve their software updates from the server on your local network rather than over the Internet, which will also result in faster downloads for your users. The service can be configured to automatically download and make the update available, or the updates can be manually enabled.

The process of manually controlling which updates can be downloaded and made available to your users can be particularly useful when a software update might be incompatible with some software you're using or the update hasn't gone through testing in your environment.

GOALS

▶ Understand the concepts of the Software Update service (SUS)

▶ Configure the server to provide software updates

▶ Configure a client to use the Software Update service

▶ Configure which updates are provided to the clients

▶ Learn to troubleshoot the Software Update service

If you have set the service to automatically download and enable updates, obsolete updates will be removed automatically. If you set the service for Manual, you will need to cull outdated updates manually.

Clients can be configured to utilize the update service by a manual change to a preference list, by managed preferences, or by a configuration profile. Configuration profiles with a software update payload are only available for devices and device groups.

For situations in which multiple Software Update service implementations are appropriate to use, such as for load balancing across a large number of client computers, a cascade of servers can be created. One main server is created and others are pointed at it to get their updates. This prevents having many Software Update servers from using additional network bandwidth. Refer to Apple Support article HT3765, "OS X Server: How to cascade Software Update Servers from a Central Software Update Server."

Reference 17.2
Troubleshooting the Software Update Service

If the Software Update service doesn't work as expected, you can troubleshoot the issue by looking into the following areas:

▶ Check the network. The client must be able to contact your Software Update server and be able to communicate with it. The default port the service uses is 8088.

▶ Are the updates listed in SUS? If the updates haven't been downloaded, they won't be available to the client devices. The Software Update service can't work through an authenticated proxy if you are using one.

▶ Is space available on the server's disk? Logs will indicate that Software Update will stop synchronizing if the server's volume has less than 20 percent of its total storage space available.

▶ Is the Software Update service profile installed on the device? If the computer doesn't have a profile containing the Software Update service information, it won't know to look for your Software Update server.

▶ Is the specific update enabled? Check in the list of updates.

▶ Check the Software Update logs (Service, Access, and Error logs).

Exercise 17.1
Configure Software Update

Setting up your Software Update server is easy. Here's how:

1   Perform these exercises on your administrator computer. If you do not already have a connection to your server computer with Server app on your administrator computer, then connect to it with the following steps: Open the Server app on your administrator computer, choose Manage > Connect to Server, click Other Mac, select your server, click Continue, provide administrator credentials (Administrator Name ladmin and Administrator Password ladminpw), deselect the "Remember this password" checkbox, and then click Connect.

2   In the Server app sidebar, select the Software Update service.

3   Click the Settings tab.

4   Select Automatic to download the updates and enable them unless you are in a classroom situation, in which case select Manual.

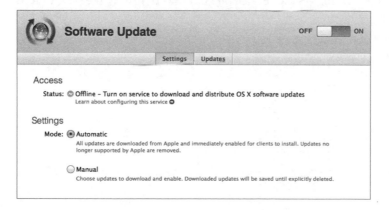

TIP If you want to control which updates are available to the clients, select Manual. This will download the updates but not automatically enable them.

TIP If you have another storage volume, you may want to consider changing the location of the update packages. The default location is on your startup volume, and the updates can take a considerable amount of room on the volume. You can change the location through the Settings pane for the server in the Server app.

5 Click the On switch. After a period of time, the list of available updates appears in the Updates pane. If you have chosen Manual, the choice "Automatically download new updates" becomes visible in the pane.

This begins mirroring the software updates from Apple. If you have a slow Internet connection, this initial sync takes quite some time, possibly a number of hours. A common situation is turning on the service one day and returning the next to fully downloaded updates.

Enable Individual Updates

You can select which updates to make available to your users from within the list of updates if you use the Manual choice in Settings.

1 In the Server app, select the Software Update service.

2   Select Manual if originally configured as Automatic.

3   In the toolbar, click the Updates button.

This screen lists all the updates currently available from the Apple servers.

4   Select which updates you want to be downloaded and enabled.

If the list of updates is empty, it is still being copied down from Apple.

Voice Update – Ioana	3.0.5	07/16/13	105.89 MB	Available ▾	
iPhoto Update	9.2.3	07/17/12	373.51 MB	Available ▾	
Multi-Lingual Voices	2.0.0	05/13/12	199.41 MB	Download	
Voice Update – Ya-Ling	2.0.0	05/13/12	377.83 MB	Download and Enable	
Voice Update – Daniel	2.0.0	07/23/13	344.89 MB	Available ▾	
Voice Update – Monica	3.0.8	08/22/13	376.01 MB	Available ▾	

NOTE ▸ The update must be copied down before you can enable it.

You can enable or disable the update by selecting its status entry or by using the Action (gear icon) pop-up menu at the bottom of the pane.

✿ ▾	743 updates	
Download		⌘↓
Download and Enable		⇧⌘↓
Enable		⌘E
Disable		⌘H
Remove…		⌘T
View Update		↵
Check for Updates…		

Exercise 17.2
Configure Computers for Your Software Update Service

▶ **Prerequisites**

- ▸ Exercise 11.1, "Enable Profile Manager"
- ▸ Exercise 17.1, "Configure Software Update"

As with other settings, you'll be using profiles to tell your computer to utilize your local Software Update server instead of Apple's. This preference can be set at the device or device group level. Refer to Lesson 12, "Managing with Profile Manager," for more information on how to build profiles.

1 On your administrator computer, open the Profile Manager web app, and log in with administrator credentials.

2 In the left column, select Device Groups.

3 Click Add (+) to create a new device group. In the device group name field, enter LabGroup, and press the Tab key to save the name change.

4 Under Settings for LabGroup, click Edit.

5 For the Profile Distribution Type, select Manual Download so that you can download this profile on your administrator computer, which is unmanaged.

6 In the Description field, enter Software Update Service Settings.

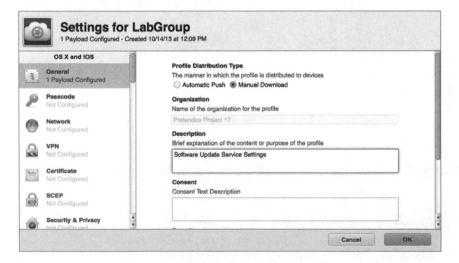

7 Leave the other settings in this pane at their defaults.

8 In the Profile Manager web app sidebar, select Software Update and click Configure.

9 In the Software Update server field, enter http://servern.pretendco.com:8088/index.sucatalog (where n is your student number).

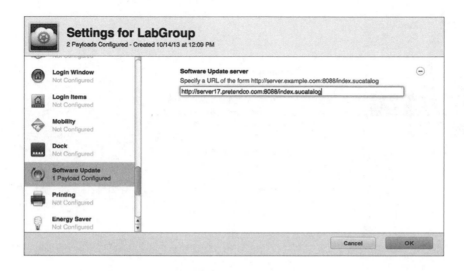

10 Click OK to exit the Software Update payload pane.

11 Click Save to save the changes. In the Save Changes dialog, click Save again.

12 On your administrator computer, in the Profile Manager web app view of the Lab-Group configuration profile, click Download.

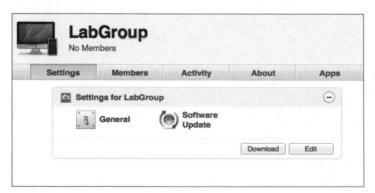

13 System Preferences automatically opens the .mobileconfig file and asks if you want to install it. Click Install, then provide administrator credentials.

14 After the configuration profile is installed, inspect the settings in the Profiles pane of System Preferences.

15 On your administrator computer, from the Apple menu, choose Software Update.

16 On your server, check in the Software Update service logs in the Server app. Look for the administrator computer's IPv4 address in the Access log to show that your Software Update service is being used.

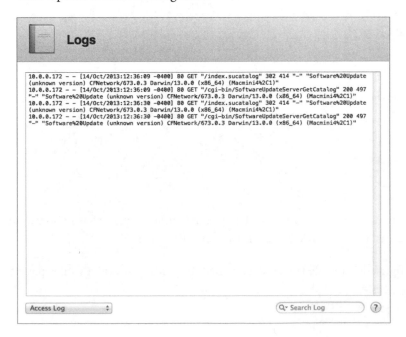

If you are not using Profile Manager, you can use the defaults command in Terminal to point unmanaged client computers to a Software Update server. You must be an administrator to use the defaults command:

sudo defaults write /Library/Preferences/com.apple.SoftwareUpdate CatalogURL*URL*

Replace *URL* with the URL of the Software Update server, including the port number and the name of the catalog file:

sudo defaults write /Library/Preferences/com.apple.SoftwareUpdate CatalogURL
http://servern.protendco.com:8088/index.sucatalog

Clean Up

Remove the SUS profile from your client computer and turn off the SUS service.

In this lesson you learned how to store software updates on your local network and serve them to your clients. You also learned how to configure your clients to use this service.

Providing Network Services

Lesson 18

Offering Time Machine Network Backup

A powerful feature of Time Machine is its ability to use network-based share points as a backup location. You can use OS X Server to provide a centralized destination for backups and to quickly monitor your users' backups, including information about how large each backup is, the progress of a backup, and the last time a backup was successfully completed.

In order to use your server as a Time Machine backup destination, users simply select your server's Time Machine destination from a list; your server uses Bonjour to advertise the shared folder or folders it offers for the Time Machine service. It couldn't get much simpler than that.

GOALS

▶ Enable the Time Machine service

▶ Configure OS X Server to offer Time Machine services

▶ Restore from Time Machine

Reference 18.1
Configuring Time Machine as a Network Service

Time Machine is a powerful backup and restore service available to users of OS X (Mavericks, Mountain Lion, Lion, Snow Leopard, and Leopard); you can use the Time Machine service with OS X Server to provide a backup destination on your server to Time Machine users.

You can now configure a limit to the size of each client backup, but only Macs running OS X Mavericks or newer will obey this limit. Apart from this limitation, Time Machine will by design eventually fill up the destination volume with backup files, so it's a good idea to use a volume (or volumes) that you dedicate to Time Machine only.

The File Sharing service must be turned on in order for clients to use the Time Machine service.

TIP The Server app provides no warning that if you turn off the File Sharing service, you will interrupt active Time Machine backups or restores; so, if you offer the Time Machine service, be sure not to turn off the File Sharing service until you have confirmed that no client computers are actively backing up or restoring with the Time Machine service.

After you use the Server app to choose a destination for Time Machine backups, click the On/Off switch to turn on the Time Machine service. On the Time Machine destination, each client computer gets its own sparse disk image (a sparse disk image can grow in size), and there is an automatically configured ACL to prevent anyone from accessing or deleting Time Machine files from the sparse disk image.

If you later change the backup volume, users who use your server's Time Machine service will automatically use the new volume. However, OS X Server does not automatically migrate existing backup files. The next time a client's Mac runs a Time Machine backup, the user sees a warning that the identity of the backup disk has changed since the previous backup. After the user agrees to use the disk, OS X uses Time Machine to back up all the non-excluded files, not just the files that have changed since the last time a successful Time Machine backup completed, so it may take a long time, depending on how much data is backed up.

Remember that you can use the Server app's Users pane or Groups pane to configure user and group access to the Time Machine service; to do so, secondary (or Control-) click an account, choose Edit Access to Services, and then select or deselect the checkbox for Time Machine.

Exercise 18.1
Configure and Use the Time Machine Service

▶ **Prerequisites**

- ▶ Exercise 7.1, "Use Time Machine to Back Up OS X Server."
- ▶ Exercise 10.1, "Create and Import Network Accounts"; or create a user with Full Name **Barbara Green**, Account Name **barbara**, and a password of **net**.
- ▶ You must have a folder named Shared Items, owned by the Local Admin user, and located at the root of the startup disk; you can use the section "Create a New Location for Shared Folders" in Exercise 13.1, "Explore the File Sharing Service," to create that folder and modify its ownership. Alternatively, you could use an extra disk if you have one available.

You will configure your server to be a network destination for Time Machine backups so client computers can keep a Time Machine backup in a centralized location.

In a production environment, you should use a disk other than your startup disk as a Time Machine backup destination. In this exercise, you will create a new folder to use on the startup disk for testing purposes. Be sure to follow the instructions to stop the Time Machine service at the end of the exercise; otherwise, your server's startup disk might become filled with backup files.

1   Perform these exercises on your administrator computer. If you do not already have a connection to your server computer with Server app on your administrator computer, then connect to it with the following steps: Open the Server app on your administrator computer, choose Manage > Connect to Server, click Other Mac, select your server, click Continue, provide administrator credentials (Administrator Name ladmin and Administrator Password ladminpw), deselect the "Remember this password" checkbox, and then click Connect.

2   In the Server app sidebar, select Time Machine.

3   Below the Destinations field, click Add (+).

4   Next to the "Store backups in" field, click Choose.

5   Select your startup disk.

6   Open the Shared Items folder.

7   Click New Folder.

8   Enter the name **Time Machine Backups** and click Create to create the new folder.

9   Select the folder you just created.

10   Click Choose.

11   Confirm the details of the shared folder you are about to create.

12   Click Create.

Note that the Server app displays which volume is used as the backup destination, and how much space is available on that volume.

13   Click the On/Off switch to start the service.

When you turn on the Time Machine service, the Server app automatically starts the File Sharing service if it is not already running.

Configure an OS X Computer to Use the Time Machine Destination

Verify that network-based Time Machine works as expected. Configure your administrator computer to use the Time Machine service.

Configure Time Machine to Exclude Most Files

Since this is a learning environment, you can reduce the amount of space required for a Time Machine backup by excluding your Documents folder, as well as system files such as the system applications and UNIX tools. Configure this before setting a Time Machine destination, to ensure that you don't back up files that are unnecessary for the exercise.

1   On your administrator computer, from the Time Machine status menu, choose Open Time Machine Preferences.

2   Click Options.

3   Ensure that the "Show Time Machine in menu bar" checkbox is selected.

4   Click Add (+) to add a folder to be excluded.

5   In the sidebar, select Documents, then click Exclude.

6   Click Add (+).

7   Click the pop-up menu in the center of the top of the window, and choose your startup disk.

8   Hold the Command key and select each of the visible folders except the Users folder.

9   Click Exclude.

10 At the notice that you've excluded the System folder, click Exclude All System Files.

11 If you have any other disks or volumes on your administrator computer, add those to the list of excluded items.

12 Review the list of exclusions, then click Save.

Leave the "Back up while on battery power" checkbox unselected (it appears only for portable Macs).

Configure Time Machine to Use Your Server's Time Machine Service

Now that you've configured your administrator computer's Time Machine preferences to exclude most files, select your server's Time Machine network volume.

1 In the Time Machine preferences, click Select Backup Disk.

> **NOTE** ► If you are in a classroom environment, do not select another student's server, as this will create unexpected results when their Time Machine service stops.

2 Select the item named Time Machine Backups with your server's computer name.

For the sake of keeping things simple for this exercise, leave the "Encrypt backups" checkbox unselected.

3   Click Use Disk.

4   Provide credentials for a user on the server and click Connect. Use Barbara Green's user name (**barbara**) and password (**net**).

5   Click Connect.

6   Note that Time Machine preferences displays the server name, how much space is available, and information about backup dates.

7   From the Time Machine status menu, choose Back Up Now.

8   Once the backup has completed, click Close at the notification.

Inspect the Status of the Backup at the Server

The Time Machine service allows you to monitor the status of the backups.

1   On your administrator computer, in the Server app, connect to your server.

2   In the Server app sidebar, select Time Machine.

3   Click Backups.

4   Double-click the entry for the backup of your administrator computer, or select it and click Edit (pencil icon).

5   Note all the information displayed, then click View Share Point.

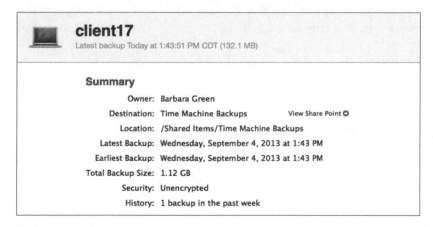

6 Note that the Server app opened the File Sharing pane, with details about the Time Machine Backups shared folder.

MORE INFO ▶ There are no normal network users or groups listed in the Access field. A user account has access to the Time Machine service if it's a member of the com.apple.access_backup group. This group is normally not visible; you add members to this group when you use the Users pane or Groups pane to manage access to services for an account, and select the checkbox for access to the Time Machine service.

7 Click View Files.

8 Note that the Server app opened the Storage pane, and that the disk image's name uses the client's computer name.

9 Click File Sharing in the Server app sidebar.

10 Note that the Time Machine destination is listed with a special icon.

Restore from a Network Time Machine Destination

To confirm that the network Time Machine service works, simulate accidentally deleting a file and using Time Machine to restore it. Use the following steps to create a file
with TextEdit, initiate a Time Machine backup, delete the file, empty the Trash, and then
restore the file using Time Machine.

1 On your administrator computer, open Launchpad from your Dock and open
TextEdit.

2 Enter some text, like This file will be deleted and then restored.

3 Press Command-S to save the file.

4 Press Command-D to choose the desktop as the location to save the file.

5 Name the file DeleteMe (TextEdit automatically adds an appropriate extension, such as
.rtf or .txt) and click Save.

6 Quit TextEdit.

Make a backup with the newly created text file on the desktop. You will use the Time
Machine preferences to monitor the status of the backup.

1 From the Time Machine status menu, choose Open Time Machine Preferences.

2 From the Time Machine status menu, choose Back Up Now.

While a backup is in progress, the Time Machine menu icon includes an additional arrow.

3   Wait until the backup has completed; wait until the progress indicator (spinning striped cylinder) stops and the Time Machine menu icon returns to its idle state.

4   Quit System Preferences.

Delete the file and empty the Trash.

1   Drag the DeleteMe file to the Trash (or select DeleteMe and press Command-Delete).

2   In the Dock, click the Trash.

3   If there are any files you do not want to permanently erase, drag them to your desktop or otherwise relocate them from the Trash.

   NOTE ▸ Time Machine does not back up your Trash, so once you empty the Trash, you will not be able to restore files that were in the Trash before you made your first Time Machine backup.

4   Choose Finder > Empty Trash (or press Shift-Command-Delete).

5   At the message asking if you are sure, click Empty Trash.

Enter Time Machine and restore the text file.

1   From the Time Machine status menu, choose Enter Time Machine.

2   In the Finder window sidebar, click Desktop.

3   Click the arrow to go backward in time until you see your DeleteMe file.

4   Select the DeleteMe file, then click Restore.

5   Open the DeleteMe file to confirm that this was the file you originally created.

6   Quit TextEdit.

7   Delete the DeleteMe file and empty the Trash.

Clean Up

Since this is a test environment, stop using Time Machine from your server.

1   On your administrator computer, from the Time Machine status menu, choose Open
Time Machine preferences.

2   Click Select Disk.

3   Under Backup Disks, select the Time Machine destination you just used and click
Remove Disk.

4   At the message asking if you are sure, click Stop Using This Disk.

5   If the On/Off switch for Time Machine is not already set to Off, click the On/Off
switch to turn Time Machine off.

6   Quit System Preferences.

If necessary, eject the Time Machine Backups shared volume from your client computer.

1   On your administrator computer, in the Finder, press Command-N to open a new
Finder window.

2   In the Finder window, if the Time Machine Backups volume appears in the sidebar,
click Eject.

Configure the Time Machine service to stop offering your server's volume.

1 In the Server app, connect to your server.

2 In the Server app sidebar, select Time Machine.

3 Select the Time Machine Destinations shared folder, then click Remove (–).

4 At the message asking if you are sure, click Remove.

The Server app automatically turns off the Time Machine service (but it does not turn off the File Sharing service).

In this exercise you configured your server to be a network destination for Time Machine backups so client computers could keep a Time Machine backup in a centralized location. You made a limited backup, deleted a file, and then verified that you could restore that file from the Time Machine backup provided by your server.

Lesson 19

Providing Security via the VPN Service

A virtual private network (VPN) connection is like having an impossibly long Ethernet cable from a user's computer or device somewhere else in the world to your organization's internal network; your users can use VPN to encrypt all traffic between their computers or devices and computers inside your organization's internal network.

Don't confuse a firewall and VPN; a firewall can block network traffic based on several different possible criteria—such as the port number and source or destination address—and there is no authentication involved, but a user must authenticate in order to use the VPN service.

GOALS

▶ Understand the benefits of virtual private network (VPN)

▶ Configure the VPN service

Your organization may already have a network device that provides VPN service, but if you don't, consider using the OS X Server VPN service, which is both powerful and convenient, especially considering its tight integration with AirPort devices.

Reference 19.1
Understanding VPN

Even though your server can offer many of its services using SSL to secure the content of data being transferred, some services, like AFP, do not use SSL. In general, for services offered by OS X Server, authentication is almost always secure and encrypted over the network, but the payloads may not be. For example, without a virtual private network connection to encrypt traffic, the content of files transferred over AFP are not encrypted. So if an eavesdropper can capture unencrypted network traffic, he might not be able to reassemble credentials, but he can reassemble information to which you probably don't want him to have access.

If your organization does not have a dedicated network device that provides VPN service, you can use OS X Server to provide VPN service using the Layer 2 Tunneling Protocol (L2TP) protocol or using L2TP and the Point to Point Tunneling Protocol (PPTP) protocol. PPTP is considered less secure, but it is more compatible with older versions of Mac and Windows operating systems.

Regardless of what you use for VPN, you can configure your users' computers and devices to use VPN so that when they are outside of your organization's internal network, they have a secure connection to your internal network. If you provide VPN service for your users, you can use a firewall to allow services that you provide to all users, like the web and wiki service, but configure your firewall to block outside access to mail and file services. When your users are on the other side of the firewall from your server, they can use the VPN service to establish a connection as if they were on your internal network, and the firewall will not affect them; they can access all the services as if they were not remote.

The most difficult part of establishing a VPN connection falls outside the scope of this guide; you need to be sure that the router passes the appropriate traffic from outside your network to your server so that VPN clients can establish and maintain a VPN connection. See Apple Support article TS1629 for more information about well-known ports.

Reference 19.2
Configuring VPN with the Server App

The VPN service is configured and ready for you to start with the default options; just click the On/Off switch. This lesson explains the configuration options.

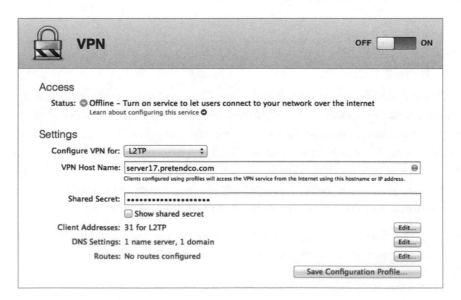

If you have older clients that aren't compatible with L2TP, click the "Configure VPN for" pop-up menu and choose L2TP and PPTP, to allow either protocol.

To allow you the flexibility of using an alternate DNS host name that clients use to access your server's VPN service, you can change the VPN Host Name field. When you modify the field, the status indicator is red if your server has no DNS record available for the host name your enter, and the status indicator is green to indicate the existence of a DNS record. Keep in mind that the host name you specify here will likely be used by people that are external to your local network; the host name you specify should have DNS records available outside of your local network as well.

For example, if your server is behind an AirPort device that provides DHCP and NAT, make sure that the host name you specify in the VPN Host Name field has a publicly accessible DNS record that matches the public IPv4 address of the AirPort device. The following figure from AirPort Utility's Network tab illustrates that the VPN service appears if you use the Server app to manage your AirPort device and make the VPN service available.

Selecting the VPN entry and clicking Edit results in the following dialog, which displays the VPN-related public UDP and TCP ports that are sent to your server.

To ensure confidentiality, authentication, and communications integrity, both the OS X Server VPN service and the VPN clients must use the same shared secret, which is like a passphrase. In order to establish a VPN connection, a user must still authenticate with her user name and password. By default, the Server app generates a random string of characters for the shared secret. You can change the string to something else, but it's best if this is a random string. This shared secret is included if you create a configuration profile to distribute to users. If you change the shared secret later, each of your users needs to update their VPN client configuration. Some ways of accomplishing this include:

▶ Save the configuration profile again, distribute it to your users, and have them install the new configuration profile.

▶ Use the Profile Manager service to distribute a configuration profile that includes VPN configuration, which automatically updates the shared secret in the configuration profile when it is installed or reinstalled.

▶ Instruct your users to manually enter the new shared secret at their VPN client.

Understanding Advanced Configuration Options

You could simply turn on the VPN service without configuring these advanced options, but if you have more than a few networked devices on your local network, you should at least review the configuration of the Client Addresses field, to ensure that local clients and VPN clients never accidentally get assigned the same IPv4 address.

The Client Addresses field shows the number of IPv4 addresses the VPN service hands out to VPN clients; click Edit to configure the range. If you've enabled both L2TP and PPTP, you can use a slider to distribute the number of clients available for each protocol.

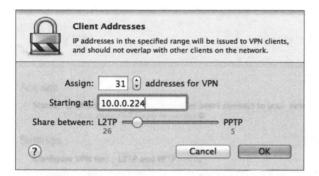

When you hover the pointer over the "Starting at" field, the Server app displays the effective IPv4 address range for each protocol, as shown in the following figure.

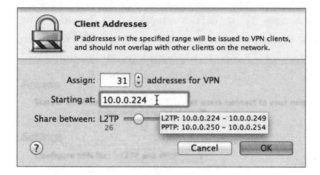

When a VPN client successfully connects to your server's VPN service, the VPN service assigns the VPN client an IPv4 address for your local network. Be sure that no other devices on your local network use an IPv4 address in the range that the VPN service issues to clients; you should configure your local network's DHCP service to not offer IPv4 addresses in the same range, and ensure that there are no devices with manually assigned IPv4 addresses in the same range.

Similarly, you can assign one or more default search domains that are appropriate for clients on your internal network.

By default, the VPN service configures VPN clients to use the same DNS server or servers, and the same search domain or search domains, that your server uses. This means that VPN clients have access to DNS records that are available for clients on your internal network only.

Click Edit next to the DNS Settings field to confirm that the DNS Settings are valid.

For example, for clients in your local network, server17.pretendco.com should resolve to 10.0.0.171, but clients not on your local network should have server17.pretendco.com resolve to a publicly accessible IPv4 address. Of course, pretendco.com is a domain intended for training purposes, and you should use a domain that you control instead of pretendco.com.

If you have a complex network configuration, you can specify additional routes and whether they are private or public. One example would be if you have multiple private subnets, as shown in the figure below.

Saving a Configuration Profile

After you've configured your VPN settings, you can create a configuration profile for your users; just click the Save Configuration Profile button in the VPN pane.

The configuration profile uses the VPN Host Name that you specify in the Server app's main configuration pane for the VPN service.

Having a configuration profile for a computer (a Mac with OS X Lion or later) or an iOS device makes it easy to set up a VPN connection; a user needs to provide only a user name and password, and doesn't need to enter the information that she would otherwise need to manually enter, such as the service type, VPN server address, and shared secret. By default, the configuration profile file name has a suffix of .mobileconfig and works with both Macs (Lion and later) and iOS devices.

You can also use the OS X Server Profile Manager service to create and distribute a configuration profile that contains VPN configuration information. If the VPN service is started, it is automatically included in the "Settings for Everyone" configuration profile. See Lesson 12, "Managing with Profile Manager," for more information.

Reference 19.3
Troubleshooting

The VPN service writes log messages to /var/log/ppp/vpnd.log, but when you use the Server app to view the logs, you don't need to know the log locations; just open the Logs pane and choose Service Log in the VPN section of the pop-up menu.

You might not understand all the information, but you might compare information about a trouble-free connection with information related to someone experiencing problems. In general, it is a good idea to keep examples of "known good" logs, so that you can use them as a reference when you are using logs to troubleshoot problems.

Exercise 19.1
Configure the VPN Service

▶ **Prerequisite**

    ▶ Exercise 10.1, "Create and Import Network Accounts"; or create a user with Full Name Barbara Green, Account Name barbara, and a password of net.

The VPN service is easy to configure and turn on. You will configure the VPN service on the server, save a profile with that configuration information, install the profile on your administrator computer, and start a VPN connection. In the instructor-led environment, we do not have the ability to configure the classroom router to allow VPN service for each student's server, so you will make a VPN connection from inside the classroom network, which is still a valid connection.

1   Perform these exercises on your administrator computer. If you do not already have a connection to your server computer with Server app on your administrator computer, then connect to it with the following steps: Open the Server app on your administrator computer, choose Manage > Connect to Server, click Other Mac, select your server, click Continue, provide administrator credentials (Administrator Name ladmin and Administrator Password ladminpw), deselect the "Remember this password" checkbox, and then click Connect.

    Be sure you are using your administrator computer so that you can install the configuration profile in the next exercise.

2   In the Server app sidebar, select VPN.

3   In the instructor-led environment, confirm that the VPN Host Name is your server's host name.

If you are performing the exercises independently and your router forwards all traffic, or all traffic on VPN-related ports, to your server's IPv4 address, you could configure the VPN Host Name to be a host name that maps to your server's publicly available IPv4 address.

4   Select the "Show shared secret" checkbox to view the shared secret.

Assign the range of client addresses.

You will assign addresses between 10.0.0.n6 and 10.0.0.n9, where n is your student number. For example, student 1's range is 10.0.0.16 through 10.0.0.19, and student 16's range is 10.0.0.166 through 10.0.0.169.

1   Next to Client Addresses, click the Edit button.

2   Enter 4 in the "Assign addresses for VPN" field.

3   Enter 10.0.0.n6 (where n is your student number) in the "Starting at" field.

4   Hover your pointer over the "Starting at" field until the range of IP addresses appears. Confirm that the range is what you expect.

5   Click OK to save the changes.

Turn on the VPN service.

1   Click the On/Off switch to turn on the service.

Save the configuration profile. The Save Configuration Profile button appears only when the service is on.

1   Click Save Configuration Profile.

2   Press Command-D to change the destination folder to your desktop.

3   Click Save.

See Lesson 12, "Managing with Profile Manager," for more information about distributing configuration profiles to computers and devices.

Install the VPN Profile on Your Administrator Computer

On your administrator computer, open and install the VPN configuration profile, and then open a VPN connection.

1   On your administrator computer, from the desktop, open the mobileconfig file (the default name is VPN.mobileconfig).

2   When System Preferences opens the mobileconfig file, click Show Profile.

3   Scroll through the profile and inspect its settings.

There are two things to note in the following figure (the window was resized in order to display all the information without scrolling). The configuration profile is not signed. And if you have configured your server to provide device management in the Profile Manager pane of the Server app, the configuration profile's Description field reflects the organization name you specified, rather than the server's host name.

4   Click Continue.

5   When asked to confirm, click Continue.

6   In the "Enter settings for 'VPN'" pane, leave Username blank, so that each user of this computer will be required to enter his own user name, and click Install.

7   When prompted, provide local administrator credentials and click OK.

The profile appears in the Profiles preferences' list of profiles.

NOTE ▶ If you have already completed Exercise 9.1, "Configure Your Server as an Open Directory Master," then the Description field will contain "VPN settings for Pretendco Project *n*," (where *n* is your student number).

Configure the VPN icon to appear in the menu bar so that users can start a VPN connection without opening System Preferences.

1   Click Show All to return to the list of all preferences.

2   Click Network.

3   In the list of interfaces, select the newly installed VPN entry.

4   Select the "Show VPN status in menu bar" option.

5   Click Connect.

6   At the VPN Connection pane, provide credentials for a local user or a local network user on your server and click OK.

You can use the user name barbara, and a password of net.

If you successfully authenticate and make a VPN connection, Status is shown as Connected, and you see connection information (Connect Time, IP Address, and Sent and Received traffic meters). As a reminder: In the figure below, the Account Name field is blank, so that each user of this Mac must provide both a user name and a password.

7   If you are not in an instructor-led environment and your Mac is outside your local network, confirm that you can access internal resources. For example, if your server's

Websites service is not already on, then on the server computer, use the Server app's Websites pane to turn the service on. Then on your administrator computer, open Safari, and in the Location field, enter your server's private IPv4 address. Confirm that the page opens as expected.

8   Click Disconnect.

Examine Logs

Use the Server app to inspect information related to the VPN service. You'll examine the information for a successful connection.

1   On your administrator computer, if you are not already connected to your server, open the Server app, connect to your server, and authenticate as a local administrator.

2   In the Server app sidebar, select Logs.

3   In the pop-up menu, choose Service Log under the VPN section.

   When you enter text in the search field, the Server app highlights entries that contain the text you entered.

4   In the search field, enter the name of the user you specified when making a VPN connection earlier.

   Note that the text you enter is highlighted as you type it.

5   Press Return to go to the next instance of your search term.

In this exercise you configured the VPN service with the Server app, used a configuration profile to quickly configure a VPN client, used System Preferences to quickly establish a VPN connection, and used the logs to view the VPN service log.

Exercise 19.2
Clean Up

On your administrator computer, remove the VPN profile to prepare for the other exercises.

1   In the Network preferences, deselect the "Show VPN status in menu bar" checkbox.

2   Click Show All.

3   Open Profiles.

4   Select the VPN profile.

5   Click the Remove (–) button.

6   Click Remove to remove the profile.

7   If asked, provide your local administrator credentials and click OK.

     Note that when there are no profiles, Profiles is not displayed in the available preferences.

8   Quit System Preferences.

9   In the Server app, click the On/Off switch for the VPN service to turn it off.

10   In the Finder, drag VPN.mobileconfig to the Trash, choose Finder > Empty Trash, and click Empty Trash.

Lesson 20

Understanding DHCP

You can use the OS X Server DHCP (Dynamic Host Configuration Protocol) service to dynamically configure network settings for computers and devices, so that you don't have to manually configure them. The word "Host" in "Dynamic Host Configuration Protocol" refers to the computers and devices that are DHCP clients. Although many networks now provide DNS and DHCP service as part of their basic infrastructure, you may want to use the OS X Server DHCP service because it is easier or more convenient to administer DHCP with the Server app than it is to administer with your network router's interface. Additionally, you can dedicate one or more of your server's network interfaces to providing DHCP, DNS, and NetInstall services to an isolated or dedicated NetInstall subnet (as Lesson 15, "Leveraging NetInstall," explains, NetInstall clients require DHCP service on the network in order to successfully start up from a network image).

Warning: If your network's infrastructure already provides DHCP service, *do not* turn on the OS X Server DHCP service; otherwise, client computers on your local network may no longer be able to function on the network (for instance, they may obtain an IPv4 address from your server's DHCP service that another DHCP service has already assigned, or they may start using a DNS server that isn't configured properly). You should not have more than one DHCP service active on the same network. Of course, it is possible for multiple DHCP servers to coordinate with each other, but the OS X Server DHCP service is designed as a standalone service.

GOALS

▶ Learn the function of DHCP

▶ Use the Server App to configure and manage the DHCP service

▶ Understand static addresses

▶ Identify current clients of OS X Server DHCP services

▶ Display the log files for the DHCP service

Reference 20.1
Understanding How DHCP Works

The process followed by a DHCP server granting an address to a client is well documented. The interaction occurs in this order:

1. A computer or device (host) on the network is configured to obtain network configuration information via DHCP. It broadcasts a request over its local network to see if a valid DHCP service is available.

2. A DHCP server receives the request from the host and responds with the appropriate information. In this example, the DHCP server proposes that the host use an IPv4 address of 172.16.16.5, along with some other network settings, including a valid subnet mask, router, DNS servers, and default search domain.

3. The host replies to the first DHCP offer it sees on the network; it sends a request for the IPv4 address of 172.16.16.5, the setting that the DHCP server just offered it.

4. The DHCP server formally acknowledges that the host can use the settings it requested. At this time, the host has a valid IPv4 address and can start using the network.

A key benefit provided by the DHCP server in this example is the assignment of configuration information to each host on the network. This negates the need to manually configure the information on each computer or device. When the DHCP server provides this configuration information, you are guaranteed that users will not enter incorrect information when configuring their network settings. If a network has been engineered properly, a new user can take a new Mac out of the box, connect to either a wired or wireless network, and automatically configure the computer with appropriate networking information. The user can then access network services without any manual intervention. This capability provides a simple way to set up and administer computers.

Understanding DHCP Networks

You can use OS X Server to offer DHCP service on multiple network interfaces. It is likely that each network interface will have different network settings, and that you will want to offer a different set of information to DHCP clients depending on what network they are on.

OS X Server uses the term "network" to describe a set of DHCP settings; a network includes the network interface on which you offer DHCP service, the range of IPv4 addresses you offer on that interface, and the network information to offer, including lease time, subnet mask, router, DNS server, and search domain. For clarity, this guide refers to this kind of network as a DHCP network. The DHCP network is the foundation of the DHCP service in OS X Server.

If you need to offer multiple ranges of IPv4 addresses per network interface, you can create multiple DHCP networks per network interface.

> **MORE INFO** ▶ Other DHCP services use the word "scope" to describe DHCP networks.

As part of your planning process, you should decide whether you need multiple DHCP networks or whether a single DHCP network will suffice.

Understanding Leases

A DHCP server leases an IPv4 address to a client for a temporary period, the lease time. The DHCP service guarantees that the DHCP client can use its leased IPv4 address for the duration of the lease. Halfway through the lease time, the host requests to renew its lease. The host relinquishes the address when the network interface is no longer in use, such as when the computer or device is shut down, and the DHCP service can assign that IPv4 address to another host if necessary. In the Server app, you specify a lease time of 1 hour, 1 day, 7 days, or 30 days.

If mobile computers and devices use your network, it's likely that they don't all need to be on your network at the same time. Leasing allows an organization to support a larger number of network devices than there are available IPv4 addresses by reusing IPv4 addresses over time. If this is the case for you, the lease time is one of the key options to consider when implementing a DHCP service; if network devices come and go often, consider a short lease time, so that once a network device leaves the network, its IPv4 address becomes available for a different network device more quickly.

Even if you have more available IPv4 addresses than devices, the fact that hosts need to periodically renew their DHCP leases means that you can make a change to the DHCP information you hand out, and hosts will eventually receive updated information when they renew their lease. If it is a big change, like an entirely different set of network settings, you can force a lease update by rebooting clients or by briefly disconnecting and then reconnecting their network connections.

Understanding Static and Dynamic Assignments

You can use the DHCP service to dynamically or statically assign an IPv4 address to individual computers and devices. Each computer or device's network interface has a unique MAC (Media Access Control) address, which is a physical attribute that cannot be easily changed; it uniquely identifies the network interface. The DHCP service associates a lease with a MAC address. The MAC address is also known as a physical or network address; an example of a MAC address is c8:2a:14:34:92:10. Understand the difference between a dynamic and a static address:

▶ Dynamic address—An IPv4 address is automatically assigned to a computer or device on a network. The address is typically "leased" to the computer or device for a specific period of time, after which the DHCP server either renews the lease of the address to that computer or device, or makes the address available to other computers and devices on the network.

▶ Static address—You assign an IPv4 address to a specific computer or device on the network and rarely change it. Static addresses can be applied to a computer or device manually, or by configuring the DHCP server to provide to a MAC address the same IPv4 address every time the computer or device with that MAC address connects to the network.

It is possible that you will have a combination of statically and dynamically assigned addresses on your network. One of the determining factors as to which address type is most appropriate is the use of the computer or device. For example, if the computer or device is a server, network appliance, or printer, you should consider a static address, whereas mobile computers and devices that come and go on your network would likely be assigned dynamic IPv4 addresses.

Understanding Serving Multiple Subnets

The location of the DHCP server has a direct impact on the viability of a DHCP implementation. When a network client asks for DHCP service, it uses the BootP (Bootstrap Protocol) network protocol. By default, most routers do not forward BootP traffic beyond network borders, whether physically separate subnets or programmatically separated VLANs (virtual local area networks). In order for network clients to receive DHCP service, the DHCP server must be providing DHCP service on the subnet via a network interface on that subnet, or the router must be configured to relay BootP traffic between subnets; this is sometimes referred to as configuring a helper address or a DHCP relay agent.

Reference 20.2
Configuring DHCP Service

This section details the necessary steps for using the Server app to configure OS X Server.

NOTE ▶ Do not turn on the DHCP service at this time; refer to the optional exercise for complete instructions.

The process for configuring DHCP with the Server app involves the following steps:

1. Configuring your server's network interface(s)
2. Editing and creating networks
3. Starting the DHCP service
4. Monitoring the DHCP service

NOTE ▶ You have to show the Advanced section of the Server app sidebar in order to select the DHCP service (or you could choose DHCP from the View menu).

Configuring Your Server's Network Interface

Before you can offer any services on a network interface, it needs to be configured and active. Use the Network preferences on your server to configure each network interface on which you intend to serve DHCP. The following figure shows a Mac mini configured with two extra USB to Ethernet adapters, so it can offer DHCP service on multiple networks.

Editing a Subnet

Your next step is to edit one or more subnets. This process includes the configuration of any optional settings, such as DNS information.

By default, when you open the DHCP pane in the Server app, the Networks tab displays one DHCP network, based on your server's primary network interface.

If you double-click this default DHCP network to edit it, you'll see that the name is based on the IPv4 address of your server's primary network interface, and the starting IPv4 address and ending IPv4 address is just a starting point. You need to edit the range of IPv4 addresses that DHCP service offers; your server's own IPv4 address is included in the range, and you do not want to hand out your server's IPv4 address to a client for the client to use. One default DHCP network's settings are shown in the following figure.

As you can see, the information you can specify for a DHCP network includes:

▶   Name

▶   Lease duration

▶   Network interface

▶   Starting IP address

▶ Ending IP address

▶ Subnet mask

▶ Router

Also, if you click the Edit button next to DNS, you can specify the following:

▶ DNS name server(s)

▶ Search domain(s)

When you create a new network, the Router, name server, and search domain fields are automatically populated from the values of the network interface that the new network uses.

> **NOTE** ▶ If you specify your server's IPv4 address to be a name server, be sure to configure your DNS service to perform lookups for all appropriate networks. Also note that OS X Server does not perform routing; it will not pass traffic from an otherwise isolated network out to the Internet.

In the Networks pane, you can configure multiple subnet ranges. For example, you can add an additional subnet range for a second range on an existing network interface or for a range on a different network interface. When you create a new DHCP network, the Server app will not allow you to specify a range of IPv4 addresses that another DHCP network already includes.

Click Add (+) to create a new DHCP network, and click Remove (–) to remove an existing DHCP network. Here's an example of the Server app displaying three DHCP networks, with two on the same subnet:

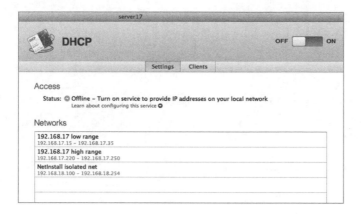

Starting the DHCP Service

To start the DHCP service; click the On/Off button to turn on the service.

> **NOTE ▶** Do not turn on the DHCP service at this time; refer to the optional exercise for complete instructions.

Monitoring and Configuring the DHCP Service

You can use the Server app to view information about the DHCP clients associated with the DHCP service. To view the DHCP client information, click the Clients tab.

> **TIP▶** You can change the size of the columns in the Server app window to display more information for a particular column.

The Clients pane provides the following information:

▶   Client (for Macs, this is the client's computer name)

▶   Type (Dynamic or Static)

▶   IP Address

▶   Network (DHCP network)

Assigning Static Addresses

In the Clients pane, the DHCP service allows you to create a static IPv4 address for a client; the Server app refers to this as a static address (some other DHCP servers call this a reservation). This allows you to benefit from the ease of using DHCP to configure network settings like subnet mask and DNS servers, while assigning static IPv4 addresses to key equipment (such as servers, printers, and network switches) automatically.

If you already know a network device's MAC address, it's simple to create a static address for it. In the Clients pane, click Add (+), assign a name, choose the DHCP network, assign an IPv4 address, and specify the MAC address:

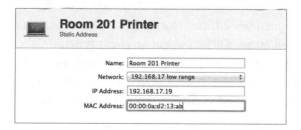

But what if you don't know the MAC address? You can create a static address for a DHCP client that already has a lease. In the Clients pane, select the client in the list, click the Action (gear icon) pop-up menu, and choose Create Static Address. In the following figure, the Unknown entry is a printer.

After you choose Create Static Address, you can specify the Name, Network, and IP Address; the MAC Address is pre-populated.

Reference 20.3
Troubleshooting DHCP

As with many network services, it is sometimes difficult to exactly locate the cause of a DHCP problem. At times, configuration errors will be present on client systems. Other times, problems with the network infrastructure will prevent the computers and devices on the network from communicating with the DHCP server. On occasion, issues arise when the DHCP server has not been configured correctly or is not behaving in an expected manner.

To think through the troubleshooting process, imagine that a specific computer or device on your network is unable to obtain a DHCP address from your server. First, troubleshoot the client, and then troubleshoot the server.

Ask the following questions when you are troubleshooting DHCP issues for OS X:

▶ Is the computer or device configured correctly on the network? Check physical network issues, such as cabling, broken routers or switches, and limitations of the physical subnet. Ensure that the appropriate network interfaces are active.

▶ Can you establish any network connection? Can you ping another host? Can you see another host over Bonjour?

▶ Is the configuration properly set up? Are you using addresses dynamically assigned via DHCP or manually assigned static address? If the problem is with DHCP, would a static address work?

▶ Is an IPv4 address assigned via DHCP or is the address self-assigned (169.254.x.x range)? Can you ping another host via both IPv4 address and host name? Can you perform a DNS lookup?

In this imaginary situation, you were able to connect to an external website by manually configuring the network interface with a static address, so you have concluded that the issue must lie with the server.

Ask the following questions when you are troubleshooting DHCP issues for OS X Server:

▶ Is the DHCP server configured correctly on the local network? Is the server reachable on the network via ping? Does the server have the proper IPv4 address?

▶ Is the DHCP service configured properly? Is the DHCP service turned on?

▶ Does the Server app show the expected DHCP client activity?

▶ Do the DHCP log entries match the expected DHCP client activity?

Examining the Logs

DHCP log entries are contained in the main System Log file. You can view the System Log using other utilities such as the Console app, but if you use the Server app's Logs pane to view the DHCP Service Log, only the DHCP entries will be displayed.

> **TIP** You can change the size of the Server app window to display log entries on a single line.

Apple's implementation of DHCP relies on BOOTP. That's why the DHCP process that runs on the server is listed as the bootpd process.

You can look for specific events by entering them in the search box at the top right of the pane. Note the specific DHCP entries and the general flow of the events for DHCP:

▶ DHCP DISCOVER—A DHCP client sends a discover message to look for DHCP servers.

▶ OFFER—A DHCP server responds to a client DHCP DISCOVER message.

▶ DHCP REQUEST—A DHCP client requests DHCP configuration information from the DHCP server.

▶ ACK—A DHCP server responds with DHCP configuration information for the DHCP client.

You can remember this chain of events with the acronym DORA: Discover, Offer, Request, Acknowledge.

You can also determine whether a client has received an IPv4 address from a DHCP server. If the DHCP server has run out of available network addresses, or no DHCP service is available, the client will automatically generate a self-assigned link-local address. Link-local addresses are always in the IPv4 address range of 169.254.x.x and have a subnet mask of 255.255.0.0. The network client will automatically generate a random link-local address and then check the local network to make sure no other network device is using that address. Once a unique link-local address is established, the network client will be able to establish connections only with other network devices on the local network.

Exercise 20.1
Configure DHCP Service (Optional)

> **NOTE** ▶ Skip this exercise if you do not have an additional isolated network and an additional network interface, or if you cannot disable DHCP on the router for the isolated network you are using with this guide.

Do not enable the DHCP service on a network that already has DHCP service.

Follow along with the steps in this exercise to configure an additional network interface on your server computer, disable the default DHCP network, and create a new DHCP network for an additional isolated network.

You will use your administrator computer as a DHCP client on an isolated network, as shown in the following figure.

Start out by making sure your extra isolated network is ready.

1   If you have a Mac Pro with multiple Ethernet ports, you can use the Ethernet port that you are not already using. Otherwise, connect the USB to Ethernet adapter, or the Thunderbolt to Gigabit Ethernet adapter, to your server computer.

2   Use an Ethernet cable to connect the Ethernet adapter (or your Mac computer's other network port) to an isolated network Ethernet switch.

Now that your server computer's other network interface is connected to an Ethernet switch, configure that network interface.

1   On your server computer, log in as a local administrator if you are not already logged in as a local administrator.

2   Open System Preferences.

3   Select Network.

4   Select the newly added, or unconfigured, network interface.

5   Click the Configure IPv4 pop-up menu and choose Manually.

6   Enter the following information:

IP Address: 192.168.n.1 (where n is your student number)

Subnet Mask: 255.255.255.0

Router: 192.168.n.1 (where n is your student number)

7   Click Advanced to set the DNS server and search domains.

8   Click the DNS tab.

9   For the DNS Server field, click Add (+) and enter 192.168.n.1 (where n is your student number).

10   For the Search Domains field, click Add (+) and enter pretendco.com.

11   Click OK to save the changes.

12 Click Apply.

Configure the DHCP service.

1 In the Server app sidebar, select DHCP. If the Server app does not display the Advanced services in the sidebar, then hover the pointer over the word "Advanced" and click Show.

2 Select the default DHCP network, which is based on your server's primary network interface.

3 Click Delete (–), and then click Delete.

4 Click Add (+) to create a new DHCP network.

5 Enter Extra Net in the Name field.

6 Click the Lease Duration pop-up menu, and choose 1 hour.

7 Click the Network Interface pop-up menu and choose the network interface you just configured at the beginning of this exercise.

8 Enter the following information:

Starting IP Address: 192.168.n.50 (where n is your student number)

Ending IP Address: 192.168.n.55 (where n is your student number)

9 If necessary, enter the following information:

Subnet Mask: 255.255.255.0

Router: 192.168.n.1 (where n is your student number)

10 For DNS, click Edit, and enter the following information, if necessary:

Provide these name servers to connected clients: 192.168.*n*.1 (where *n* is your student number).

Provide these search domains to connected clients: pretendco.com.

11 Click OK to dismiss the DNS Settings sheet.

12 Review the settings.

13 Click Create to save the changes.

Start the DHCP service.

1 Click the On/Off button to start the DHCP service.

2 At the notice that another DHCP service might be runnning, click Enable DHCP.

Use the following steps to connect your administrator computer to the extra isolated network, and allow it to obtain a DHCP address. Create a new network location for your administrator computer to use DHCP, and prepare to switch networks. A network location is a collection of all the settings for all your network interfaces, and switching between network locations allows you to quickly change network settings. See Lesson 23,

"Advanced Network Configuration," in *Apple Pro Training Series: OS X Support Essentials 10.9* for more information on network locations.

1   On your administrator server, quit the Server app if it is open.

2   In the Finder, press Command-N to open a new Finder window.

3   If there are any eject icons for network volumes in the Finder window sidebar, click them to eject all network volumes.

4   Connect your administrator computer's Ethernet cable to the isolated network's Ethernet switch.

Preserve your current network location so you can quickly return to it.

1   On your administrator computer, open System Preferences.

2   Choose View > Network.

3   If the current network location already has an appropriate name, move on to the next steps.

    If your current network Location is still named Automatic, click the Location pop-up menu, choose Edit Locations, double-click Automatic, enter Server Essentials, press Return to save the name change, click Done, and then click Apply.

Create a new network location.

1   Click the Location pop-up menu, and choose Edit Locations.

2   Click Add (+).

3   Enter DHCP as the new Location name, then click Done.

4   In the Location pop-up menu, choose the location named DHCP.

5   Confirm that the Location pop-up menu is set to DHCP.

6   Click Apply.

7   Leave the Network pane open so you can change locations again at the end of this exercise.

Without any configuration of your new location, each network interface is set to use DHCP. Wait for your administrator computer's Ethernet interface to receive a new IPv4 address assigned by DHCP.

Monitor the service and view the logs.

1   On your server computer, in the DHCP pane, click Clients.

2   From the View menu, choose Refresh (or press Command-R).

     Confirm that your administrator computer is listed.

3   In the Server app sidebar, select Logs.

4   Click the Logs pop-up menu and choose the Service Log under the DHCP section.

     Confirm that you can see the Discover, Offer, Request, and Acknowledge (Ack) traffic.

Clean Up

Change back your administrator computer's network location, reconnect to the network for the rest of the exercises, and turn off the DHCP service.

1   On your administrator computer, click the Location pop-up menu and choose Server Essentials.

2   Click Apply.

3   Disconnect your administrator computer's Ethernet cable from the isolated network switch.

4   Connect your administrator computer's Ethernet cable to the network switch you were using before this lesson.

5   In the Server app sidebar, select DHCP, and click the On/Off switch to turn off the service.

     Confirm that the status indicator next to DHCP in the Server app sidebar disappears, indicating that the service is off.

You enabled the DHCP service on a network interface that's connected to an isolated network. You confirmed that a client (your administrator computer) can obtain an IPv4 address from your server's DHCP service, and you viewed the DHCP service logs.

Lesson 21
Hosting Websites

OS X Server provides a simple interface for providing web hosting services. Based on open source, popular, and well-understood Apache, the OS X Server hosting facilities allow even a new administrator to bring a website online.

Reference 21.1
Web Service Software

This lesson helps you understand, manage, and secure the various aspects of the Apple web services, including managing high-bandwidth connections, sharing files, and locating log files for access, viewing, and troubleshooting.

The OS X Server web service is based on Apache, open source software commonly used in a variety of operating systems. It is a well-accepted and well-understood web server that is serving more than 60 percent of all the websites on the Internet.

As of this writing, the version installed in OS X Server is Apache 2.2.24.

To provide web hosting that is available to users on the Internet, proper DNS entries for external hosts must be registered and the OS X Server must be exposed to the Internet via a DMZ (demilitarized zone), also known as perimeter networking or port forwarding.

Reference 21.2
Understanding Basic Website Structure

Before you manage any websites, it is important to know where critical Apache and website files are stored. Commonly used Apache and Apple configuration files for web services are located in /Library/Server/Web.

Configuration files still exist at /private/etc/apache2/, which is normally hidden from view in the Finder, but they should not be manipulated. Apache modules—including Apple-specific modules (pieces of code that perform Apple-specific functions in Apache)—are located in /usr/libexec/apache2/, which is also normally hidden from view in the Finder. Apache modules will not be covered in this guide, but additional information can be found in external Apache documentation. The default location for the OS X Server website is in /Library/Server/Web/Data/Sites/.

All website files and the folders in which they normally reside must be at least read-only for Everybody or the "_www" user or group; otherwise, users won't be able to access the files with their web browsers when they visit your site.

Enabling and Disabling Websites

When managing websites on OS X Server, you use the Server app. You also use the Server app to manage file and folder permissions, thus allowing or restricting access to folders that are to be seen by web browsers, such as Safari.

Because OS X Server has preconfigured web services for the default website, all you need to do to start exploring is turn on the web service.

To disable a website, you simply remove it from the list of websites in the Server app. This does not remove the site files, just the reference to the site in the web service configuration files.

Managing Websites

To allow multiple websites to be hosted on one server, domain name, IP address, and port are used to separate sites from one another. For example, you can have two sites on the same IP address as long as their ports are different. You can also have two sites with the same IP address and different domain names. By editing and ensuring that one of these three parameters is unique, you are logically separating your sites. The URL to reach a server's webpage is its IP address or fully qualified domain name (FQDN), such as:

▶   http://10.0.0.171
    or
▶   http://server17.pretendco.com

This can be modified by adding a port definition, such as:

▶   http://server17.pretendco.com:8080
    or
▶   http://server17.pretendco.com:16080

Users visiting the site may need to be told the port value in order to access the site. Ports 80 and 443 are known by most browsers and do not require additional typing when entering the address.

Reference 21.3
Monitoring Web Services

Apache has excellent logging capabilities and uses two main files when logging website information: the Access log and the Error log. The log files can store all kinds of information, such as the address of the requesting computer, the amount of data sent, the date and time of transaction, the page requested by the visitor, and a web server response code.

Log files, named access_log and error_log, are located inside /var/log/apache2/ and are readable via the Server app. The Apache logs are parsed to display the access and error logs per site. While the logs are also viewable in the Console app, they are not parsed and they will need to be filtered to find entries for specific sites.

Reference 21.4
Troubleshooting

To troubleshoot web services, it helps to understand how the service works and what pieces control what aspects of the service. Here are some areas to investigate:

▶   Check if the Websites service is running by verifying that a green status indicator dot appears next to the service in the Server app.
▶   Check that the website is pointing to the location where the website files are stored.

▶ Verify that the website files and directory can be read by the _www user or group or by the group Everybody.

▶ Check if there are site restrictions as to who can access the site.

▶ Check that the appropriate networking ports aren't blocked to the server (80 for http, 443 for https, and any others that may have been defined for a specific website).

▶ Check that the proper IP address has been set for the website.

▶ Use Network Utility to check that DNS resolves properly for the website's fully qualified domain name (FQDN).

Exercise 21.1
Enable Web Services

▶ **Prerequisites**

▶ Exercise 3.1, "Configure DNS Services"

▶ Exercise 10.1, "Create and Import Network Accounts"

The Websites service is very easy to configure and use. This exercise will get OS X Server prepared to host websites.

Start the Websites Service

To use the Websites service, you must first enable it as a service in the Server app.

1   Without having turned on the Websites service, open Safari on your administrator computer and connect to http://10.0.0.*n*1 (where *n* is your student number). Observe the page, and then in the Location field, enter the FQDN (http://server*n*.pretendco.com, where *n* is your student number), and make sure you can observe the page again. Refresh the page if necessary.

2   Note that even though you haven't turned on the Websites service, a basic webpage appears telling you that the web service is not on.

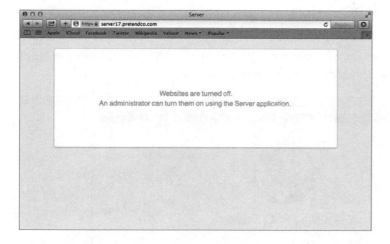

3   Perform these exercises on your administrator computer. If you do not already have a connection to your server computer with Server app on your administrator computer, then connect to it with the following steps: Open the Server app on your administrator computer, choose Manage > Connect to Server, click Other Mac, select your server, click Continue, provide administrator credentials (Administrator Name ladmin and Administrator Password ladminpw), deselect the "Remember this password" checkbox, and then click Connect.

4   In the Server app, select Websites in the sidebar. Click the On/Off switch at the top of the window to turn on the service.

5 Again, open Safari on your administrator computer and connect to http://10.0.0.*n*1 (where *n* is your student number). Observe the page, and then enter the FQDN (http://server*n*.pretendco.com, where *n* is your student number), and make sure you can observe the page again. Refresh the page if necessary.

NOTE ▶ Notice that you did not configure the website in any way. The OS X Server web service is set to serve up the default webpage automatically.

6 Once more, open Safari on your administrator computer, and connect to https://10.0.0.*n*1 (where *n* is your student number). Observe the page, and then enter the FQDN (https://server*n*.pretendco.com, where *n* is your student number), and make sure you can observe the page again. Refresh the page if necessary. This connects to the SSL-protected version of the site.

View Website Parameters

Understanding what parameters OS X Server sets for the default website is helpful, as you will often want to adjust or change some of them on your other sites.

1 In the Server app on your administrator computer, select the Websites service.

2 Select the default website, and click the Edit (pencil icon) button below the Websites field.

Although you are looking at the default website, items to be defined and entered for any new websites would include:

▶ Store Site Files In—The location of the files served up by the selected site. The arrow button opens a Finder window at the location where the site files are stored.

▶ Who Can Access—Allows the site to require authentication for access.

▶ Additional Domains—Alternate domain names for the site.

▶ Redirects—Redirects requests to other URLs.

▶ Aliases—Makes folders accessible via multiple URLs.

▶ Index Files—The index files used when not defined when entered in a browser.

▶ Edit Advanced Settings—Set site advanced preferences.

3   Click Cancel to return.

Create a New Website

Now that you have viewed the general parameters, you will create a secondary website based on a second IP address, FQDN, and port number.

> **NOTE** ▶ OS X Server can have multiple IP addresses on a single interface, or more than one network interface. Therefore, it is important to distinguish IPv4 addresses as mapped to certain sites. Entering this information limits the site to just the entered parameters.

> **NOTE** ▶ Port 443 assumes SSL access to a site, which you will enable later.

1   On your server, open System Preferences, click Network, click Add (+), choose your primary network interface in the Interface pop-up menu, and click Create.

2 Select the new interface, click the Configure IPv4 pop-up menu, and choose Manually. Assign the IP Address of 10.0.0.*n*5 (where *n* is your student number) with a Subnet Mask of 255.255.255.0, Router 10.0.0.1, DNS Server 127.0.0.1, and Search Domain pretendco.com. Click Apply.

3 Still on the server, open TextEdit and create a new document. In the document, add the text My New Website! Press Command-S to save the file. In the Save As field, enter index.html. Press Command-D to set the Where pop-up menu to Desktop. Click the File Format pop-up menu and choose Web Page (.html). Click Save.

4 Use the Finder to navigate to /Library/Server/Web/Data/Sites and make a new folder called MyNewWebsite.

5 Drag index.html into /Library/Server/Web/Data/Sites/MyNewWebsite. Provide administrator credentials if prompted.

6 On your server, in the Server app Websites pane, click the Add (+) button to create a new site, and enter the following information:

▶ Domain Name: server*n*.pretendco.com (where *n* is your student number)

▶ IP Address: Any

▶ Port: 8080

▶ SSL Certificate: None

▶ Store Site Files In: Select Other, navigate to /Library/Server/Web/Data/Sites/MyNewWebsite, and then click Choose.

▶ Who Can Access: Anyone

7   Click Create to serve the new webpage.

8   On your administrator computer, in Safari, enter http://server*n*.pretendco.com:8080 (where *n* is your student number) in the address bar and press Return to contact the site.

Your edited webpage appears from your directory over the port you chose, 8080.

NOTE ▶ You can see the proper site because you have defined a different port from the default server website.

9 If you try accessing http://server*n*.pretendco.com (where *n* is your student number), you'll see that it defaults back to the original OS X Server default page.

Modify the website so that it responds to a different host name. Lesson 3, "Providing DNS," contains directions for creating the appropriate DNS records for www.pretendco.private at 10.0.0.*n*5 (where *n* is your student number). The following figures illustrate the necessary DNS records.

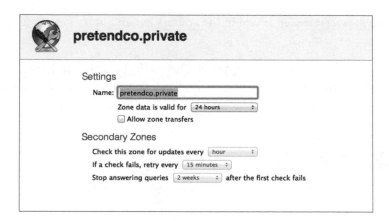

10 Click the Edit button for the website and change the following:

▶ Domain Name: www.pretendco.private

▶ IP Address: 10.0.0.n5 (where n is your student number)

▶ Port: 80

▶ Click Done and when prompted, click Use 10.0.0.n5 (where n is your student number).

NOTE ▶ You may need to quit and reopen the Server app to recognize the new network interface.

11 In Safari, enter http://www.pretendco.private in the address bar and press Return to contact the site.

Your edited webpage from your directory appears. This works because you have defined a specific IP for that site to respond to and a DNS record that responds with that IP address when using the FQDN for www.pretendco.private.

12 Quit Safari.

Verify Folder Access

For proper website behavior, it is imperative that folder permissions (and file permissions, to some extent) be set up with adequate access, as well as appropriate controls. At a minimum, the Everyone group must have read access for Apache to serve the files. It is also acceptable for the www (shown as _www) user or group to have read-only access.

To check if permissions are read-only for All:

1   Open the Server app on the server computer and navigate to the Websites service.

2   Select any site, click the Edit (pencil icon) button, and then click the arrow icon.

    This opens a Finder window at the site folder.

3   View the standard permissions on the folder via Get Info (Command-I or Control-click) in the lower half of the window. Notice that for everyone, permissions are set to Read Only. This allows all users, including _www, to access that folder.

Manage Website Access

OS X Server provides a mechanism to control access to a whole website or portions of the site that can only be accessed by certain users or groups.

Controlling access can be incredibly useful when dealing with websites that contain sensitive information or sections of a site that should only be accessible to one person or group. For example, you could set up a website so that only those users in a given group can access the site. You could also set up a portion of the site so that only a department has access to those particular pages. In most cases, access limitations are set up after users and groups are created, because the access to certain web directories is based on users, groups, or both.

1   In the Server app, use the Groups pane to create a new group with the Full Name of WebAccess. Edit the WebAccess group to add Sue Wu as a member.

2   In the Server app, use the Websites pane to select the www.pretendco.private site. Click the Edit button.

3   Set the Who Can Access menu to WebAccess. Click OK and accept the IP warning if one is given.

4   In Safari, enter http://www.pretendco.private in the address bar and press Return to contact the site.

5   Authenticate with Sue Wu and her password net. Members of the WebAccess group will be able to access the site. Try again with a user who isn't a member of the WebAccess group. You may need to quit Safari and reopen it to allow another login attempt.

6   Quit Safari.

Exercise 21.2
Secure Your Website

▶ **Prerequisite**

- ▶   Exercise 21.1, "Enable Web Services"

Most web traffic travels across the network in clear text, meaning that the content can be viewed by anyone who captures the web data. For many situations this is acceptable, but any time sensitive information is sent across the wire a method of protection is required.

It's very easy to encrypt the web traffic using SSL (Secure Sockets Layer) and a certificate.

Use SSL

OS X Server makes it easy to turn on SSL for a website. During the process of turning on SSL, the default port of the website changes from 80 to 443. You will create a new website using the host name ssl.pretendco.private. Lesson 3, "Providing DNS," contains directions for creating the appropriate DNS records for ssl.pretendco.private at 10.0.0.n3 (where n is your student number).

1   Using the same technique as you did with Exercise 21.1, use the Network system preferences to create a new IPv4 address using your primary network interface. Assign the address of 10.0.0.n3 (where n is your student number).

2   Open the Server app and connect to your server again.

3 Open TextEdit and create a new document. In the document, add the text My New SSL Website! Press Command-S to save the file. In the Save As field, enter index.html. Press Command-D to set the Where pop-up menu to Desktop. Click the File Format pop-up menu and choose Web Page (.html). Click Save.

4 Use the Finder to navigate to /Library/Server/Web/Data/Sites, and make a new folder called MyNewSSLWebsite.

5 Drag index.html into /Library/Server/Web/Data/Sites/MyNewSSLWebsite. Provide administrator credentials if prompted.

6 In the Websites service, click the Add (+) button to create a new site, and enter the following information:

NOTE ▶ You may need to close and reopen the Server app for the new IP address to show up in the list.

▶ Domain Name: ssl.pretendco.private

▶ IP Address: 10.0.0.n3 (where *n* is your student number)

▶ Port: 80

▶ Store Site Files In: Select Other, navigate to /Library/Server/Web/Data/Sites/MyNewSSLWebsite, and then click Choose.

▶ Who Can Access: Anyone

7 Click Create.

8 In Safari, enter http://ssl.pretendco.private in the address bar and press Return to contact the site.

Your edited webpage from your directory appears.

NOTE ▶ Notice that the site isn't protected by SSL yet, as you haven't provided an SSL certificate for the website to use.

9 In the Server app, select the SSL website you just made and click the Edit (pencil icon) button.

10 Choose the available SSL certificate in the SSL Certificate pop-up menu.

NOTE ▶ In the example shown, a self-signed certificate that was automatically generated by the server is being used, but this will cause a certificate warning to appear in users' browsers since it is untrusted. To prevent this, consider buying a certificate from a known certificate authority, using the host name of the server requested.

11 View the details of the ssl.pretendco.private website in the Server app, and notice that the port has been changed to 443 from 80. Click Done.

12 In Safari, access https://ssl.pretendco.private. Click the lock to the left of the URL and click Show Certificate to see the details of the certificate used to secure the website.

Exercise 21.3
Monitor Web Services

When administering a website, it is important to understand how OS X Server handles Apache log files, where they are stored, and how to view them.

To view Apache log files for a given site:

1   Open the Server app and select Logs. Choose Access Log (www.pretendco.private) from the pop-up menu.

2   On your administrator computer, open the Terminal app (click LaunchPad, click Others, and click Terminal). Then enter

ab -n 10000 -c 50 http://www.pretendco.private/

and press Return.

This is an Apache test tool that tells your OS X computer to ask for 10,000 (the -n parameter) requests run concurrently by 50 (the -c parameter) pretend users' concurrent connections.

3   View the log and watch the requests get logged.

4   On your administrator computer, open Safari and type the following:

http://server*n*.pretendco.com/nada.html (where *n* is your student number)

This page does not exist; therefore, it will log an error.

5   Using Logs, check the error log for the error by searching for "nada." You will see an error generated by the bad request.

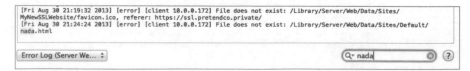

Exercise 21.4
Disable a Website

There is no button or checkbox to disable a website. You must remove the website from the Websites service, but when you do that, it leaves the files in place.

1   Open the Server app and select Websites.

2   Select the ssl.pretendco.private site and click the Remove (–) button at the bottom of the pane. Click Remove to confirm.

3   In the Finder, navigate to /Library/Server/Web/Data/Sites/MyNewSSLWebsite and confirm that the files still exist for the site.

Clean Up

No changes are required for this lesson, as the work you have just done turning on the Websites service and configuring website hosting will not impact other lessons.

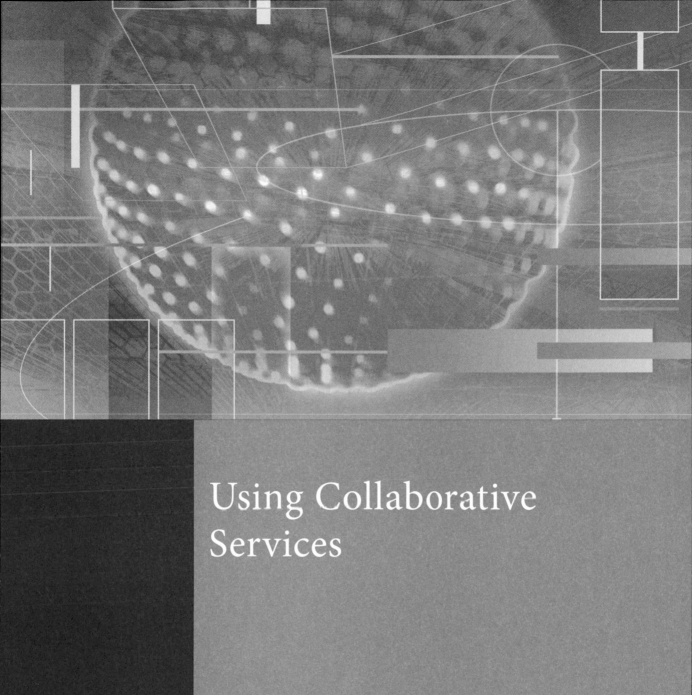

Using Collaborative Services

Lesson 22
Providing Mail Service

OS X Server provides a simple interface for setting up a capable and standards-based email service. While setting up email servers in the past has been fraught with complication, the configuration of this service in OS X Server has been simplified, yet still allows administration of the deeper details.

GOALS

▶ Set up the Mail service

▶ Configure email accounts for users

▶ Filter email for viruses and spam

Reference 22.1
Hosting Mail Services

Email is one of the fundamental services on the Internet. OS X Server includes a feature-rich email service you can use to send, receive, and store email for your organization. Aside from the obvious reason of hosting an email server to gain an Internet identity, a number of other factors make hosting your own mail service advantageous. If you have a small office with a slow Internet connection, you may find that keeping all of your email within the building rather than using external email servers makes better use of your network bandwidth. This is especially true if typical messages within your organization include large attachments. Additionally, many organizations are required to keep the information held in their email messages secure for regulatory or competitive reasons. Hosting your own email server in-house can keep confidential data from falling into the wrong hands. You may also find that various third-party email services don't offer the exact services you want. By running your own mail servers, you can customize various options to meet the needs of your organization.

The Mail service in OS X Server is based on two open-source email packages:

▶ Postfix handles acceptance and delivery of individual messages.

▶ Dovecot accepts connections from individual users downloading their messages to their mail client. Dovecot is a replacement for Cyrus, found in 10.5 and earlier versions of OS X Server.

In addition to these programs, the Mail service in OS X Server makes use of a number of other packages to provide features, such as spam and virus scanning. Each of these is discussed in this lesson, but first you must learn how email works.

Understanding Mail

Although email is one of the oldest and simplest systems on the Internet, it is composed of a number of different protocols. The primary protocol is Simple Mail Transfer Protocol (SMTP), which is responsible for delivering a message from the sender to the sender's email server and between email servers. When a message is sent, the outgoing mail server first looks up the address of the destination's Mail exchange (MX) server using DNS. A given Internet domain can have multiple MX servers to help balance the load and provide redundant services. Each MX server is assigned a priority. The highest-priority servers are assigned the lowest number and are tried first when delivering mail via SMTP. In the following image, the priority number follows right after the record type (for example, the first MX record has a priority of 20).

To look up information about a domain's MX servers, you can use the Terminal app by entering dig –t MX apple.com.

```
server17:~ ladmin$ dig -t MX apple.com

; <<>> DiG 9.8.3-P1 <<>> -t MX apple.com
;; global options: +cmd
;; Got answer:
;; ->>HEADER<<- opcode: QUERY, status: NOERROR, id: 32711
;; flags: qr rd ra; QUERY: 1, ANSWER: 11, AUTHORITY: 8, ADDITIONAL: 1

;; QUESTION SECTION:
;apple.com.                     IN      MX

;; ANSWER SECTION:
apple.com.              3011    IN      MX      20 mail-in24.apple.com.
apple.com.              3011    IN      MX      100 mail-in100.apple.com.
apple.com.              3011    IN      MX      10 mail-in6.apple.com.
apple.com.              3011    IN      MX      20 mail-in22.apple.com.
apple.com.              3011    IN      MX      10 mail-in4.apple.com.
apple.com.              3011    IN      MX      20 mail-in25.apple.com.
apple.com.              3011    IN      MX      20 mail-in23.apple.com.
apple.com.              3011    IN      MX      10 mail-in7.apple.com.
apple.com.              3011    IN      MX      10 mail-in2.apple.com.
apple.com.              3011    IN      MX      10 mail-in5.apple.com.
apple.com.              3011    IN      MX      20 mail-in21.apple.com.

;; AUTHORITY SECTION:
apple.com.              15944   IN      NS      adns1.apple.com.
apple.com.              15944   IN      NS      nserver5.apple.com.
apple.com.              15944   IN      NS      nserver.apple.com.
apple.com.              15944   IN      NS      adns2.apple.com.
apple.com.              15944   IN      NS      nserver2.apple.com.
apple.com.              15944   IN      NS      nserver4.apple.com.
apple.com.              15944   IN      NS      nserver6.apple.com.
apple.com.              15944   IN      NS      nserver3.apple.com.

;; ADDITIONAL SECTION:
adns1.apple.com.        15944   IN      A       17.151.0.151

;; Query time: 0 msec
;; SERVER: 127.0.0.1#53(127.0.0.1)
;; WHEN: Sat Aug 31 10:10:22 2013
;; MSG SIZE  rcvd: 502

server17:~ ladmin$
```

An individual email message may travel through many servers while en route to its final destination. Each server that a message passes through will tag a message with the name of the server and the time it was processed. This is done to provide a history of which servers handled a given message. To examine this trail using the Mail application, you can choose View > Message > Long Headers while viewing the message.

```
Received:  from cooper ([127.0.0.1]) by localhost (cooper.pretendco.com [127.0.0.1]) (amavisd-new, port
           10024) with ESMTP id 09379-03 for <david.pugh@pretendco.com>; Sat, 21 Sep 2002
           15:31:32 -0400 (EDT)
Received:  from mail-out4.apple.com (mail-out4.apple.com [17.254.13.23]) by cooper (Postfix) with
           ESMTP id 5D5B9B7C672 for <david.pugh@pretendco.com>; Sat, 21 Sep 2002 15:31:32
           -0400 (EDT)
Received:  from relay14.apple.com (relay14.apple.com [17.128.113.52]) by mail-out4.apple.com (Postfix)
           with ESMTP id 292BD251CA2; Sat, 21 Sep 2002 15:31:31 -0700 (PDT)
Received:  from relay14.apple.com (unknown [127.0.0.1]) by relay14.apple.com (Symantec Mail Security)
           with ESMTP id 0E96B20A4C; Sat, 21 Sep 2002 15:31:31 -0700 (PDT)
Received:  from [17.09.21.02] (sep21-2002.apple.com [17.09.21.02]) (using TLSv1 with cipher AES128-
           SHA (128/128 bits)) (No client certificate requested) by relay14.apple.com (Apple SCV relay)
           with ESMTP id E1B20A24685; Sat, 21 Sep 2002 15:31:30 -0700 (PDT)
```

Once the email message is delivered to the recipient's mail server, it will be stored there for the recipient to receive the message using either of the two available protocols:

▶ Post Office Protocol (POP) is a common email retrieval protocol used on mail servers where disk space and network connections are at a premium. POP is preferred in these environments because a mail client will connect to the server, download the email, remove it from the server, and disconnect very quickly. Although good for the server, POP mail servers are typically less user-friendly because they don't support server-side folders and may cause difficulties for a user connecting from multiple devices.

▶ Internet Message Access Protocol (IMAP) is commonly used by mail services that want to provide more features to the user. IMAP allows the storage of all email and email folders on the server, where they can be backed up. Additionally, a mail client will often remain connected to the mail server for the duration of the user session. This can result in quicker notification of new messages. The downside to using IMAP is that it puts more load on the resources of the mail server.

Configuring DNS for Mail

When you send an email, you'll need to ensure that DNS is configured for your domain so that mail can be delivered to the proper address. DNS can be provided by a DNS hosting company or by using your own DNS servers. While the examples here will rely on the basic DNS service provided by the OS X Server, additional DNS would be needed for a "real-life" email server setup.

Specifically you will need to set up an MX record for the domain. The MX record is how the sending email server knows where to send the email. Without an MX record, the server will utilize an A record for the domain listed. Considering that often the email server will be a different server than that used for hosting a domain's website, this may not be a good situation, as the mail might be delivered to the wrong location.

Relaying Outgoing Mail

The OS X Server email service has the option to relay outgoing email through another SMTP server. This can be important if you don't want to run your own SMTP service with the attendant issues with blacklists, or if the ISP you use doesn't allow you to host your own SMTP server.

Most likely you'll need user credentials to connect to the ISP's SMTP server. If your ISP allows non-authenticated connections to the SMTP server, it will most likely be tagged an open relay at some point in the blacklists. If your ISP doesn't require credentials to connect, find a new SMTP service that does to prevent problems down the line.

Enabling Mail Quotas for Users

To enable a mail storage quota for a user, the Server app provides a simplified management tool as compared to earlier versions of Server. A difference with OS X Server is that the same quota is applied to all users.

A quota can be helpful to manage the amount of mail users can retain on the email server, but it can also limit them if they exceed their limit and they miss email because of full mailbox errors.

Enabling Incoming Mail Virus Scanning

A common concern when running a mail server is how to protect your users from viruses. The OS X email service uses the ClamAV virus scanning package for this purpose. The virus definitions are updated on a regular basis using a process called freshclam. Any email that has been identified as containing a virus is stored in the /Library/Server/Mail/Data/scanner/virusmails folder and is deleted after a period of time. An alert is sent to the defined recipients in the Server app Alert notifications.

Enabling Incoming Mail Blacklists, Greylists, and Junk Filtering

Blacklists are lists of domains known to host junk mail or other unwanted email servers. By subscribing to a blacklist, your email server will scan the incoming email, compare the host IP from where it came, and allow it to pass or not based on whether or not that host IP is listed. By default, the OS X Server email service utilizes the blacklist hosted by the Spamhaus Project, but you can change this to any other blacklist.

The danger of using a blacklist is that sometimes innocent hosts can get listed, and thus proper and desired emails can get blocked from delivery to your users. Getting off black-lists can be daunting and may result in lost email.

Greylists are a method of spam control that tosses out the initial attempt of a sender to send an email to an email server. A legitimate email sender will try sending the message again, whereas a spam producer usually only tries once.

The OS X Server email service can also use the SpamAssassin software package to scan incoming email and rank its likelihood of being spam. The text of the message is analyzed using a complex algorithm given a number that reflects how likely it is to be spam. This can be remarkably accurate unless the email contains terms and words commonly applied to spam. To counteract this, you can manage the service by adjusting what score is con-sidered spam. Certain types of organizations, such as a school, might need to use higher scores, while others, like a medical office, might use a lower score.

The levels of score are:

▶ Aggressive—The filter tolerates few signs of being junk mail.

▶ Moderate—The filter tolerates some signs of being junk mail.

▶ Cautious—The filter tolerates many signs of being junk mail.

Messages that are tagged as spam have the subject line appended by ***JUNK MAIL*** and are sent on to the recipient. The recipient can then either delete the mail, open it, or possibly configure a filter in the mail client to move it to a junk folder.

Reference 22.2
Troubleshooting Mail Services

To troubleshoot the Mail service as provided by OS X Server, it helps to have a good understanding of how email works in general. Review the previous sections to make sure you understand each of the working pieces.

Here are some common problems and suggestions for rectifying them:

▶ DNS problems—If the domain doesn't have proper MX records associated with it, other email servers may not be able to locate your email server to deliver the messages. You can utilize Network Utility to do a DNS lookup of your domain.

▶ Service issues—Utilize the Logs tab in the Server app to review the Mail log for clues as to why the service might not start or work properly.

▶ Can't send or receive email—Review the SMTP log for problems with users not being able to send mail, and the POP and IMAP logs for problems with users not being able to receive mail.

▶ Too much spam being sent to the users—Increase the spam filtering rating in the filtering preferences in the Mail service in the Server app.

▶ Too many real emails being marked as spam—Decrease the spam filtering rating in the filtering preferences in the Mail service in the Server app.

Exercise 22.1
Enable the Mail Service

▶ **Prerequisites**

  ▶ Exercise 3.1, "Configure DNS Services"
  ▶ Exercise 10.1, "Create and Import Network Accounts"; or use the Server app to create users Barbara Green and Todd Porter, each with an account name that is the same as their first name in lowercase, and a password of net.

The OS X Server email service is configured using the Server app. The interface is very elegant and relatively complication-free.

1   Perform these exercises on your administrator computer. If you do not already have a
     connection to your server computer with Server app on your administrator computer,
     then connect to it with the following steps: Open the Server app on your administra-
     tor computer, choose Manage > Connect to Server, click Other Mac, select your server,
     click Continue, provide administrator credentials (Administrator Name ladmin and
     Administrator Password ladminpw), deselect the "Remember this password" checkbox,
     and then click Connect.

2   Select your server. Click Certificates, and check that the default SSL certificates apply
     to all services.

3   Select the Mail service in the left column. Click Edit next to "Provide mail for" and
     enter the domain (pretendco.com). In this situation we want to use the pretendco.com
     domain and not a subdomain such as server17.pretendco.com. Click OK.

4   Turn on the Mail service. This may take a few minutes while the virus definitions are downloaded.

Relay Outgoing Mail

To set up the option to relay outgoing email through another SMTP server:

1   In the Mail service pane in the Server app, select the "Relay outgoing mail through ISP" option.

2   Click the Edit button.

3   If needed, fill in the SMTP server information provided by your ISP, including the user credentials, and click OK. This is not needed for the exercise. If you are performing this exercise in an instructor-led environment, this is not necessary, so click Cancel.

Enable Mail for a User

Unlike in earlier versions of OS X Server, enabling email services for a user is a one-step process. You simply need to provide an email address for the user in the user's record.

1   When editing an existing user or making a new user, add an email address for the user in the Email Address field and save the change. Enter email addresses for Barbara Green and Todd Porter (barbara@pretendco.com and todd@pretendco.com).

Enable Mail Quotas for Users

Setting up quotas for the Mail service is very simple and quick:

1   In the Mail service pane in the Server app, select the "Limit mail to" checkbox.

2   Enter a quota in MB, and click outside the checkbox to make it active.

Enable Incoming Mail Virus Scanning

Almost every email server will have some level of virus scanning enabled. This is how to enable it in OS X Server:

1   In the Mail service pane in the Server app, click the Edit Filtering Settings button.

2   Select the "Enable virus filtering" option to make it active if it is not active already.

Enable Incoming Mail Blacklists, Greylists, and Junk Filtering

Here's how to enable blacklists, greylists, and junk mail filtering for the OS X Server Mail service:

1   In the Mail service pane in the Server app, click the Edit Filtering Settings button.

2   Select the "Enable blacklist filtering" and "Enable greylist filtering" options to make them active. You can use the default zen.spamhaus.org blacklist service or replace it with another. Deselect the checkbox to turn off blacklist filtering.

3 Select the "Enable junk mail filtering" option to make active. Move the slider to the
score desired for junk mail sensitivity. Move it between Aggressive and Moderate.
Click OK when done.

Exercise 22.2
Send and Receive Mail

▶ **Prerequisite**

▶ Exercise 22.1, "Enable the Mail Service"

In this exercise you'll use the Internet Accounts preferences to configure the Mail app for
Todd Porter, so you will create an account for, and log in as, Todd Porter on your admin
istrator computer. You'll see how easy it is to send mail and reply to it.

Set Up the Mail Application with the Internet Accounts Preferences

Use the Internet Accounts preferences for Todd Porter.

1 On your administrator computer, create a new user named Todd Local (Name toddlocal,
Password toddlocalpw) in the Users and Groups System Preferences pane.

2 On your administrator computer, log out.

3 Log in as Todd Local; you may need to complete the OS X Setup Assistant.

4 If the iCloud preferences open automatically, click Show All in the System Preferences
toolbar.

5   If System Preferences is not already open, open System Preferences.

6   Open Internet Accounts.

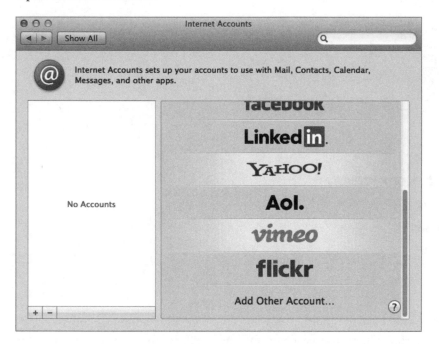

7   Scroll down in the right pane to Add Other Account and click it.

8   In the account type pane, select "Add a Mail account" and click Create.

9   Provide the following information:

▶   Full Name: Todd Porter

▶   Email Address: todd@pretendco.com

▶   Password: net

10   Click Create.

11   If you have not provided an MX record, the server responsible for email for Todd's account won't be found. Click Next.

12   In the Incoming Mail Server Info pane, enter the following information and then click Next. Accept the certificate warning if you get it:

▶   Account Type: IMAP

▶   Mail Server: server*n*.pretendco.com (where *n* is your student number)

▶ User Name: todd

▶ Password: net

13 In the Outgoing Mail Server Info pane, enter the following information and then click
Create:

▶ SMTP Server: server*n*.pretendco.com (where *n* is your student number)

▶ User Name: todd

▶ Password: net

14 Repeat this process on your server computer using the Barbara Green account. You don't have to log in as Barbara; just configure the email account. Now you have two computers with two accounts that are configured and ready to communicate with each other.

Use the Mail Application as Todd Porter

Use the Mail application as Todd Porter to send mail to Barbara Green.

1 On your administrator computer, open Mail by clicking it in your Dock. Accept the certificate error if you get it.

2 In the toolbar, click the "Compose new message" button (looks like a pencil and paper).

3 In the To field, enter barbara@pretendco.com.

4 In the Subject field, enter Hi Barbara!

5   In the Main mail window, enter Hi Barbara, Hope you are having a great trip! –Todd.

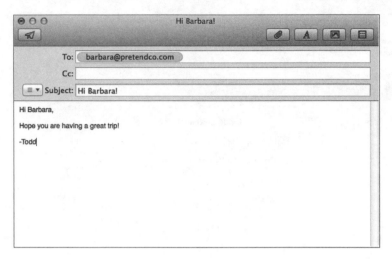

6   Click the "Send message" button in the upper-left corner of the message window.

7   Leave Mail open and running.

Use the Mail Application as Barbara Green

Use the Mail application as Barbara Green to send mail to Todd Porter.

1   On your server computer, open Mail by clicking it in your Dock.

2   See that the message from Todd was received.

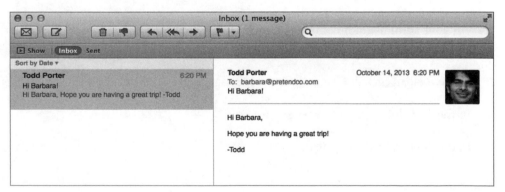

3   Select the message from Todd Porter.

4 In the toolbar of the Mail window, click "Reply to sender" (a tab with a curved arrow pointing to the left).

5 In the main body of the message, enter the message Hi Todd, Thanks! I'm staying an extra week since I can work remotely. See you soon, Barbara.

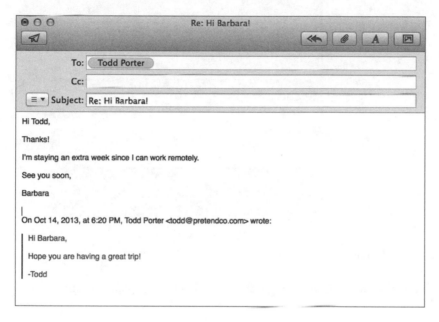

6 Click the "Send message" button.

7 Once the message is sent successfully, quit Mail.

Check the Reply as Todd Porter

In the Dock on your administrator computer, note that Mail has a red badge with the number 1 in it to indicate that you have one new mail message.

1 In Mail, click the new message from Barbara Green.

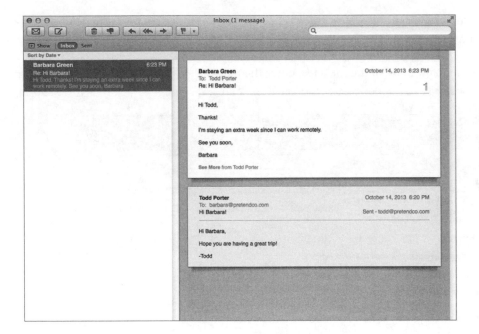

2   Press Command-Q to quit Mail.

3   On your administrator computer, log out and log back in as Local Admin.

Clean Up

Log out of the Todd Local account on your administrator computer, and log back in as the local administrator.

In this lesson you learned how to configure and use the Mail service.

Configuring the Wiki Service

OS X Server provides a simple interface for providing wiki services. Wikis are growing in popularity because they offer an easy, cross-platform method to share information to many users.

Reference 23.1
Understanding and Managing a Wiki

A wiki is a collaborative web-based tool that allows users and groups to post information in a manner that promotes the logical progression of an idea, project, theme, or any other focal point of discussion within an organization. Wikis are central to the idea of all users within a given group being able to post, edit, review, and discuss material without interference from other groups or departments within an organization. This can benefit the group whose wiki is hosting a confidential project or sensitive information. OS X Server wikis also keep a detailed history of a group's posts, so you can retrieve older information if necessary.

Wikis have a few layers of access control. You can administratively control the users and groups you allow to create wikis. Once a user creates a wiki, she can specify who can read it and who can edit it, all without any intervention from an administrator.

The user who creates the wiki becomes the default administrator for that wiki. That user can then assign administration rights to other non-server administrator users. Existing server administrators already have administration rights.

Once users have access to a wiki, they can post articles, images, and files for downloading, link pages together, and format the pages to their liking. Media such as images, movies, and audio are presented right on the webpage and do not need to be downloaded by the user.

Similar to wikis are blogs. Blogs permit users and groups to catalog their experiences surrounding a project or theme. Whereas wikis are collaborative, blogs tend to be singular in nature and organized in a chronological format; however, with group blogging, shared experiences may be posted together.

The files for the Wiki service are stored at /Library/Server/Wiki.

The wiki calendar feature is reliant on the Calendar service running. If you plan on having a group calendar, make sure Calendar is running.

Since the wiki is a web service and can be used across the Internet, it is a wise idea to SSL protect the wiki site. This will prevent the content from being readable as it passes across networks.

Files that are hosted in a wiki or blog can be viewed by the wiki users directly in the wiki itself courtesy of the Quick Look functionality of OS X Server. This is handy, as not all uses will have the appropriate applications installed on their computers.

Reference 23.2
Troubleshooting the Wiki Service

Here are some common problems and suggestions for rectifying issues with the Wiki service:

▶   If your users can't connect to the Wiki service on the server, check that the clients are using a DNS server that is providing the proper name resolution for the server.

▶   If users can't connect to the Wiki website, check that ports 80 and 443 are open to the server. Check that the Wiki service is running.

▶   If users can't authenticate to the Wiki service, check that the users are using proper passwords. Reset if needed. Check that the users are allowed access to the service as per the access controls.

For additional information on troubleshooting web issues, refer to Lesson 21, "Hosting Websites."

Exercise 23.1
Enable the Wiki Service

▶ **Prerequisites**

▶   Exercise 3.1, "Configure DNS Services"

▶   Exercise 10.1, "Create and Import Network Accounts"; or use the Server app to create a user with Full Name Carl Dunn, Account Name carl, and a password of net, who is a member of a group named Contractors.

Enabling the Wiki service on OS X Server is simply done by turning on the service in the Server app.

In this exercise, you will enable the service and then limit who can create wikis. You will ensure that your site uses SSL to protect it.

> **NOTE ▶** Make sure you have the Contractors group and users available from Lesson 10.

1   Perform these exercises on your administrator computer. If you do not already have a connection to your server computer with Server app on your administrator computer, then connect to it with the following steps: Open the Server app on your administrator computer, choose Manage > Connect to Server, click Other Mac, select your server, click Continue, provide administrator credentials (Administrator Name ladmin and Administrator Password ladminpw), deselect the "Remember this password" checkbox, and then click Connect.

2   In the Server app sidebar, select Wiki. Turn the service on by clicking the On/Off switch.

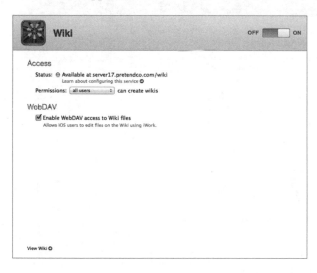

3   Wiki creation can be limited to specific groups by adding the groups to the Permissions menu. Choose "only some users."

4 In the new window that opens, add the Contractors group to the list. Click OK.

5 In Safari, navigate to **http://server***n*.**pretendco.com** (where *n* is your student number) to view the default site.

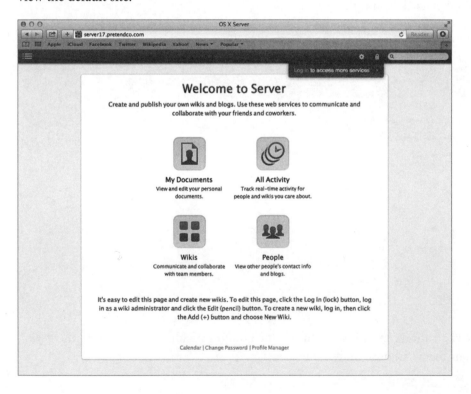

6 Click Wikis to see the interface. Note that this connection isn't protected by SSL.

7 To protect the site with SSL automatically, in the Server app select Web. Edit the non-SSL default website and set up a redirect where "This website" is redirected to "Server Website (SSL)."

This sends any requests on HTTP to the SSL-protected HTTPS site.

8 On your administrator computer in Safari, navigate to server*n*.pretendco.com (where *n* is your student number) to view the default site again, but notice that a certificate dialog appears, since a self-signed certificate was used. (You will not see this if you use a certificate signed by a known certificate authority.) Click Continue, and then click Wikis to see the interface.

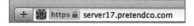

9 Log in as Carl Dunn, a member the Contractors group, click the menu in the upper-left corner of the page, and then click My Documents.

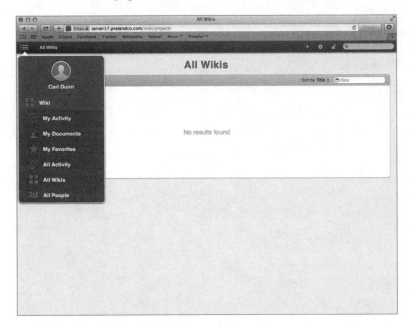

10 Click Carl Dunn's name in the list under Everything.

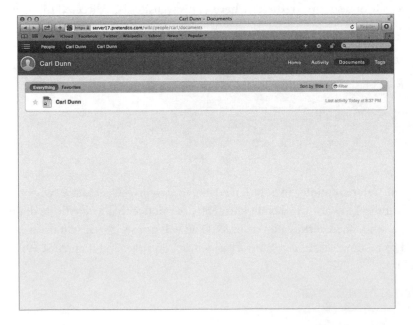

11 Click the Add (+) pop-up menu at the top of the page, and choose New Wiki.

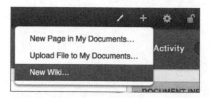

12 Give the wiki a name—such as My First Wiki!—and a description. Click Continue.

13 In the "Set permissions" pane, start typing Contractors into the Permissions field. When the Contractors group appears, choose it and set the permissions to Read and Write. For "all logged-in users," set permissions to Read Only, and for "All unauthenticated users," keep permissions at No Access. Click Continue.

14 In the "Set appearance" pane, pick the color scheme and icon you like. Click Create.

15 Click "Go to Wiki" at the "Setup complete" pane.

16 Review the various menus and choices in the wiki to get used to the interface.

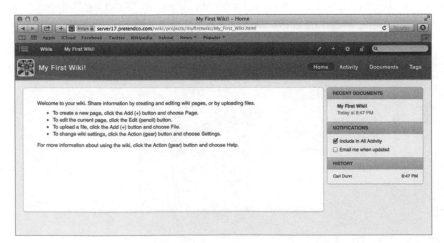

Exercise 23.2
Edit a Wiki

► **Prerequisite**

► Exercise 23.1, "Enable the Wiki Service"

Users that you authorized to create wikis can begin the process of creating a wiki. Because wikis are web based, you can use any browser on any platform to authenticate users to start the process of wiki creation. In this exercise, you'll use network user credentials to create a wiki, manage access to it, and create some content.

1 Log in to the wiki as Carl if you aren't still logged in, and then click the Edit (pencil icon) button.

2 Click at the end of the existing text, press Return for a new line, and then click the Attachment (paper clip) icon in the upper-left corner.

3 Click Choose File, navigate to your Downloads folder, select About Downloads.pdf, and then click Choose.

4 Click Upload to attach the file.

5 Click Save to save the edits to the page.

6 View the results of the edit. Additional media can be uploaded using the appropriate buttons in the toolbar. The media will be presented right on the webpage and won't

require downloading for use by the reader. Click the Quick Look (eye) icon next to the filename to view the attachment.

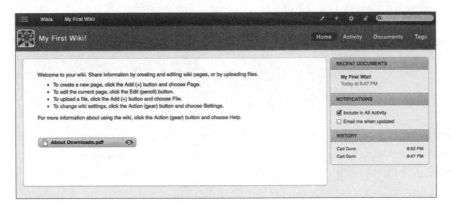

7 To turn on the blog, click the Action (gear icon) pop-up menu and choose Wiki Settings.

8 Under the General tab, select the Blog checkbox and click Save.

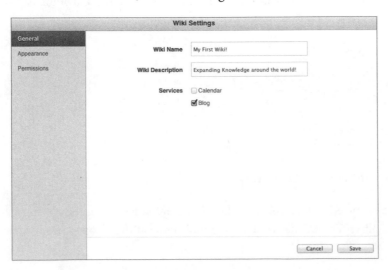

9   Once the blog is on, click the Add (+) button to add a new blog post within the wiki.

10   Give your blog post a name like My First Blog! Click Add.

11   View the resulting blog post.

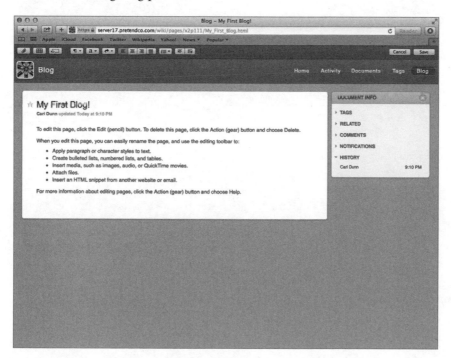

12   Enter Wiki Settings again and click the Permissions tab. Modify the permissions for "All unauthenticated users" to Read Only. Click Save.

13 To delete the wiki, click the wiki name to move back to the wiki itself, click the Action (gear icon) pop-up menu, and choose Delete Wiki. You will be asked to confirm your choice.

14 Click "log out," and then quit Safari.

Clean Up

No cleanup is needed in this section. You learned to turn on the Wiki service, edit a wiki, turn on a blog, and edit a blog.

Lesson 24

Implementing Calendar Service

One of the core collaboration services, Calendar provides a standards-based method of scheduling tasks and resources.

Reference 24.1
Calendar Service Data Locations

Like most other services, the data repository for Calendar service is located at /Library/Server. Within that directory is a folder containing data specific to the Calendar service at /Library/Server/Calendar and Contacts.

Within that folder is a Config folder that has the main configuration file, caldavd-system.plist, for the caldav daemon.

Logs are stored at /var/log/caldavd/access.log.

GOALS

► Understand features of Calendar

► Explore the usage of the service

► Understand the underlying processes of the service

Reference 24.2
Using the Calendar Service

OS X Server contains a calendaring service based on several open source initiatives, mainly the Calendar Server Extensions for WebDAV (CalDAV) calendaring protocol. The Calendar service uses HTTP for access to all of its files. Users who want to use the calendaring service can take advantage of several handy features:

► Scheduling rooms or items that can be checked out, such as projectors

► Enabling access control for delegation of scheduling and restricted viewing of your calendar(s)

► Allowing multiple calendars per user

- ▶ Permitting the attachment of files to events
- ▶ Sending invitations to events, regardless of whether or not the recipient is a user on the Calendar server
- ▶ Checking to see if users or meeting locations are available for a certain event
- ▶ Privately annotating an event with comments that only they and the event organizer can access
- ▶ Using push notification to support immediate updates for computers and mobile devices

And these under-the-hood features should make administrators happy:

- ▶ Integration with Open Directory in OS X Server, Microsoft's Active Directory, and LDAP directory services requires no modification to user records.
- ▶ Service discovery makes it easy for users to set up Calendar when you choose "Create Users and Groups" or "Import Users and Groups" during your initial server setup.
- ▶ Server-side scheduling frees up client resources for better client performance and more consistent scheduling results.

Once the Calendar service is started, users can create and manipulate their events and schedules with Calendar (v4.0 or higher), Calendar for iPhone and iPod touch, and wiki calendar pages. A number of third-party applications also work with the Calendar service; you can locate them by doing a web search for CalDAV support.

The Calendar service provides a way to create and use resources (like a projector or a set of speakers) and locations (such as a building or a meeting room). If no delegate has been set, the Calendar service automatically accepts the invitation for the location or resource if it is free, and makes the free/busy information available to users. You can also define a delegate to moderate the availability of the resource or location.

Delegates can have two functions based on whether you set Automatic or With Delegates Approval. If you set Automatic, the resource will automatically accept the invitation, but the delegate can view and modify the resource's calendar. If With Delegates Approval has been selected, the delegate must accept or deny the invitation. The delegate can also view and modify the resource's calendar.

You add locations and resources with the Server app in the Calendar pane.

Reference 24.3
Troubleshooting the Calendar Service

To troubleshoot the Calendar service provided by OS X Server, it helps to have a good understanding of how the Calendar service works in general. Review the preceding sections to make sure you understand each of the working pieces.

Here are some common problems and potential solutions:

▶ If your users can't connect to the Calendar service on the server, check that the clients are using a DNS server that is providing the proper name resolution for the server.

▶ If users can't connect to the Calendar service, check that ports 8008 and 8443 are open to the server.

▶ If users can't authenticate to the Calendar service, check that the users are using proper passwords. Reset if needed. Check that the users are allowed access to the service as per the service access controls.

Exercise 24.1
Configure and Start the Calendar Service

▶ **Prerequisites**

▶ Exercise 3.1, "Configure DNS Services"

▶ Exercise 10.1, "Create and Import Network Accounts"

▶ Exercise 22.1, "Enable the Mail Service"

You use the Server app to start and manage the Calendar service. The parameters you can adjust are limited to the following:

▶ Enabling or disabling of email invitations and various related settings

▶ Locations and resources

Starting the Calendar service with the Server app is very simple, but you will want to gather the email server information you'll use with email invitations.

1   Perform these exercises on your administrator computer. If you do not already have a connection to your server computer with Server app on your administrator computer, then connect to it with the following steps: Open the Server app on your administrator computer, choose Manage > Connect to Server, click Other Mac, select your server, click Continue, provide administrator credentials (Administrator Name **ladmin** and Administrator Password **ladminpw**), deselect the "Remember this password" checkbox, and then click Connect.

2   In the Server app sidebar, select Calendar.

3   Select the "Enable invitations by email" option, and then click the Edit button next to it if the configuration pane doesn't open.

4   There should be an email address, com.apple.calendarserver@server*n*.pretendco.com, already populating the field.

The default email account for the user com.apple.calendarserver, a system account, is filled in for you. If you like, you may use another account, but don't use an email account that is used for normal email transactions. Still, it is suggested you use the default email account. Click Next.

5   The incoming email server information should be filled in for you, but if it isn't, enter the mail server information for the account you entered in the previous step. Click Next.

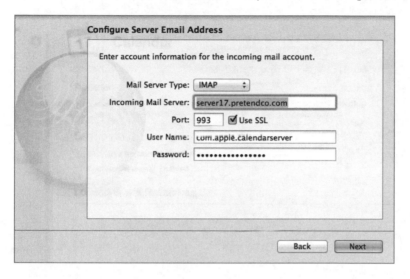

6   The outgoing email server information should be filled in for you, but if it isn't, enter the mail server information for the account you entered in step 4. Click Next.

7 Review the Mail Account Summary page and click Finish.

8 Start the Calendar service.

9 To secure communications between the Calendar service and the clients, set an SSL certificate for the service in the Server app by selecting Certificates in the Server app sidebar and assign your server's certificate to the Calendar and Contacts service. Click OK.

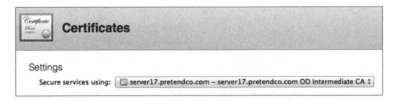

Exercise 24.2
Use the Server App to Add Resources and Locations

▶ **Prerequisite**

▶ Exercise 24.1, "Configure and Start the Calendar Service"

To add a location and a resource with the Server app:

1   In the Server app sidebar, select the Calendar service.

2   Under the Locations and Resources section, click the Add (+) button, and then choose Location from the pop-up menu.

3   Enter or change the following data for your new location:

   ▶ Name: Conference Room A

   ▶ Accept Invitations: Automatically

   ▶ Delegate: Sue Wu (It populates with choices as you type a name.)

4   Click Create to save the changes to the location.

   You have now added a location that will be visible when you add or modify an event on a calendar hosted by the Calendar service.

5   Click the Add (+) button, and then choose Resource from the pop-up menu.

6   Enter or change the following data for your new resource:

   ▶ Name: Demo iPad

   ▶ Accept Invitations: Automatically

   ▶ Delegate: Lucy Sanchez (It populates with choices as you type a name.)

7 Click Create.

You have now added a resource you can invite to an event.

Exercise 24.3
Access the Calendar Service as a User

▶ **Prerequisite**

  ▶ Exercise 24.2, "Use the Server App to Add Resources and Locations"

Users can create and modify events with Calendar, a web browser, and mobile devices. In this exercise, you will open Calendar, add a network Calendar account, change who can access the account as a delegate, create an event with a location and a resource, and then create one more event and access the free/busy feature.

1 On your administrator computer, open Calendar (in /Applications).

2 Choose Calendar > Add Account.

3 Choose Add CalDAV Account and then click Create to add a Calendar service account. Enter the following data:

▶ Account Type: Automatic

▶ Email Address: lucy@servern.pretendco.com (where *n* is your student number)

▶ Password: net

4 Click Create to add the account. You might get a certificate warning if you used a self-signed SSL certificate. If so, click Continue.

5 Choose Calendar > Preferences > Accounts. Choose Lucy's account. Delegate other users to access the calendar to edit and review the events. Click the Delegation tab. Notice that Demo iPad already is showing up in the list of accounts the user can access.

6 At the bottom of the pane, click Edit.

7 Click the Add (+) button.

8   Enter Sue, and then choose Sue Wu from the list. Make sure you click the name to choose it.

9   In the same Manage Account Access pane, click the Add (+) button, enter Carl, and then choose Carl Dunn from the list.

10   Select the Allow Write checkbox for Carl.

This setup allows Carl to edit events on behalf of Lucy, and allows Sue to view Lucy's events.

11 Click Done to close the Manage Account Access pane.

NOTE ▸ Do not confuse the Accounts I Can Access pane with the Manage Account Access pane. One shows who you have allowed to access your accounts, and the other shows who has allowed you to access their accounts.

12 Click the General tab and choose the calendar for server*n* (where *n* is your student number) to be your Default Calendar.

13 Close the Preferences window.

14 Choose File > New Event, or click the Create Event (+) button, to create a quick event.

15 Enter an event name, such as Status Update, and press Return.

16 In the location field, enter only the first few characters of Conference Room A. Choose Conference Room A when it appears, and then press Return.

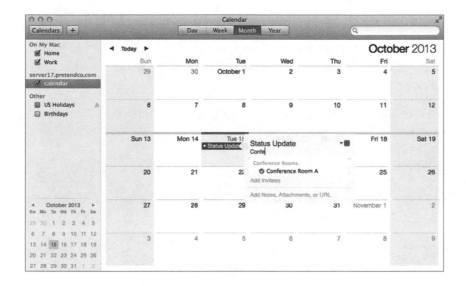

17 Click Add Invitees, and then enter only the first few characters of `Sue Wu`. Choose Sue Wu when it appears, and then press Return.

18 While still in the invitees field, enter only the first few characters of `Demo iPad`. Choose Demo iPad when it appears, and then press Return.

19 Click Add Notes, Attachments, or URL, and then select Add Attachment. Navigate to your Downloads folder, select About Downloads.pdf, and then click Open.

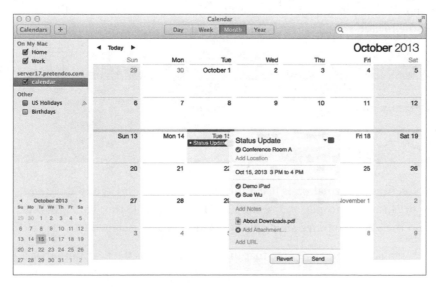

20 Click Send to save the changes to this event.

This causes Demo iPad to automatically accept the event, and Sue Wu will get an invitation to the event. The automatic accept occurred because the resource was configured to do so.

21 Click the event you just created. Choose Edit > Duplicate, which creates a new event at the same time as your original event.

22 Choose Edit > Edit Event.

23 Note that Demo iPad has an unavailable icon, because you already scheduled an event for this time that is using the Demo iPad.

24 Click Demo iPad and then click Check Availability to choose a new meeting time that works for the location and invitees (which includes people and resources).

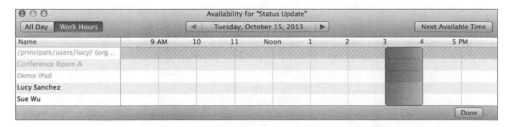

Note that free/busy information is listed for each participant invited to the event, including the location, people, and resources. The unavailable times are blocked out in gray, and the available times are displayed with the color assigned to your calendar.

25 Click Next Available Time, and note that the event moves to the next time that is not busy for each of the invitees.

26 Click Done to close the Availability window and use the new time selected.

27 Click Update to save the changes to the event and notify the invitees of the event. Locations and resources automatically accept invitations.

28 Quit Calendar, or try out some of the other features.

Even though you used Calendar in this exercise, you could also use the web calendar link available at the bottom of the default server home page (https://server*n*.pretendco.com/ webcal, where *n* is your student number). Of course, the Calendar service works with Calendar for iPhone and iPod touch through the CalDAV configuration option.

Calendars can also be added to wikis by creating a wiki and, in the General settings, selecting the Calendar checkbox.

Since the Calendar service relies on HTTP or HTTPS to transfer data from server to client and vice versa, standard web troubleshooting applies, such as checking for open and available ports. On a client, the Calendar app discovers the Calendar server via DNS lookup, so DNS problems could prevent Calendar from working as expected.

Clean Up
No cleanup is required after this exercise. You learned how to configure the Calendar service and set up accounts on a client device.

Lesson 25

Providing Messages Service

One of the common collaboration services, Messages provides a standards-based method of communicating with one or many other users.

Reference 25.1
Managing the Messages Service

Messages, previously known as iChat, allows users to collaborate in real time. Messages users can use the following features to quickly share information without the delay associated with email messages and wiki posts:

▶ Exchange text messages instantly.

▶ Send files to each other.

▶ Set up an instant audio conference (using either the microphone built into many Macs or an external unit).

▶ Initiate a face-to-face video conference using video cameras (including the iSight or FaceTime camera built into many Macs and iOS devices).

▶ Allow another Messages user to take control of a Mac (using screen sharing).

▶ Use a persistent chat (called a room) with a group of people to keep a persistent conversation going.

Unlike a telephone call, which you must either answer immediately or allow to go to voicemail, you can accept an instant text message but answer it when you are ready to process it.

By running your own Messages service, you gain these advantages, plus others like chat transcript archives and the ability to keep all messages secure and private.

Users who chat with each other can use the Messages service to keep those chats within their organization and control the text of the chats. Like many other services on OS X Server, the Messages service can be restricted to certain users or groups, permitting chats to be private and controlled. Chats can also be secured through encryption and logged, permitting them to be searched later. The Messages service is based on the open source Jabber project. The technical name for the protocol used is the Extensible Messaging and Presence Protocol (XMPP).

Configuring Messages Service Users

After the Messages service has been set up, you can permit users to join the Messages service (called Jabber in the Messages app interface). A full Messages service account consists of the following:

▶ A user's Account Name (also known as short name)

▶ The @ symbol

▶ A Messages service's host domain

For example, a user with a Full Name of Chat User1 and an Account Name of chatuser1 would configure the Messages application with a Jabber Account Name of chatuser1@ server17.pretendco.com.

There are at least three ways to configure the Messages app, including:

▶ Use a configuration profile

▶ Use the Internet Accounts system preferences and select "Add an OS X Server account"

▶ Specify a Jabber account in the Messages app

Understanding Messages Network Ports

Various ports are used for the Messages service, depending on whether the service is used internal to your network or exposed to other networks. Refer to Table 25.1 for port usage information.

Table 25.1 Messages Port Usage

Port	Description
1080	SOCKS5 protocol use for file transfers
5060	iChat Session Initiation Protocol (SIP), used for audio or video chats
5190	Only required for basic Instant Messenger (IM) use
5222 TCP	Used only for TLS connections if an SSL certificate is enabled. If no SSL certificate is used, this port is used for nonencrypted connections. TLS encryption is preferred to legacy SSL connections, as it is more secure.
5223 TCP	Used for legacy SSL connections when an SSL certificate is used
5269 TCP	Used for encrypted TLS server-to-server connections, as well as nonencrypted connections. TLS encryption is preferred to legacy SSL connections, as it is more secure.
5678	UDP port used by Messages to determine the user's external IP address
5297, 5298	Used by Messages versions older than v10.5 for Bonjour IM. v10.5 and later use dynamic ports.
7777	Used by the Jabber Proxy65 module for server file transfer proxy
16402	Used for SIP signaling in OS X 10.5 and later
16384–16403	These ports are used by OS X 10.4 and earlier for audio or video chat using RTP and RTCP. Traffic was exchanged in .Mac (MobileMe) to determine the user's external port information.

Understanding Messages Logging

The Messages service can meet the need to review the chat archive of a conversation, perhaps for auditing or administrative purposes. In addition to archiving all messages, any user can configure their Messages app to archive their own personal chats for review.

The archives are kept in plain text, even if the communications between the Messages users are encrypted. The Messages service does not archive audio or video content or files transferred using the service.

The Messages service can log all chat messages. The default folder for the archive is on the service storage volume in Library/Server/Messages/Data/message_archives/. The archive file is jabberd_user_messages.log, and it contains all the messages your users have exchanged using your server's Messages service.

The ownership and permissions of the jabberd_user_messages.log file allow only a hidden service account (named _jabberd) or the root user to access its contents.

While it is possible to change permissions on the message_archives folder and the log it contains so you can use a GUI text editor to view the file, it is safer and more secure to use the command-line tools in Terminal to view the file; you can use the sudo command in Terminal to obtain the temporary root access you need to access and view the contents of the file.

Configuring Messages Federation

Your organization may have more than one computer running OS X Server. If both of those servers use the Messages service, it is possible to join them together, allowing users and groups in both Open Directory masters to engage each other in instant messaging. The process of joining different Messages service servers together is called federation. Federation not only allows two servers running Messages services to join, it also allows any other XMPP chat service, such as Google Talk, to join. The Messages service federation is enabled by default.

> **NOTE** ▶ You can enable secure encryption for the federation if you are already using an SSL certificate. This forces all communications between the servers to be encrypted, similar to the way in which the communications between Messages and the Messages server are encrypted when using that certificate. For archiving purposes, messages are always decrypted on the server.

Reference 25.2
Troubleshooting the Messages Service

To troubleshoot the Messages service provided by OS X Server, it helps to have a good understanding of how the Messages service works in general. Review the preceding sections to make sure you understand each of the working pieces.

Here are some common problems and suggestions for rectifying them:

▶ If your users can't connect to the Messages service on the server, check that the clients are using a DNS server that is providing the proper name resolution for the server.

▶ If users can't connect to the Messages service, check that the appropriate ports are open to the server, as listed in Table 25.1 earlier in the section.

▶ If users can't authenticate to the Messages service, check that the users are using proper passwords. Reset if needed. Check that the users are allowed access to the service as per the service access controls.

Exercise 25.1
Set Up the Messages Service

▶ **Prerequisites**

▶ Exercise 3.1, "Configure DNS Services"

▶ Exercise 10.1, "Create and Import Network Accounts"; or use the Server app to create users Sue Wu and Carl Dunn, each with an account name that is the same as their first name in lowercase, and a password of net, and configure both users to be members of a group that has the option enabled to make all group members Messages buddies (such as the local network group named Workgroup).

You use the Server app to enable the Messages service like most of the other services on OS X Server. Once enabled, the service is managed in a fashion similar to that of the other services.

1 Start these exercises on your administrator computer. If you do not already have a connection to your server computer with Server app on your administrator computer, then connect to it with the following steps: Open the Server app on your administrator computer, choose Manage > Connect to Server, click Other Mac, select your server, click Continue, provide administrator credentials (Administrator Name ladmin and Administrator Password ladminpw), deselect the "Remember this password" checkbox, and then click Connect.

2   To confirm that Messages is configured to use SSL, select Certificates in the Server app sidebar.

> **NOTE ▶** If you haven't yet configured your server to be an Open Directory master, you will see a self-signed SSL certificate instead of the certificate signed by the OD Intermediate CA.

3   If the "Secure services using" pop-up menu is set to a single certificate, as shown in the following figure, you can skip to step 4, because Messages will use this SSL certificate. In the following figure, all services are configured to use the SSL certificate that was signed by the OD Intermediate CA.

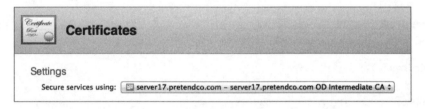

If the "Secure services using" pop-up menu is set to "Custom configuration," as shown in the following figure, click that pop-up menu and choose Custom.

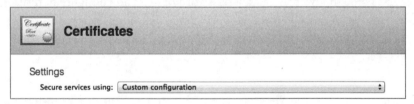

After choosing Custom, in the list of services and their corresponding certificates, next to the Messages service, click the Certificate pop-up menu, choose a certificate from the available certificates, and then click OK.

4   In the Server app, select the Messages service, then click the On/Off button to turn
the service on.

Once the service is turned on, the green status indicator is displayed. There is a link to the
Help Center for the Messages service beneath the Status field.

Enable Messages Service Archiving

To enable Messages service logging:

1   In the Server app sidebar, select Messages if necessary, then select the "Archive all
messages" checkbox.

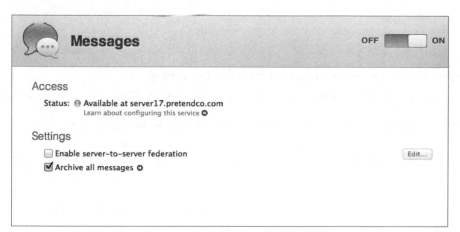

2   To view the location of the Messages archives, click the link next to the "Archive all
messages" checkbox.

The Server's Storage pane opens and displays the folder.

NOTE ▶ If you click the link next to the "Archive all messages" checkbox while using the Server app on the server, as opposed to from an administrator computer, instead of the Server app opening the folder in the Storage pane, it opens the folder in a new Finder window.

Later in this exercise you will view the logged messages.

Configure Messages on Your Administrator Computer

Now that you have the Messages service running, verify that you can connect to the service.

To enable a Messages account to use the Messages (Jabber) service:

1 On your administrator computer, open the Messages app by clicking the Messages icon in your Dock.

2 At the iMessage Setup dialog, click Not Now, and then at the confirmation dialog, click Skip.

3 At the Account Setup dialog, select "Other messages account" from the menu and click Continue.

4 In the Account Type pop-up menu, choose Jabber.

5 Enter sue@server*n*.pretendco.com (where *n* is your student number) in the Account
Name field, and enter the password net in the Password field.

6 In the Server Options section, leave the Server and Port fields blank, and leave the
checkboxes unselected. Messages will automatically use the appropriate server and port.

7 Click Create.

> **NOTE ▶** If you get a message that the login ID or password is incorrect, confirm that the
> file /Library/Server/Messages/Config/jabberd/sm.xml refers to server*n*.pretendco.com
> rather than server*n*.local (where *n* is your student number).

8 If you see the message that Messages can't verify the identity of your server, click
Show Certificate, select the "Always trust" checkbox, click Continue, and then provide
local administrator credentials.

The Messages (Jabber) service Buddies window for Sue We automatically opens.

> **MORE INFO ▶** In the header at the top of the Buddies window, Messages displays the
> full name of the user logged in on OS X, not the full name of the account you used to
> authenticate to the Messages service.

TIP ▶ If you close your Buddies window, you can display it again by choosing Window > Buddies (or by pressing Command-1).

Configure the Messages App on Your Server Computer

Now that you have the Messages app configured on your administrator computer with the Sue Wu user account, configure the Messages app on your server computer as another user, Carl Dunn, so you can use Messages to communicate between the two computers.

1   On your server computer, if you aren't already logged in with the Local Admin account, log in now (Name **Local Admin** and Password **ladminpw**).

2   On your server computer, open the Messages app by clicking the Messages icon in your Dock.

3   At the iMessage Setup dialog, click Not Now, and then at the confirmation dialog, click Skip.

4   At the Account Setup dialog, select "Other messages account" and then click Continue.

5   In the Account Type pop-up menu, choose Jabber.

6   Enter the following information:

▶   Account Name: carl@server*n*.pretendco.com (where *n* is your student number)

▶   Password: net

7   In the Server Options section, leave the Server and Port fields blank, and leave the checkboxes unselected. Messages will automatically use the appropriate server and port.

8   Click Create.

The Messages (Jabber) service buddy list for Carl Dunn automatically opens.

You can add Jabber buddies (other users with whom you want to chat and whose names you want to appear in a list for easy access) to your buddy list as you normally would when using Messages for any non-Jabber account. You can optionally add a buddy who exists in your Open Directory database. Be sure to include the person's full name when adding a Messages (Jabber) service buddy.

Send Messages from One Mac to Another Mac

When using Jabber accounts, you need to get permission from another person before you can use Messages with them. However, both users are members of the Open Directory group named Workgroup; this group automatically has the "Make group members Messages buddies" option selected.

However, you may need to connect and reconnect to the Messages service for the Messages app to populate the Workgroup buddy list.

If these two users are not members of the Open Directory group named Workgroup, which automatically grants authorization, you must take the following steps to authorize the users to chat with each other: As Sue Wu, use Messages to click Add (+) in the Buddies window, choose Add Buddy, and specify carl@server*n*.pretendco.com (where *n* is your student number) as the Jabber account; then as Carl Dunn, click Accept at the notification asking if he would like to be added to Sue Wu's buddy list.

Simulate a chat between the users.

1 Disconnect Sue Wu from the Messages service. On your administrator computer, in the lower-left corner of the Messages window, click the Available pop-up window and then choose Offline (or press Control-Command-O).

2 On your server computer, disconnect Carl Dunn from the Messages service (press Control-Command-O).

3 Wait a moment, then reconnect Sue Wu to the Messages service. On your administrator computer, in the lower-left corner of the Messages window, click the Offline pop-up window and then choose Available (or press Control-Command-A).

4 On your server computer, wait a moment, and then reconnect Carl Dunn to the Messages service (press Control-Command-A).

5 If Workgroup does not appear in the Buddies window for a user, disconnect and reconnect again.

6 From either computer, in the Buddies window, click the Workgroup disclosure triangle to reveal its contents.

7 Double-click a buddy, enter some text in the Jabber field of the Messages window, and then press Return.

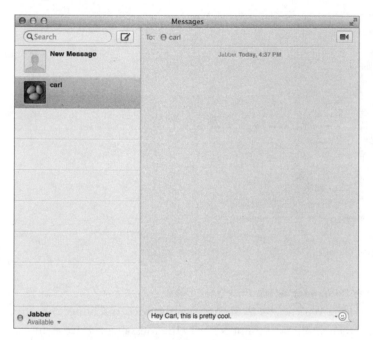

8 On the other computer, reply to the message.

Restrict Messages Service Users

You can restrict who is permitted to use the Messages service by using service access controls. As with many other services, you restrict user access via the Server app.

To restrict the user Sue Wu from chatting with others on the Messages service:

1 On your administrator computer, in the Server app sidebar, select Users.

2 Select Sue Wu, and then click the Action (gear icon) pop-up menu and choose Edit Access to Services.

3 Deselect the Messages checkbox to disable the user's access to the Messages service.

4   Click OK to save the change.

Disconnect and Attempt to Reconnect as the Restricted User

Now that you've restricted Sue Wu's access to the Messages service, disconnect her from the Messages service and then attempt to connect her to the Messages service again.

1   Disconnect Sue Wu. On your administrator computer, in the lower-left corner of the Messages window, click the Available pop-up window and then choose Offline (or press Control-Command-O).

2   On your administrator computer, Quit the Messages app.

3   Wait about a minute before reconnecting.

4   On your administrator computer, open the Messages app.

5   Reconnect Sue Wu. On your administrator computer, in the lower-left corner of the Messages window, click the Offline pop-up window and then choose Available (or press Control-Command-A).

     If you are automatically reconnected, disconnect again and wait another minute before attempting to reconnect.

6   When you are prompted for Sue Wu's password, enter net and click Log In.

Even after providing a valid password, you still can't log in as Sue Wu, because you removed her access to the Messages service.

7   Click Cancel as many times as is necessary to close any authentication dialog.

Re-enable Sue Wu's access to the Messages service, and connect to the Messages service again as Sue Wu.

1   On your administrator computer, in the Server app sidebar, select Users.

2   Select Sue Wu, and then click the Action (gear icon) pop-up menu and choose Edit Access to Services.

3   Select the Messages checkbox to enable her access to the Messages service.

4   Reconnect Sue Wu. On your administrator computer, in the lower-left corner of the Messages window, click the Offline pop-up window and then choose Available (or press Control-Command-A).

   If you are prompted for the password, click Cancel and then try again after a moment.

5   Confirm that you can chat between the two computers again.

Restrict Messages Federation

By default, federation is not allowed with any other Messages service running on any other server or Jabber server. However, you can institute federation and then restrict the Messages service federation to approved Messages servers only. To do so:

1   On your administrator computer, in the Server app sidebar, select the Messages service. Make sure that "Enable server-to-server federation" is selected, and then click the Edit button.

2   Select the "Restrict federation to the following domains" option and click the Add (+) button to add only those domains you want to participate within the federation.

3   As an example, enter the hypothetical server18.pretendco.com. It does not matter that this server is not online.

4   Click OK.

5   To keep communication secure between federated servers, apply an SSL certificate to the Messages service and select the "Require secure server-to-server federation" option. Click OK to close the dialog.

View Messages Service and Chat Logs

To view the connection logs for the Messages service, you will use the Server app to view the Messages Service log. Then, to view the archive of messages, you will use sudo in a Terminal command.

1   On your administrator computer, in the Server app, select the Logs pane.

2   Click the pop-up menu and choose Service Log.

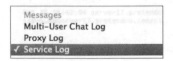

3   Browse the contents of the Service Log.

4   Enter session started in the search field, then press Return. This displays the date, Jabber account name, and computer name from which a new jabber session started.

Each time you press Return, the Logs pane displays another entry.

The Messages service reports in the system log can also log any errors that may occur, and you can search for them using the search field in the toolbar.

Additional logs are available in the Logs section of the Server app.

5   To view the chat transcripts, on your server computer, open Terminal (click Launch-Pad, click Other, and click Terminal).

6   In the Terminal window, enter the following command, all on one line:

sudo more /Library/Server/Messages/Data/message_archives/jabberd_user_messages.log

Then press Return to issue the command.

The sudo command gives you root permissions for the command that follows it.

The more command displays the contents of a file one screen at a time; if there is more than one screen full of text in the file, press the Space bar to view the next screen full of text, or press q to exit the more command.

7   You are prompted for the password of the currently logged-in user; enter ladminpw and press Return.

The chat transcripts appear; look for the conversation Carl and Sue had.

```
● ○ ○                    ⌂ ladmin — bash — 80×24
Last login: Fri Oct 25 16:11:34 on console
server17:~ ladmin$ sudo more /Library/Server/Messages/Data/message_archives/jabb
erd_user_messages.log

WARNING: Improper use of the sudo command could lead to data loss
or the deletion of important system files. Please double-check your
typing when using sudo. Type "man sudo" for more information.

To proceed, enter your password, or type Ctrl-C to abort.

Password:
# This message log is created by the jabberd router.
# See router.xml for logging options.
# Format: (Date)<tab>(From JID)<tab>(To JID)<tab>(Message Body)<line end>
Fri Oct 25 16:37:57 2013        sue@server17.pretendco.com/client17    carl@ser
ver17.pretendco.com    Hey Carl, this is pretty cool.
Fri Oct 25 16:38:18 2013        carl@server17.pretendco.com/server17    sue@serv
er17.pretendco.com/client17    Yeah, I could see how my organization could use
this.
Fri Oct 25 16:43:07 2013        sue@server17.pretendco.com/client17    carl@ser
ver17.pretendco.com    Let's see what this text looks like in the archive.
server17:~ ladmin$ █
```

Lesson 26
Managing Contacts Service

OS X Server provides a simple interface for providing Contacts services. Contacts allows the central storage of information and makes it available to many clients.

GOALS

► Configure Contacts service

► Understand protocols used

► Connect to the Contacts service

Reference 26.1
Understanding the Contacts Service

The Contacts service enables users to store contacts on the server and to access those contacts with multiple computers and devices. In addition to any application that can use CardDAV, the following Apple applications are compatible with the Contacts service:

► Contacts and Address Book

► Mail

► Messages

Another feature of Contacts allows you to enable the Contacts service to provide LDAP searches of the directory servers your server may be bound to, so your users do not have to configure their Contacts preferences to include various LDAP servers. This option is not available for configuration unless the server is bound to another directory service.

The Contacts service uses open source technologies, including CardDAV (an extension to WebDAV), HTTP, and HTTPS, as well as vCard (a file format for contact information).

When you create a contact with the Contacts service, you use CardDAV, not LDAP, to copy the changes to the server.

Reference 26.2
Troubleshooting the Contacts Service

Here are some common problems with the Contacts service and how they might be rectified:

▶ If your users can't connect to the Contacts service on the server, check that the clients are using a DNS server that is providing the proper name resolution for the server.

▶ If users can't connect to the Contacts service, check that the ports 8800 and 8843 are open to the server.

▶ If users can't authenticate to the Contacts service, check that the users are using proper passwords. Reset if needed. Also check that the users are allowed to use the service based on the service access controls.

Exercise 26.1
Configure the Contacts Service with the Server App

▶ **Prerequisites**

  ▶ Exercise 3.1, "Configure DNS Services"

  ▶ Exercise 10.1, "Create and Import Network Accounts"

There is very little to configure in the Contacts service. The Server app allows you to:

▶ Turn the service on and off.

▶ Enable directory contacts for search.

In this exercise, before you start the Contacts service, you will specify an SSL certificate for the service to use.

This exercise requires that the OS X Server computer be set up as an Open Directory master with the sample users imported.

1 Perform these exercises on your administrator computer. If you do not already have a connection to your server computer with Server app on your administrator computer, then connect to it with the following steps: Open the Server app on your administrator computer, choose Manage > Connect to Server, click Other Mac, select your server, click Continue, provide administrator credentials (Administrator Name ladmin and

Administrator Password **ladminpw**), deselect the "Remember this password" checkbox, and then click Connect.

2   To protect Contacts with SSL, select Certificates in the Server app sidebar. Apply the server certificate and click OK.

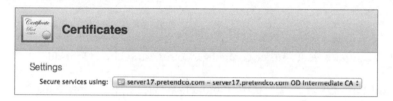

3   In the Server app, select the Contacts service.

4   Select "Allow users to search the directory using the Contacts application."

NOTE ▸ This box will be dimmed if the server is not bound to another directory service or is not an Open Directory master. If it is dimmed, you can still use the Contacts service, but it will be limited to local users resident on the server.

5   Turn on the Contacts service.

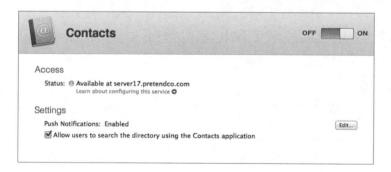

Exercise 26.2
Configure OS X to Use the Contacts Service

▶ **Prerequisite**

   ▸   Exercise 26.1, "Configure the Contacts Service with the Server App"

The Contacts application in OS X is designed to work with the Contacts service on OS X Server.

1   From Launchpad, open Contacts on your client computer and choose Contacts > Preferences.

2   Click Accounts.

3   Click the Add (+) button, select "Other contacts account," and click Continue.

4   Leave the Account type as CardDAV, as the Contacts service implements CardDAV.

5   In the User Name field, enter gary.

    You must use the user's short name.

6   In the Password field, enter the proper password, net.

7   In the Server Address field, enter servern.pretendco.com (where *n* is your student number).

8   Click Create.

9   If a Verify Certificate dialog appears, click Show Certificate, select the "Always trust" checkbox, and authenticate with administrative credentials.

    The new account appears in the Accounts list.

Of course, in a production environment, you would populate client computers to trust your known good SSL certificates, and then train users to alert an administrator when they see an unknown-certificate message.

10 Close the Preferences window.

11 Notice in Contacts the two sections under All Contacts: server*n*.pretendco.com (where *n* is your student number) and Directories. The latter one is due to the Contacts service having the "Include directory contacts in search" option configured.

> **NOTE** ▸ If the Contacts pane isn't showing on the left side, click the leftmost view button at the bottom of the left pane.

12 Choose server*n*.pretendco.com (where *n* is your student number) and click the Add (+) button to create a new contact that will be stored on the server.

13 Enter sample information for a user, including email and Jabber addresses. You can use the following values:

> ▶ First: Jet
>
> ▶ Last: Dogg
>
> ▶ Email (work): jet@pretendco.com
>
> ▶ Chat (work): jet@jabber.pretendco.com

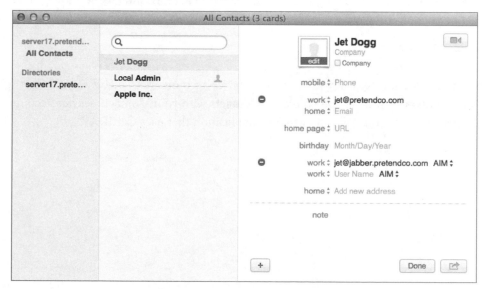

14   Click Done to save your changes.

The contact you just created is synced locally on your OS X computer for offline use, and it is also stored with the Contacts service, so you can access it from other computers and devices.

Messages also supports your Contacts service account. Use the following steps to demonstrate that you can use your Contacts service account with Messages. If you haven't already configured Messages with your network user account, refer to "Managing the Messages Service" in Lesson 25.

15   If Messages is not already running, open Messages (in /Applications).

16   If the server*n* List window is not already displayed, choose Window > server*n*.pretendco.com List (where *n* is your student number).

17   Click the Add (+) button, and choose Add Buddy.

18   Click the disclosure triangle to reveal additional choices.

19   Click the entry you created (Jet Dogg).

20   Click Cancel.

In a production environment, you would click Add to add this user to your buddy list. Do not click Add now, because this would create an authorization request for the foreign Jabber server, and you are on an isolated network.

21   Quit Messages.

The contacts you create with your Contacts service account are available to you on other OS X computers, as long as you configure Contacts with your Contacts service account. You can also access your contacts with any application that uses CardDAV.

Index

Differentiate yourself.
Get Apple certified.

Stand out from the crowd. Differentiate yourself and gain recognition for your expertise by earning Apple Certified Pro status to validate your OS X Server skills.

This book prepares you to pass the OS X Server Essentials 10.9 Exam and in conjunction with the OS X Support Essentials 10.9 Exam, earn Apple Certified Technical Coordinator (ACTC) status. The exam is available at Apple Authorized Training Centers (AATCs) worldwide. ACTC certification verifies knowledge of OS X and OS X Server core functionality, including the ability to configure key services and perform basic troubleshooting on OS X and OS X Server.

Three Steps to Certification

1 Choose your certification path.
   More info: training.apple.com/certification.

2 All Apple Authorized Training Centers (AATCs) offer all OS X and Pro Apps exams, even if they don't offer the corresponding course. To find the closest AATC, please visit training.apple.com/locations.

3 Register for and take your exam(s).

"Knowing that I am Apple Certified gives my clients the confidence to trust me with their most complex projects. It makes my life easier: my Apple Certifications open a whole new world of trust. Apple Certified professionals have already proven that they know their craft."

— Luisa C. Winters, Multimedia Specialist/Graphic Artist, VideoTrainers

Reasons to Become an Apple Certified Pro

- Raise your earning potential. Studies show that certified professionals can earn more than their non-certified peers.

- Distinguish yourself from others in your industry. Proven mastery of an application helps you stand out from the crowd.

- Display your Apple Certification logo. Each certification provides a logo to display on business cards, resumes and websites.

- Publicize your certifications. Publish your certifications on the Apple Certified Professionals Registry (apple.com//certification/verify) to connect with

Training Options

Apple's comprehensive curriculum addresses your needs, whether you're an IT or creative professional, educator, or student. Hands-on training is available through a worldwide network of Apple Authorized Training Centers (AATCs). Self-paced study is available through the Apple Pro Training Series books, which are also accessible as eBooks via the iBooks app. Video training and video training apps are also available for select titles. Visit training.apple.com to view all your learning options.

The Apple Pro Training Series

Apple offers comprehensive certification programs for creative and IT professionals. The Apple Pro Training Series is both a self-paced learning tool and the official curriculum of the Apple Training and Certification program, used by Apple Authorized Training Centers around the world.

To see a complete range of Apple Pro Training Series books, videos and apps visit: **www.peachpit.com/appleprotraining**

Apple
Certified